T0330097

THE FOREIGN PUBLIC DEBT OF CHINA

THE FOREIGN PUBLIC
DEBT OF CHINA

By

ARTHUR GARDINER COONS, Ph.D.
ASSISTANT PROFESSOR OF ECONOMICS
OCCIDENTAL COLLEGE

PHILADELPHIA

UNIVERSITY OF PENNSYLVANIA PRESS

LONDON

HUMPHREY MILFORD: OXFORD UNIVERSITY PRESS

1930

LANCASTER PRESS, INC.
LANCASTER, PA.

TO MY MOTHER

PREFACE

During the time in which the manuscript of this book has been prepared China has been unsettled politically, being torn by civil strife. In 1927 the Peking Government was the recognized central government of China, although its power was admittedly weak. Since that time numerous developments have occurred in the internal political situation. The Peking Government, such as it was, has ceased to exist and a government by the Nationalist party under the leadership and presidency of General Chiang Kai-Shek has been established at Nanking, largely representative of the dominant military leaders of China Proper, which promises to become the nearest to a government for all of China, as well as the strongest government, that has been formed since 1912. Speculation as to the outcome of internal political and military activity is not the purpose of this book or within its scope. Interest centers chiefly upon the origin and size of the foreign financial commitments of the Chinese Government, and the financial and economic position of China as regards repayment and the restoration of Chinese public credit abroad. As a whole our concern is with economic factors only, although the consideration of such cannot be complete without reference to the political problems. The economic elements in the Chinese problem of reconstruction aid in understanding the political problems. On the other hand an uncertain political future would seem to render futile economic speculations. Something, however, can be said of the financial situation quite apart from reference to recent political changes.

The Chinese Government referred to throughout means the Central Government, referring to the Peking Government and its successor in responsibility and authority, acting as the government of China recognized by foreign powers. The commitments of one government in good faith become the obligations of succeeding governments which would represent the same state, both by recognized principles of international law and the requirements of financial stability. The Peking Government under the Republic accepted the indebtedness of the Imperial Government in 1912. Conflict has arisen as to the legally and morally binding character, upon the Nanking Government, of debts contracted by a government which, although officially recognized, was not representative of all China. It is not our purpose to attempt to decide this question. Subsequent diplomatic activity will arrive at a solution of this mooted problem. Suffice it here to outline all the contracted obligations of former recognized Chinese governments, which would appear to be the public debt of China. By the very nature of the case no complete or final statement of this debt can be given, but an attempt will be made to state it as definitely as possible. Paucity of statistics in regard to many phases of Chinese economic life and the fact that current information is scarcely available make it impossible to avoid a large measure of speculation. However, though in some respects China is undergoing comparatively rapid changes, these changes are not so rapid or so divergent in their character as to render futile a presentation of material available.

These foreign loans to China fall into two broad classes, secured loans and unsecured loans. Before making a survey of China's capacity to repay her outstanding foreign public debts, it is important to observe what these obligations are.

The historical treatment of the Chinese Government's foreign financial obligations will consider principally the financial elements involved, such as the amount of the loans that were contracted, the amount available to China, the interest cost and discounts necessary to obtain these loans, the revenues of China that have been pledged as security, and other relevant commitments which have resulted in foreign financial control in China, as well as the extent to which these loans were contracted for productive and other purposes.

Although the loans are bound up almost inextricably with both internal and external political factors, both in origin and in present position they will be considered more from the economic and financial points of view.[1] Some portions of the financial aspects have already been treated, but attempt has been made to introduce elements not stressed as much by other writers.[2]

China is regarded as including all the eighteen Provinces of China Proper, and the three Manchurian provinces; also Mongolia, Sinkiang and Tibet, since the sovereignty or suzerainty of China over these latter areas is recognized.

Throughout this book the use of the dollar symbol, unless specifically marked " G " or " gold " or " U. S." refers to Chinese currency. As is customary with other writers and with the Chinese Government itself in official publications various kinds of Chinese dollars, principally the Yuan and Mexican dollars are grouped together. Hence the dollar

[1] The relation of these foreign loans to the Open Door Policy has been admirably treated by Dr. M. J. Bau in *The Open Door Doctrine in Relation to China.*

[2] Cf. F. H. Huang, *Public Debts of China*, 1919. T. W. Overlach, *Foreign Financial Control in China*, 1919. W. W. Willoughby, *Foreign Rights and Interests in China*, 1920. S. R. Wagel, *Finance in China*, 1914.

symbol unless otherwise noted can be taken to refer to the
Yuan, or to the Mexican dollar as current in the Far East.
Such grouping is not done for taels. There is a wider
divergence among the various kinds of taels, as to weight
and fineness of silver, than between the dollars of the Chinese currency.

It is needless to state that even though care has been
given to acknowledge the sources of material, it is impossible for me to acknowledge in detail all those writers on
Far Eastern questions to whom I am indebted for an interest in the Orient. Particularly, however, do I wish to
thank Professor Ernest M. Patterson of the University of
Pennsylvania for the stimulating instruction which led me
to become interested in this phase of international economics. To him I am also indebted for many helpful
criticisms.

ARTHUR G. COONS

Los Angeles, Calif.,
  July, 1929

CONTENTS

Part III

Chinese Government Indebtedness and Financial Capacity

Part IV

Trade and Industrial Development

TABLES

INTRODUCTION

China's use of foreign funds for governmental purposes dates from 1865, when the first loan to China was made by an English bank, for about £ 1,400,000 to pay a war compensation to Russia after the Treaty of Ili. From that time until 1887, which can be set off as the first period in China's loan history, there were negotiated at least twelve loans.[1] Most of these were negotiated with British banks which by that time were well organized and operating in far eastern markets. The Hongkong and Shanghai Banking Corporation, through its offices in Shanghai, or Hongkong, or London, made eight loans, five to the total amount of £ 4,486,000, and three in taels to the total amount of 7,550,700, or say a total of both sterling and tael loans of approximately £ 5,500,000. The Oriental Bank, and Jardine Matheson and Co., English firms, loaned to the extent of 3,000,000 taels, while Baring Bros. loaned £ 1,500,000.

The other loans during this period were from German banking firms, one from the Deutsche Asiatische Bank for 2,500,000 taels,[2] and another from a syndicate of Berlin and Hamburg bankers for 5,000,000 marks.

[1] The exact number is not known. Dr. Lee lists 12 prior to 1894. The *Encyclopedia Sinica* gives 7. The *Encyclopedia Britannica* lists 8. The latter includes one not given by Dr. Lee, namely the loan of 1878 by Deutsche Asiatische Bank of taels 2,500,000 at 5½ per cent, as well as two prior to 1874, namely one in 1865, and one in 1866, which Dr. Lee does not include, his table beginning in 1875. A. W. Ferrin lists 12 loans 1875–1887. The *China Year Book*, 1912, p. 297, lists of loans prior to 1894 to a total of £ 4,912,000.

[2] This loan is mentioned in *Encyclopedia Britannica*, XI Edition, VI, 188, and by Dr. Pan in *The Trade of the United States with China*.

1

Altogether the loans to the Chinese Government in this early period probably did not much exceed £ 9,000,000.[3] Interest rates varied from 8 per cent in 1874 to 5½ per cent in 1887. The most characteristic rate was 8 per cent, though the loans in the later years, 1885, and 1886, bore 7 per cent and 6 per cent. The highest rate was 15 per cent in 1877 on a loan by the Hongkong and Shanghai Bank, reported by the *Encyclopedia Britannica*.[4] One writer states, however,[5] that this was obtained not because the bank wanted to charge this interest, but because the Chinese themselves offered the terms. The loans contracted in the latter part of this period not only bore the lower rates of interest, but also were for longer periods of duration. No security seems to have been pledged. It is not possible to state the amounts of these loans which were finally available to the Chinese Government. The issue of 1875, for example, is reported to have been issued at 95, but for the other loans no statement of discounts by bankers for commissions and expenses was found. All of these loans have long since been repaid.

The funds obtained from these loans were mainly spent on military and naval expenditure. Of the $57,000,000 (Chinese) borrowed during the period from foreigners, $4,500,000 were spent for navy, $27,900,000 for military and post-bellum expenditure, and $24,200,000 for reorganization. Thus China began her use of external credits for military and administrative rather than for productive purposes.

[3] Only an approximation is possible.
[4] Also by the *China Year Book*, 1912, p. 297. Dr. Lee gives the loan of that year as bearing 8 per cent, and cites a different principal amount.
[5] S. R. Wagel, *Finance in China*, p. 23.

PART I

SECURED LOANS

CHAPTER I

WAR AND INDEMNITY LOANS

The Sino-Japanese War Loans

After a period of no foreign borrowing, 1887 to 1894, China found herself in 1894 forced to obtain funds abroad. The Sino-Japanese War of 1894 and 1895 found China quite unprepared, especially in a financial way, for the prosecution of a war. The treasury contained little and revenues were just about sufficient to cover ordinary administrative expenditures. Attempts to float internal loans, such as the " Merchants Loan of 1894," having failed, China was compelled to seek external credits for the prosecution of the war, as had been done in a smaller way earlier in her history.

With this need the Chinese Government negotiated two loans with the Hongkong and Shanghai Bank, one for 10,000,000 Kuping taels (in £ sterling 1,635,000) and the other for £3,000,000. Though the contracts do not specify the purposes for which the funds were to be used, these two loans have been generally referred to as the " war loans." [1] The repayment of the principal of the first loan was to be accomplished in ten equal annual installments beginning November 1, 1904. In the loan of 1895 the Chinese Government reserved the right to redeem the whole amount at any time at par. Both were redeemed by 1914.

[1] Contracts are in MacMurray, *Treaties and Agreements with and Concerning China*, pp. 11–18; No. 1895/1 and No. 1895/2.

2

The Sino-Japanese War Indemnity and Indemnity Loans

At the conclusion of the Sino-Japanese war, with China defeated by Japan, the Treaty of Shimonoseki, April, 1895, required from China, in addition to the recognition of the independence of Korea and the cession to Japan of the Liaotung Peninsula, an indemnity of 200,000,000 Kuping taels (roughly $150,000,000 in gold); 50,000,000 to be paid within six months, the second installment to be paid within twelve months after exchange of ratifications, and the balance to be paid in six equal annual installments. Interest at 5 per cent per annum on all unpaid portions was to be charged, but if China paid the whole indemnity within three years the interest item was to be waived and included as a part of the principal.[2]

This increased demand on China was sufficient to cause further financial embarrassment, but, in addition 30,000,-000 Kuping taels were added to the indemnity as a price to be paid for the retrocession to China by Japan of the Liaotung Peninsula which had just been ceded to Japan by the treaty. This retrocession came about through the opposition of Russia, France and Germany, to the retention by Japan of this territory so strategically located in relation to Manchuria and Korea. China received it back upon agreeing to the additional indemnity.[3]

The Franco-Russian Gold Loan

This new need upon the part of China for funds gave Russia an opportunity. Fearing that Great Britain would obtain an overwhelmingly strong prestige in the matter of financial control over the Government of China through the contemplated appointment of Sir Robert Hart by the Chi-

[2] MacMurray, p. 18, No. 1895/3.
[3] MacMurray, p. 52, No. 1895/10.

nese Government to take charge of financial arrangements with foreign nationals for the purpose of obtaining foreign loans, and fearing that the British would secure most of these, Russia proposed to make a loan to China. With the assistance of a syndicate of French bankers cooperating with the Russian interests, a loan of 400,000,000 francs was negotiated and signed by China. The French syndicate was composed of six French banks and the Russian of four banks.

The competition among rival foreign interests in serving China in her need for funds is evidenced by several features of this loan agreement. In addition to being secured by the deposit of customs bonds of China—the Maritime Customs revenue—the Imperial Russian Government undertook to guarantee the issue and thus sought to bind China to Russia. In Article IV a part of Russia's purpose is disclosed:

" In consideration of this loan the Chinese Government declares its resolution not to grant to any Foreign Power any right or privilege under any name whatsoever concerning the supervision or administration of any of the revenues of the Chinese Empire. But in case the Chinese Government should grant to anyone Power rights of this character, it is understood that from the mere fact of their being so granted, they should be extended to the Russian Government." [4]

Furthermore, the Chinese Government agreed not to issue any other bonds until January 15, 1896, and to make these bonds tax-exempt in China. The maturity of the loan was set at 1931, a period of 36 years, with redemption by annual drawings out of a sinking fund of 1.288 per cent yearly, plus 4 per cent of total amount of bonds redeemed.

[4] MacMurray, p. 41, No. 1895/7, article IV.

The interest rate was the lowest of any loan up to that time, 4 per cent. The amount of the loan was 400,000,000 francs, or 100,000,000 gold roubles, which equalled £15,820,000. The bonds were to be issued in sterling, francs, marks, florins, and roubles. In July, 1926 £3,719,041 remained outstanding.[5] Of all the bonds now outstanding, these 4 per cent's of 1895 hold priority on the Maritime Customs revenue of China, the most assured income of the Chinese Government.

The Cassel Loan and the Nanking Loan

In the same year, 1895, two other loans, for smaller amounts, each for £1,000,000, were negotiated by China, one with British and the other with German interests, under pressure from these Powers, respectively, when the terms of the Franco-Russian loan became known. The British loan, known as the Cassel loan, was obtained from the Chartered Bank of India. The German loan was concluded with Arnhold, Karberg & Co. and is commonly called the Nanking loan of 1895. Both the Cassel and Nanking loans were secured by the customs revenue, and the Nanking loan had the added security of the Kiangsu *likin*[6] and salt taxes. The repayment of principal was not to begin until after the fifth year had elapsed from the year of issue.

In this respect the terms were more favorable to China than the Franco-Russian loan, which had provided for amortization of principal by annual drawings over the thirty-six years of the period of the loan. These British and German loans were redeemed by the close of the loan

[5] J. R. Baylin in *Foreign Loan Obligations of China*, published by the Chinese Government Bureau of Economic Information, 1925, pp. 6–7, 85.

[6] *Likin* is a tax levied against goods in inland transit.

period. The purposes of these three loans are not mentioned in the loan agreements, nor is it known definitely for what purposes the funds were expended, but they are regarded by all writers as indemnity loans and were probably used largely for this purpose.

In 1895, the largest British and German banking interests in the far East made an agreement for the mutual sharing of all Chinese business which might be obtained by either. German and British cooperation was evidenced by the negotiations of the following year, when in the spring of the year the second installment of the indemnity fell due. This Anglo-German group, composed of the Hongkong and Shanghai Bank and the Deutsche Asiatische Bank, offered to the Chinese Government to provide it with sufficient funds at an interest rate of 5 per cent, but an issue price of 89½. These terms China declared were severe. They seemed to reflect the desire of these interests to take advantage of China's desperate situation. China turned to other financial interests probably hoping for competition to act to reduce the disadvantageous nature of the terms. Other offers were made by other interests, but were all rejected, since none of them proved satisfactory to China. The French Minister at Peking, supported by the Russian Minister there, offered to relieve China, and thus allow her to meet the rapidly approaching payment to Japan, on the condition that the Imperial Customs Service (which was organized under foreign supervision and at the time under the inspector generalship of Sir Robert Hart, British) should be turned over to the French; and further on the condition that France was to receive special privileges in the three southern provinces of Kwangsi, Kwangtung and Yunnan. For all of these concessions the French Government would be willing to guarantee the loan to the Chinese

Government. Such a guarantee would have made the flotation of the loan easier and less costly to China, because the additional security would have caused the bonds sold to command a higher price. The final choice of China was to accept the modified terms of the Anglo-German group. The reduction in terms in favor of China is quite noticeable.

The Anglo-German Loan of 1896

The Anglo-German Loan, often called the 5 Per Cent Sterling Loan of 1896, was concluded for a nominal principal of £16,000,000. It was agreed that "the price of 94 per cent net" was to go to the Chinese Government and such "net proceeds, namely £15,040,000 sterling," were to be held to the order of the Chinese Government in London. This net to China was £720,000 more than would have been received had the first offer of 89½ been accepted. As in almost all former loans definite arrangements for repayment of principal had been stipulated, so here, but with this difference—a sinking fund arrangement was added, whereby through monthly rather than yearly installments paid to the banks a fund was to be available for payment on principal. This was a further safeguard for the investor of the bonds of this issue since the Maritime Customs revenue already had been pledged for five previous loans, and this sinking fund rendered impossible the diversion of the funds during the year to other purposes. The provision for the sinking fund also stipulated that no conversion or redemption could take place other than through the action of the sinking fund, thus limiting redemption. The Chinese Government further agreed not to issue any other loan until six months should have elapsed after the issue of the total amount of the loan.[7] An interesting stipulation,

[7] MacMurray, pp. 55–59, No. 1896/2.

in the light of the attempts of other nations to control the Imperial Maritime Customs, reads as follows: " The administration of the Imperial Maritime Customs of China shall continue as at present constituted during the currency of this loan." This loan matures in 1932.

The Anglo-German Loan of 1898

Further international rivalry was evidenced in the negotiations of 1898 attending the efforts of China to obtain funds to pay off the balance of the Japanese indemnity before the conclusion of the three years stipulated as a condition for waiving the interest on the deferred payments and allowing all interest to that time paid to be counted as a part of the principal sum.[8] Various financial interests offered attractive financial arrangements provided China would grant to the country in question, represented by each of these interests, railway rights, or concessions, or a changed or closer financial control over China, as the particular nation's interest might require. China finally, however, did conclude a loan with the Anglo-German group, but on rather harsh terms, for £16,000,000, bearing 4½ per cent interest, with an issue price to the public of 90, but with the amount available to China at 83 per cent of the principal, in amount £13,280,000.[9] The duration of the loan was set at 45 years, the longest loan period contracted for up to that time, and the principal was to be repaid by annual payments from a sinking fund built up by monthly installments, which with interest made a monthly payment of £69,602–. Unlike the loan of 1895, in which China reserved the right to redeem at any time at par, in this Anglo-German Loan of 1898, it was agreed that " dur-

---

[8] Cf. above, p. 6.

[9] A. W. Ferrin, *Chinese Currency and Finance*, p. 48.

ing the 45 years the amortization shall not be increased nor the loan redeemed or converted by the Chinese Government." [10]

Other clauses in the agreement point out further burdens. " In reimbursement of expenses incurred in connection with the distribution of the service to Bondholders of the principal and interest of the loan, the Banks shall receive from the Chinese Imperial Government a commission of a quarter per cent on the annual loan service, say an amount of £2,088–." [11] This amount of ¼ per cent on the annual loan service through the 45 years of the loan, will amount to over £114,000, which is in addition to the original discount on the nominal principal. Furthermore, these payments were to be made at the Chinese offices of the banks in Shanghai sycee to meet payment in sterling in Europe, the rate of exchange to be agreed upon on the same day with the two banks. This is mentioned because it brings out one of the factors in the problem of the cost to China not only of this loan but of all of her foreign loans. With China paying in silver and the price of silver in the London market accepted as the basis for exchange rates, it is evident that a decline in the price of silver in London would bring an increasing cost of obtaining sterling exchange, and thus increase the real cost to the Chinese Government, whose currency is on a silver basis, and whose funds with which to pay would be available in silver.

The loss to China on this financial operation was real. The interest waived on the indemnity amount to 10,000,000 taels. The interest on the loan, however, which made redemption of the indemnity possible, was 21,500,000 taels, during just the first five years. In addition the low yield

[10] MacMurray, pp. 107–112, No. 1898/3, Clause 3.
[11] Clause 4 of the agreement. MacMurray, p. 108, No. 1898/3.

of 83 meant a further loss of about 10,000,000 taels, and the annual service charge of $\frac{1}{4}$ per cent, as well as the losses due to fluctuations of exchange rates, brought still further losses.[12]

The security given on this loan of 1898 was the Maritime Customs revenue, and certain salt revenues, as well as the likin receipts of certain ports of the Yangtze and Chekiang. These latter revenues were to be placed under the control of the Inspector General of Maritime Customs. The Maritime Customs were already serving as security for six previous issues of Chinese Imperial Government bonds. It was further agreed that in case the security pledged at any time should become insufficient, further revenue sufficient to complete the required amount should be forthwith placed under the Inspector General. Further, it was agreed that if China should enter negotiations for revision of the customs tariff accompanied by a decrease or abolition of likin, such revision should not be barred because likin was pledged for this loan, but the bank's agreement must be obtained for any downward change in the likin dues pledged on this loan. As in the Anglo-German loan of 1896, so here, the administration of the Maritime Customs was not to be changed during the currency of the loan. Since China could not redeem this loan before 1943 foreign control of the customs revenue was thus further imposed. Definite statement of the purpose of the loan is in the agreement, China promising to pay off the entire indemnity out of the proceeds.

Summary

The loans discussed thus far in this chapter make up a second period in the loan history of the Chinese Govern-

12 Cf. F. H. Huang, *Public Debts of China*, p. 24.

ment, a period in which foreign loans were contracted for unproductive purposes. No material income-yielding assets could China claim from the use of these funds. By this time the Chinese Government had obligated itself for funds received from foreign loans for war and indemnity purposes, and mainly for the Sino-Japanese War and its consequences in indemnity, to the amount of £54,455,000. This total of war loans was $561,080,000.[13] Three of these loans, namely, the Franco-Russian of 1895, and the Anglo-German loans of 1896 and 1898, had certain amounts outstanding on the dates given as follows:[14]

Franco-Russian Loan, maturity 1931, July, 1926 . £3,719,041
Anglo-German, 1896, maturity 1932, April, 1926 . 4,907,950
Anglo-German, 1898, maturity 1943, March, 1926 . 9,778,225

making a total of £18,405,216 of the loans growing out of the war with Japan in 1894 and 1895 yet unpaid. These loans have always been regularly met in the past and will probably always be met until maturity since they constitute first charges on the Maritime Customs revenues, the foremost of the Chinese Government's resources. The amortization installments and interest added together for 1926 were as follows:

Franco-Russian Loan of 1895 .... £   833,670
Anglo-German Loan of 1896   949,778
Anglo-German Loan of 1898   826,730
                                              _____
Total £2,610,178

There is little likelihood that the Maritime Customs collections, which continue today (1927) under foreign admin-

[13] Chia Sze-Yi, *Financial History of the Republic*, Part IV, ch. 2, sec. a, pp. 1069–76. Translated for me by a Chinese student at the University of Pennsylvania.
[14] J. R. Baylin, *op. cit.*, pp. 7, 9, 11, and 85.

istration, and which in 1925 totalled 70,725,600 Haikwan taels (or at 5½ taels to the £ sterling, £ 12,859,200) would fail to be sufficient to provide for these obligations.

The Boxer Indemnity

At the close of the Boxer War an indemnity was imposed upon China by the Powers. This indemnity added a very heavy financial burden to the Chinese Empire, creating what is probably the greatest external debt in history which is not the result of borrowing or foreign wars. The Boxer uprising of 1900 was internal warfare against the foreigners in China. Japanese, Russian, British, American, French and German troops landed and fighting their way inland captured Peking. Then China had to agree, 1901, not only to respect certain privileges of foreigners in China, but also to pay an indemnity of 450,000,000 Haikwan taels or £ 67,500,000 (at 6.66 taels = 1 £) (about $325,000,-000G). It was arranged as if a loan of that amount had been made, with interest on the unpaid amounts, to be charged at 4 per cent per annum. The fractional bonds of the total amount were divided into five series, all to run for 39 years, until 1940: [15]

A	£ 11,250,000,	repayment beginning	1902
B	£ 9,000,000,	"	"	1911
C	£ 22,500,000,	"	"	1915
D	£ 7,500,000,	"	"	1916
E	£ 17,250,000,	"	"	1932

Thus amortization of principal was to run from 1902 to 1940, in an increasing scale of annual payments, so that, with interest, the total amount of the indemnity paid by 1940 would have amounted to 982,238,150 Haikwan taels

[15] *China Year Book*, 1913, p. 333.

(or £ 147,335,722, which is a little over $717,000,000 gold), nearly a billion taels.

The apportionment of the indemnity among the several powers was declared in the Protocol of June 14, 1902, to be as follows: [16]

Russia	130,371,120 Taels
Germany	90,070,515
France	70,878,240
Great Britain	50,620,545
Japan	34,793,100
United States	32,939,055
Italy	26,617,005
Belgium	8,484,345
Austria-Hungary	4,003,920
Other nations, including the Netherlands, Spain, Norway, Sweden, and International Claims	1,222,155
	450,000,000 Taels

It is well known that the United States in 1908 remitted a substantial portion of the American share in the indemnity, the portion which had not been required to meet claims presented, thus reducing China's obligations by some $11,961,121.76 (gold). These funds were applied by China to the founding and endowing of Tsing Hua College at Peking, where students are prepared for entrance to American universities. The balance of the American indemnity amounting to $6,137,553 (gold) has since been remitted. In May, 1924, Congress decided that these funds should be applied to educational and cultural activities as decided by a Board of Trustees composed of 10 Chinese and 5 Americans.

The indemnity was secured on the balance of the Im-

[16] Table arranged from a table in MacMurray, p. 311, No. 1901/3, note 3.

perial Maritime Customs revenues, above that used for previous loans; also on the revenues of the native customs, administered by the Imperial Maritime Customs in the open ports, and on the revenues of the salt tax, excluding that portion pledged for previous foreign loans.

In the treaty it was stated that " capital and interest shall be payable in gold or at the rates of exchange corresponding to the dates at which the different payments fall due," and a commission of bankers appointed by the Powers was to receive such payments in Shanghai.[17]

The price of silver had steadily declined since 1880 and it continued to decline after 1900. In 1901 at the time of the Boxer Protocol 1 £ = 6.66 taels while in 1903 it had a value of 7.5 taels at the time to make payment. Since the customs revenue which was pledged and in fact all of China's resources were receivable in silver it meant an increasing burden on China. It was a matter of dispute as to whether the indemnity was a gold debt or a silver debt. The United States, it appears, " always understood it to be the meaning of the agreement that the indemnity was payable in silver." [18] But not all Powers agreed to this view.

By 1905, accordingly, it was necessary to make a " more definitive arrangement respecting both the liquidation of the arrears and the payments to be made in the future." The Powers undertook to " extinguish by a lump sum of 8,000,000 taels the whole of the debt incurred by China towards all of the Powers collectively on account of the payment in silver during the years up to January 1, 1905." [19] It was further set forth that China was to make

[17] MacMurray, p. 281, No. 1901/3.

[18] Mr. Hay to Mr. Conger, July, 1902, *Foreign Relations*, 1904, p. 184.

[19] MacMurray, pp. 319–20, No. 1901/3, Note 6.

the future payments in one of three ways as each Power should choose, either in silver, at the London market price, or in gold bills, or in telegraphic transfers.

To adjust the exchange on the indemnity as just mentioned, amounting to 8,000,000 taels, China negotiated a loan of £1,000,000 with the Hongkong and Shanghai Banking Corporation and the Deutsche Asiatische Bank, the Anglo-German group, with interest at 5 per cent, price of issue 97, to run for twenty years, with the Peking Octroi and the Shansi likin taxes pledged as security.[20]   This loan was redeemed in 1915, and was the only loan floated to pay the Boxer Indemnity.

In the period of the Revolution the indemnity payment became in arrears, so that by December 31, 1912, the arrears were estimated at about £2,000,000.[21]

At the time of the entrance of China into the war in 1917, the agreement of the Powers was obtained to the " principle of postponement, without interest, of the annual installments of the 1901 indemnity during the period of five years," but Russia pointed out that her share in the indemnity was the greatest, being 28.9 per cent.   She therefore consented to the postponement of only approximately one third of the indemnity due to her.   The other nations, parties to this agreement, were Belgium, France, Great Britain, Italy, Japan and Portugal.   In the same collective note of September 8, 1917, setting forth these conditions, it was further stated that " the German and Austro-Hungarians must not benefit from any payment on account of the indemnities of 1901, the treaty of 1901 be-

---

[20] *China Year Book*, 1913, p. 333, and *Foreign Relations*, 1904, p. 177, *et seq., Ibid.*, 1905, p. 145, *et seq.*

[21] *China Year Book*, 1914, p. 397.

ing, as regards the Central Empires, forever abrogated as to this point." [22]

In September, 1922, at the close of the five year period, the amount outstanding on the Boxer indemnities was £ 72,-031,432.[23] Had they not been postponed and regular payments made the amount outstanding probably would have been less than £ 60,000,000. But other developments have lowered them. To be sure, in this figure of £ 72 million, was included none of the German portion of the indemnity or the Austrian. These were definitely cancelled by the Treaties of Versailles and St. Germain, respectively. But there are included in this figure British, Japanese, Russian, American and French portions, which have either been remitted or substantially changed.

In April, 1923, the Japanese Government decided to set aside a sum of 2,500,000 yen annually from its portion of the indemnity and from the purchase price of the Shantung Railway and properties in Tsingtao, for the promotion of education, art, sanitation, charity and culture, generally, in China or among Chinese in Japanese territory, all to be controlled by a bureau of the Japanese Foreign Office.[24]

The Japanese portion, annually, now would be about 1,886,000 taels (7.732 per cent of the annual charge of 24,483,800 taels), or at the pro forma rate of conversion of 1.407 per tael, about 2,650,000 yen. Hence, the Japanese portion is now virtually remitted, though after 1937 when the annual amount due on the indemnity will be 35,-350,150 taels, the Japanese portion will be larger than the amount to be devoted to cultural interests.[25]

[22] MacMurray, pp. 1375–6, No. 1917/7, note.
[23] *China Year Book*, 1925, p. 735.
[24] *China Year Book*, 1925, p. 770.
[25] Cf. Amortization Tables in Baylin, *op. cit.*, p. 3.

Of May 31, 1924, the Sino-Russian agreement contains the declaration of Russia renouncing the Russian portion of the indemnity, which, after all prior obligations secured upon it are satisfied,[26] shall be spent by a Commission of three, two appointed by the Republic of China, and one by the Union of Soviet Socialist Republics, the commission acting by a majority vote and the funds to be used for instruction and promotion of culture.

In March, 1925, following out a declaration of intent of December, 1922, Great Britain decided to apply the British share of the Boxer Indemnity from December, 1922, on, to educational or other purposes mutually beneficial to Great Britain and China.   An Advisory Committee of eleven, two of them Chinese citizens, will act with the Secretary for Foreign Affairs.[27]

The French Government exchanged notes with the Chinese Government in 1922 and 1923, agreeing that the French portion of the indemnity should be used to strengthen the Banque Industrielle de Chine, and for Franco-Chinese activities of a public and charitable nature. The Gold Franc controversy,[28] over whether the indemnity payment should be made in telegraphic transfers at the prevailing rate of exchange for francs, or whether the agreement called for an amount in gold, developed, and this agreement in regard to the use of the indemnity was delayed.   The settlement of the controversy on April 12, 1925, indicates that the payments, from 1922 to 1924, are to be released to China, and that the total time of payment

[26] The deferred Russian indemnity is security for four Chinese Government internal loans. The Russian indemnity, which would have been paid had not recognition of Russia been withdrawn, is security for $6,000,000 in issues of Treasury Notes and Bills of China.

[27] *China Year Book*, 1925, p. 769.

[28] Cf. *China Year Book*, 1924.

will be extended two years, i.e., 1945 to 1947. The debt of the Chinese Government to the Banque Industrielle de Chine is extinguished and the bank will receive 5 per cent gold-dollar obligations of the Chinese Government based on the Boxer indemnity and continue as a first charge on the Maritime Customs revenue. These gold-dollar obligations amount to about $43,893,000 (gold), and thus China's unsecured debt is reduced by the amount of debts owed to the Banque Industrielle, and her secured debt is not increased. More than this amount may be necessary to repay Far Eastern creditors of that bank. After this, the balance of any indemnity payments are to be used, as noted above. The Chinese Government in addition receives 10,000,000 francs in paid-up shares of the Société de Gérance, a French holding company, acting for the Banque Industrielle in its rehabilitation. The Société for its second year showed profits of 12,835,640 francs.[29] As security for advances made to the Banque Industrielle the Chinese Government is to receive the " Repartition Bonds " allotted to the creditors of the bank as evidence of their respective claims.[30]

Summary

The exact amount of the Japanese remission not appearing from the above, it cannot be stated exactly what these remissions total. But recalling that the entire American indemnity, the British indemnity from 1922 on, the balance of the Russian indemnity, a very large portion of the Japanese indemnity, and the balance of the French indemnity, have been remitted under certain conditions, as well as that the German and Austrian portions no longer stand, it ap-

[29] E. E. Groseclose in *Commerce Reports* No. 20, May 18, 1925, p. 390.

[30] J. R. Baylin, *op. cit.*, p. 5.

3

pears that the requirements of China in the way of gold exchange needed to defray these secured debts will be greatly reduced. Probably a large portion of each of these will be spent in China. The French settlement, how-- ever, makes a demand, as mentioned, for gold dollars, to the amount of 43 million, plus interest at 5 per cent. The Russian settlement requires the liquidation of certain internal obligations. If one deducts from the 1922 figure, given above, of £72,031,432, the remissions of American, Great Britain, Russia, one-half of the Japanese (to choose a conservative figure), and on the part of France to the amount of about £10,000,000, one has left a figure of between £25,000,000 and £26,000,000. In Table A, to be conservative, only the Russian portion has been deducted to show outstanding debt of the Chinese Government, namely, an estimate of £40,000,000.

But disregarding for the moment the question of the amount of the principal sum outstanding, the more significant question is the amount of the annual burden upon the government of China in obtaining, first, the revenue and, second, the gold credits abroad. According to the original Table of Amortization the annual charge for 1926 was to be 24,483,800 taels. The German and Austrian shares of 20.01 per cent and .89 per cent respectively, totalling 20.9 per cent were cancelled by the entrance of China into the War. The Russian portion of 28.9 per cent is cancelled as noted making 50 per cent outright cancelled. Thus the annual burden of the indemnity is only 12,241,900 taels. The portion of the indemnity which was owing to Russia is security for internal loans and treasury bills. Much of the other remissions probably will be spent in China. Even the French portions, though now represented by gold dollar obligations, will probably be spent in China in some measure. However, assume that all of the remissions, other than the French, will be spent by the various designated agencies on work in China according to the following table of their respective portions of the indemnity:

	Per Cent
American	7.31
British	11.24
Japanese	7.73
	26.28

Twenty six and a quarter per cent of the original annual charge is 4,407,000 which deducted from 12,241,900 taels leaves 7,834,900 taels. A conservative estimate would then be that, though the Government of China may continue to turn over to foreign agencies over 12 million taels annually, less than two thirds of that amount will act in the immediate future as do payments on the other gold debts of the government in the international balance of accounts with China.

The fiscal problem of paying the indemnity remains, but the problem of foreign payment through the channels of international trade has probably been greatly lessened, and is thus of significance to China in the problem of her capacity to pay other foreign public debts.

The Arnhold Karberg Loans

The period of the Revolution in 1912 found the Republic of China in great need of funds for military purposes, as well as for constructive economic and even administrative purposes. While negotiations were going on in 1912 with certain foreign financial interests China secured secretly certain loans from other sources. Of these other loans, those for military purposes probably included some, if not all, of the Arnhold-Karberg and Company loans. Altogether during the years 1912 to 1914 inclusive, the Chinese Government concluded six loans through this firm and certain Austrian banks, for a total sum of £ 4,750,000.[31]

With respect to two of them, those of 1914 for £ 2,000,-000 and £ 1,200,000, the agreements were in consideration of the purchase of twelve torpedo boats and six torpedo-boat destroyers, to be built in Austrian dockyards. The former at £ 66,150 apiece and the latter at £ 145,057 apiece would make only £ 1,664,000. How much of the total amount of the loans was actually available to China is not known. They were not well secured. They were to run for short periods, for four and five year periods, with one for ten years. For the first two the Peking Octroi was pledged as security, while for the three of 1914 the transfer of title deeds tax, a stamp tax, was pledged. The loan of £ 300,000 of 1913 was backed only by Treasury notes. These loans demonstrate the results of international rivalry in supplying funds to a weak government, where other than strictly financial considerations are involved. The pressure of financial necessity was also proving itself too strong in the early days of the Republic.[32]   It seems certain that much of these Arnhold-Karberg Loans went for military purposes.[33]

In 1916 an extension loan of £ 1,233,000, bearing 8 per cent interest, was made necessary to cover the December,

[31] MacMurray, pp. 1004, 1007, No. 1913/4. Also Chia Sze-Yi, *op. cit.*, II, 1099.

[32] Further reference to this same period will be made in the chapter on Administrative Loans.

[33] W. W. Willoughby classifies them under General and Administrative Loans, where indeed they could be placed. In fact, considering the weak nature of the security, it is doubtful whether to consider them under secured or unsecured loans.

1915 installment on the three loans contracted in 1914. By 1916 £ 430,000,000 had been paid on the three loans contracted in 1912 and 1913.[34] Since 1916 no payments have been made because of the interruption of the war, and though subsequently agreements have been negotiated for their repayment, they have not been put into effect (1925). The amount outstanding on the six loans and the renewal loan, on September 1, 1922, was approximately £ 4,266,-314.[35]

Summary

In this chapter fifteen secured loans to the Chinese Government for war, indemnity or military purposes, have been considered. Of these, the three loans of 1895, 1896, and 1898 were outstanding in 1926 to an amount of £ 18,-405,216, and the Arnhold-Karberg loans and the Austrian loans to an amount at least of £ 4,266,314. The status of the Boxer indemnity has been summarized.

Ten of these loans bore 6 per cent, one 7 per cent, three 5 per cent, one 4½ per cent, and one 4 per cent. The average discount below par at which the bankers received the bonds from the Chinese Government was 7 per cent. Calculating each loan, however, at its own price as stipulated to the bankers,[36] one discovers that out of £ 61,438,-000 which China had borrowed in principal sum and was obligated to repay, £ 55,778,335 were received by China and available for expenditure. This is a discount of 9.3 per cent (i.e. 90.7 per cent of the amount to be repaid),

[34] A. W. Ferrin, *op. cit.*, p. 48.

[35] F. E. Lee, *op. cit.*, p. 189, and *China Year Book*, 1925, p. 737. Baylin, *op. cit.*, gives £ 5,200,000. No explanation is given of this figure.

[36] And taking an arbitrary discount of 4 per cent on the loan of 1894 and 5 per cent on the loan of 1905, since "price to bankers" not known.

which represents what China had to pay the banks for underwriting her bonds of this classification. This is conservative. Many of the agreements do not stipulate whether expenses of flotation were to be borne by the banks or by China; most do not specify who was to bear the expenses of the annual service of interest payments to the bondholders, and amortization payments for redemption or sinking fund. The former when borne by China would diminish the original amount available, the latter when borne by China would increase the annual interest burden.

Some of these loans may have been ill-advised. The Anglo-German loan of 1898, as pointed out, was costly, and part of the burden remains. The Cassel and Nanking loans, as some have said, were forced by Great Britain and were not needed. Certainly the war with Japan and the Boxer strife were costly to China financially, largely because of the indemnities which were imposed.

Title	Interest Rate	Date	Maturity	Price to Public	Price to Bankers	Original Principal	Original Principal in £ Sterling
1. Chinese Imperial Government.......	7	1894	1914	98		10,000,000 taels	1,635,000
2. Chinese Imperial Government......	6	1895	1914	96½	92		3,000,000
3. Chinese Imperial Government (Franco-Russian Loan)..........	4	1895	1931	{ 99.2 { 99.8	94¼	400,000,000 francs	15,820,000
4. Chinese Imperial Government (Cassel Loan)......................	6	1895	1915	106	95½		1,000,000
5. Chinese Imperial Government (Nanking Loan)..................	6	1895	1915	{ 104.5 { 99	96		1,000,000
6. Chinese Imperial Government (Anglo-German Loan)................	5	1896	1932	{ 98⅞ { 99	94		16,000,000
7. Chinese Imperial Government (Anglo-German Loan)................	4½	1898	1943	90	83		16,000,000
8. Chinese Imperial Government (Exchange Adjustment Loan)........	5	1905	1915	97			1,000,000
9. First Arnhold Karberg Loan.......	6	1912	1916		95		300,000
10. Second Arnhold Karberg Loan......	6	1912	1921		95		450,000
11. Third Arnhold Karberg Loan.......	6	1913	1917		95		300,000
12. First Austrian Loan...............	6	1913	1917		92		1,200,000
13. Second Austrian Loan.............	6	1913	1917		92		2,000,000
14. Fourth Austrian Loan.............	6	1913	1917		92		500,000
15. Austrian Loans Extension Loan.....	8	1916	1920		92		1,233,000
16. Austrian Loans Interest Deferred....	9	1916	1917		92		66,314
TOTAL—Original Principal of Loan Obligations Signed.............							61,504,314 66,314
TOTAL—Original Principal of Loans Nos. 1–15, Exclusive of No. 16....							61,438,000
TOTAL—Amount Available to Chinese Government Nos. 1–15, Exclusive of No. 16.............							
17. The Boxer Indemnities.............	4	1901	1945–47			450,000,900 taels	
TOTAL—War, Military and Indemnity Foreign Secured Debt........							

¹ Arbitrarily taking 4 per cent as commission to bankers, since not definitely known.
² Arbitrarily taking 5 per cent as commission to bankers, since not definitely known.
³ J. R. Baylin in "Foreign Loan Obligations of China," p. 22, gives £ 5,983,000 outstanding on all these obligations. F

Amount Available to Chinese Gov.	Outstanding	Date	Outstanding in £ Sterling	Security	Remarks
1,536,900 [1]	Repaid	1914		Maritime Customs	Hongkong and Shanghai Bank
2,760,000	Repaid	1914		Maritime Customs	Hongkong and Shanghai Bank
14,890,575	3,719,041	July, 1926	3,719,041	{ Guarantee of Russian Government and Maritime Customs	
955,000	Repaid			Maritime Customs	Chartered Bank of India
960,000	Repaid			Maritime Customs and Kiangsu likin and Salt taxes	Arnhold Karberg & Co.
5,040,000	4,907,950	April, 1926	4,907,950	Maritime Customs	Hongkong and Shanghai Bank and Deutsche Asiatische Bank
3,280,000	9,778,225	March, 1926	9,778,225	Maritime Customs and certain Salt and likin taxes	½%—on annual debt service
920,000 [2]	Repaid	1915		Peking Octroi and Shansi likins	{ Hongkong and Shanghai Bank and Deutsche Asiatische Bank
285,000 ⎫				{ Peking Octroi	
427,500 ⎪				{ Peking Octroi	
285,000 ⎪					
1,004,000 ⎬	4,266,314	Sept., 1922	4,266,314	{ Title, deeds, tax and Treasury notes	{ Agreement made in 1922 for repayment not yet in effect due to subsequent disagreement [3]
1,840,000 ⎪					
460,000 ⎪					
1,134,360 ⎭					
5,778,335			22,671,530		
5,778,335	or 90.7%			Maritime Customs and Salt Revenues	
	£ 72,031,432 as of Sept., 1922 Estimated 1926		40,000,000		
			62,671,530		

m F. E. Lee, op. cit.

CHAPTER II

RAILWAY LOANS

A treatment of the foreign loans contracted by the Chinese Government for railway construction, or to finance government-owned railways cannot review the entire history of railway development in China by either private Chinese firms or foreign enterprise or cover in detail the struggle for concessions principally in the period immediately following the Sino-Japanese War. It may be stated, however, that so active was the scramble for concessions that by 1899 preliminary contracts totalling 6420 miles of railway had been signed by China with foreign companies as follows:[1]

England	2,800
Russia	1,530
Germany	720
Belgium	650
France	420
United States	300

In this calculation half interests are given on half the estimated mileage of the line. Some of these concessions replaced rights once granted by provincial or national authorities to Chinese companies. Not all of these have involved the financial liability of the Chinese Government, although most of them have.

Over forty secured foreign loans have been made since 1897 on Chinese Government railways, in reference to

[1] Cf. *Correspondence re Affairs in China*, 1899, CIX, No. 1, pp. 344-7.

some seventeen or more railway projects, which in principal total £ 61,000,000, as shown by rates of conversion
adopted in Table B, or roughly $300,000,000 (gold).

It is impossible to summarize all the financial details of
these loans in a general statement. Table B presents data
on each loan. Mention should, however, be made of the
differing provisions for " control " occurring in the various
contracts for railway loans.

The first two foreign loans floated were for the Lukow-
kiao-Hankow project and for the Imperial Railways of
North China. The former loan for 16,500,000 francs
was obtained through the Société de Chemins de Fer en
Chine, a Belgian company, and the latter loan for £ 2,300,-
000 from the British and Chinese Corporation, a syndicate
composed of the Hongkong and Shanghai Bank and Jardine, Matheson and Company.

The provisions of the contract for the latter loan in
regard to control by the financial and construction agencies
are typical of the earlier loans made to the Chinese Government for railway construction.[2]   These included a guarantee by the Chinese Government, a first charge on the
railway and new lines constructed, a promise of non-
alienation by China until the term of the loan ended, a
provision that foreign capital for further construction of
branch lines or extensions, if needed, was to be sought for
through the corporation holding the concession, and a provision that a British Chief Engineer, a European chief
accountant, and a railway staff composed principally of
capable and experienced Europeans were to be appointed
by the administrator general of the railway.

After the Boxer difficulty, a supplementary contract was
concluded in regard to the management of the road.[3]   By

[2] MacMurray, p. 173, No. 1898/20.
[3] C. C. Wang, *Railway Loan Agreements*, p. 123.

this agreement there was to be a Chinese managing director, a foreign director, a British general manager, and a representative of the British bank interested, all of which officials were to constitute a board of directors, which it will be seen was apparently under Chinese administration but actually under British control.

The contract [4] with the Belgian construction company provided for company control of operations. During the period of the loan the Société was to operate the line and receive 20 per cent of the net profits and was to fix rates and control purchases. The ownership remained nominally in the Chinese Government.

The loan on the Belgian line was for 20 years, the loan on the British line was for 45 years. In the former case repayment was to commence in 1909 with regular annual installments, the Chinese Government having the right to pay off the contract at any time after 1907 and cancel the contract, an option of which the Chinese Government later took advantage. In the latter contract repayment was to be in 40 annual installments after the fifth year of issue.

In 1902 a final agreement was signed for a loan of 40,-000,000 francs from the Russo-Asiatic Bank acting for a Franco-Russian syndicate composed of the Comptoir National d'Escompte, the Société General, the Russo-Asiatic Bank and others. The proposed railway was to run from Chengting to Taiyuanfu. Into this contract similar provisions for security and control were placed as in the former loans mentioned. The general revenues of the government, a first mortgage on the entire railway property, the net revenues of the line, together with the operating contract with the bank, whereby the latter would receive 20 per cent of the net profits of the railway were stipulated

---

[4] MacMurray, pp. 145–52, No. 1898/13, notes I and II.

as security. The chief engineer was to be appointed by the Chinese director-general upon recommendation of the bank. China reserved the right to pay off the loan after 1911 and cancel the agreement.[5]

Arrangements to float a loan for £ 3,250,000 in connection with a contract held by the British and Chinese Corporation for the construction of a railway from Shanghai to Nanking were not completed until 1903, although the preliminary agreement had been signed in 1898.[6] In this loan agreement certain new and interesting provisions were incorporated. The loan was not to be amortized, but was to fall due in full in fifty years, i.e. 1953. The Chinese Government after 12 years might redeem the bonds in whole or in part at 102½ or at par after 25 years. The administration of both construction and operation was placed in a board of commissioners, appointed by the director-general, composed of two Chinese members, a British chief engineer and two other British members, selected by the corporation. There was to be a British chief accountant. In the earlier contract for the North China railway provision had been made for but one Chinese official, while this agreement called for two. Actually, however, the project was under British control. In addition to the usual 20 per cent corporation share of the profits a 5 per cent commission of the cost of all materials purchased was to go to the corporation as purchasing agent. Of the principal sum stipulated only £ 2,900,000, £ 2,250,000 in 1904 and £ 650,000 in 1907 were borrowed. The Chinese Government later did not allow the balance of the loan to be floated, ordering any further outlays to come from the National Treasury.

[5] MacMurray, p. 357, No. 1902/8.
[6] MacMurray, p. 387, No. 1903/2.

In 1907 the final loan contract for the Canton-Kowloon railway, an 1898 concession was signed with the British and Chinese Corporation for £1,500,000. Repayment was to be accomplished in the last 17½ years of the 30 year loan period, with the right of redemption at 102½, after 12½ years and up to 25 years, and at par thereafter, reserved by China.[7] No percentage commission on materials purchased was to go to the corporation but rather a lump sum of £35,000 for supervision of construction was to go to the company. The corporation was also to receive £1000 for acting as trustee for the bondholders and for handling all debt services.

At first the British company desired the terms of the Shanghai-Nanking contract, but these were modified to permit the Chinese director-general to participate in the supervision of the funds for construction, and a head office under the control of a Chinese director, with whom the British chief engineer and British chief accountant were to be associated, was substituted for the board of commissioners provided in the Shanghai-Nanking terms. This modification, as well as the lump commission, and other features of the contract, indicate greater leniency looking toward larger Chinese participation in control.

The Shanghai-Hangchow-Ningpoo railway agreement concluded the following year for £1,500,000 also provides for the £35,000 lump commission for acting as purchasing agent, though the Chinese director had the right to use other purchasing agents provided the commission was paid to the contracting company.[8] The Shanghai-Hangchow road has an interesting history.

The concession had been obtained in 1898 by the British

7 MacMurray, p. 615, No. 1907/2.
8 MacMurray, p. 702, No. 1908/3.

and Chinese Corporation but up to 1903 no appreciable arrangements had been made. The concession was cancellable, according to the preliminary agreement. The company being informed of the intent of the Chinese Government to cancel the agreement and no reply being received in 1905 an Imperial Edict transferred the rights to a provincial company which organized two companies to build the road. The British corporation protested and after diplomatic pressure the Chinese Government acceded to the flotation of a loan for £ 1,500,000 through the British Corporation. A compromise was effected whereby the construction and control of the railroad was to be entirely in the Chinese Government. The latter left the construction with the Chinese companies. There was, however, to be a British chief engineer.

Interestingly enough, the security pledged was not the railway in question but the surplus revenues of the Imperial Railways of North China, which, it will be recalled, were under the virtual control of the same British corporation. Considering the factors of control, security and attendant rights this loan was more favorable to China than most that had been negotiated up to that time, if indeed the fact that the loan was negotiated under pressure can be overlooked. A large measure of the loan funds was not used until 1913 when together with further British funds it was used to buy out the Chinese companies, which had used much Chinese capital and some Japanese capital in construction. Upon this occasion the British obtained further privileges.[9]

There was, then, a gradual reduction in the severity of the terms of railway loans to the Chinese Government, in the years just prior to 1910. In 1909, however, the

9 MacMurray, p. 713, No. 1908/3, note.

further construction necessary to the portion of the Peking-Mukden line from Hsinmingtung to Mukden, which had been originally built by Japan, was financed through the South Manchuria railway, which was owned in part by the Japanese Government. The loan amounted to only 320,000 yen but was to run for 18 years and could not be repaid in full until this period expired. This loan was not offered to the public.[10]

The use of the surplus revenues of railways already constructed as security for loans for other railway projects as was done in the Shanghai-Hangchow railway, the use of other government revenues as security and the policy of redeeming existing indebtedness where possible, indicated a desire on the part of the Chinese Government to own outright and control as much of the railway mileage of China as possible.

In 1908 the Peking-Hankow railway was redeemed from the Belgian company with a £5,000,000 loan obtained by an Anglo-French obligation on the security of certain salt revenues and consumption taxes of Chekiang, Chihli, Kiangsu, and Hupeh provinces.[11] Even before the railway became an unimpaired asset of the Chinese Government an unsecured loan was floated for $10,000,000 (Chinese) in 7 per cent bonds of the Chinese Government with an inducement offered to the bondholders in the form of a promise of limited participation in the profits of the road.[12] In 1905, the Canton-Hankow railway project, which had originally been begun by an American concern but which had fallen into Belgian hands, had been redeemed by a loan from the government of Hongkong for £1,100,000, with

[10] MacMurray, p. 767, No. 1908/18, and p. 782, No. 1909/6.

[11] MacMurray, p. 747, No. 1908/12.

[12] Although a silver loan, the majority of these were sold to banks in foreign countries.

the opium revenues of the provinces of Hupeh, Hunan and Kwangtung pledged as security.[13]

The terms of the Tientsin-Pukow railway loan contract have been considered as the most favorable ever conceded to China. The final agreement was signed in 1908,[14] after several years of delay and fruitless negotiation. Disagreement between the German and British interests, which held the concession jointly, was largely responsible for the leniency in terms, Germany being willing to grant more liberal terms than were stated in the preliminary agreement of 1898.[15]

The railway property was not pledged as security, but instead, in addition to the revenues of the railway, a number of provincial revenues of Kiangsu, Chihli, Shantung and Anhwei were hypothecated. Construction and operation were to be in the hands of the Chinese Government, with German and British chief engineers and an auditor appointed acceptable to the syndicate. After completion of construction a European chief engineer was to be selected. Disposal of the loan funds was in the hands of the Chinese director general. Thus the Tientsin-Pukow loan contract was considered a victory for China. The share of profits to the bankers was redeemed, joint management had been abandoned in principle, the control of funds was in Chinese hands, and no mortgage had been given.[16]

Out of the prolonged negotiations for the Hukuang railways, comprising the completion of the Canton-Hankow line and the construction of the projected Hankow-Szech-

---

[13] C. C. Wang, *Railway Loan Agreements*, p. 537.

[14] MacMurray, p. 684, No. 1908/1.

[15] MacMurray, p. 694, in re No. 1908/1.

[16] Though the German portion of this debt was declared forfeited by China at the close of the war the debt is still owing to the bondholders.

uan railway, developed the first Consortium of foreign banking interests for finance in China, between the financial groups of Great Britain, France, Germany and the United States. The United States, through diplomatic efforts of President Taft and Secretary of State Knox obtained from the other three powers permission for American participation in this loan.[17]

On May 24, 1910, the British, German and French banking groups had invited the American group to enter into the quadruple understanding regarding loans to China, the agreement for which was signed November 10, 1910. The Hukuang " Four-Power " loan final contract was signed May 20, 1911, for £6,000,000. Earlier the British had held out for the more severe terms of " control " as in the Canton-Kowloon contract, but the Germans had evidenced a willingness to proceed on the basis of the Tientsin-Pukow terms,—more favorable to China. Provisions substantially similar to the Tientsin-Pukow contract were incorporated in the loan agreement with the four powers.[18] The construction and control of the railway were to be vested entirely in the Chinese Government, but auditors might be appointed by the banks. Certain foreign chief engineers were to be chosen, each to be related to a section of the proposed road. The section of the project to be supervised by each foreign nation occasioned considerable negotiation which proved irritating to China. A five per cent commission to the banks on materials purchased was incorporated in the loan terms. The security given was certain revenues of the provinces of Hupeh and Hunan, but as the Revolution in China intervened before the issuance of the bonds was consummated

[17] Cf. *U. S. Foreign Relations*, 1909, Vol. 5704, p. 152 ff.
[18] Cf. MacMurray, p. 866, No. 1911/5.

and since the governmental machinery for tax collection was in part disrupted a provisional guarantee of the unimpairment of the revenues pledged was made in the form of the railway property. Also certain other foreign officials were to be appointed, to be controlled by China.[19]

A further study of the use of the Hukuang funds by China is interesting. The Hukuang loan of 1911 at a yield of 95 had netted China £5,700,000 or, at a rate of exchange of 11, $62,700,000 (silver). By June 30, 1921, the total of unused loan funds was $2,780,644 (silver), most of which was in the form of a balance with the Deutsche-Asiatische Bank.[20] The amount paid out of the Hukuang loan funds for the creditors of the Szechuan Railway Company was 934,030 taels or $1,401,046 (silver). The balance due to the old shareholders of the company was 4,564,518 taels or $6,846,777 (silver). This balance was payable by the Chinese government.

The Hupeh-Hunan section was credited originally with $54,145,273 (silver), and subsequent additions thereto from the silver loan of 1919 and from Chinese Government advances, brought the total to $66,251,925. Of this $23,-819,287 is shown as " Interest and discount out of loan funds."

For the three sections of the Hukuang Railways the following statements of cost of property are given: [21]

[19] MacMurray, p. 888, No. 1911/5, notes.

[20] This figure is taken from, and others given subsequently are compiled from, the Capital Balance sheets of the Railway, as of June 30, 1921, as audited by G. Humphreys, acting auditor. Balance sheets courtesy of J. P. Morgan & Co.

[21] From the statements of the Chief Accountant, Mr. T. G. J. Brown, as of June 30, 1921.

Hupeh-Hunan	$57,469,711	
Han-I	9,949,861	
I-Kwei	8,900,295	
Total cost of property	$76,319,867	(Silver)
The construction accounts	$53,782,195	
The financial accounts (for interest and exchange)	25,391,027	
	$79,173,222	
Less receipts on capital account	2,853,356	
	$76,319,866	(Silver)

From these statements it appears that about 2/3 of the loan funds went into actual construction. To what extent material assets, potentially income-yielding, have resulted therefrom cannot be stated.

As a result of the entrance of China into the war with Germany, the bonds of the German issue of the Hukuang loan, together with certain other German securities were declared invalid by China, except where it could be proved that they were the property of non-enemy holders. By the Treaty of Versailles Germany ceded to China all Chinese Government bonds held by her nationals as a part of the war indemnity to China. The German bonds of the Hukuang it appears, were held mainly by American interests and China declared Americans could not prove purchase prior to the declaration of confiscation. In July, 1924, following the settlement by treaty of her indemnity claims against Germany (in part through surrender by the German government of a portion of the previously German held bonds of this issue), China announced that commencing with December, 1924 she would pay the current loan service on the German issue, as well as two coupons and one sinking fund installment annually of the ar-

4

rears. Since then, funds have been received only for the interest maturing December 15, 1924 and June 15, 1925 on all bonds of the German issue not previously validated.[22]

Other foreign loans to China secured by railways were made during the period from 1898 to 1912 but not all of these can be reviewed. The Kirin-Changchun railway, the initial loan for which was negotiated in 1908 from Japan came into prominence in 1915 when Japan demanded a 99 year lease of this railway, as a part of the second group of the Twenty One demands. This China refused to grant, but further financing, through the South Manchuria Railway, involving the extension of Japanese influence on this road until 1947, was agreed to.

In Chinese financial history the period from 1898 to 1912 was characterized by loans for productive more than unproductive purposes, chiefly composed of railway loans (cf. Table B). There were a few loans for industrial purposes, chiefly telegraph and cable installation (cf. Table C).

From the time of the Revolution and the formation of the Republic in 1912 the borrowing of foreign funds by the Chinese Government has not been as definitely for the building up of productive assets as in the earlier period. Such borrowings will be reviewed in a subsequent chapter. Other secured railway loans in this latter period include the Lung-Hai railway loans of 1913 and 1919 through Belgian interests and of 1920 through Dutch interests, the Nanchang-Kiukiang Railway loans, and the gold notes issued in compensation for the Tsingtao-Tsinanfu Railway.

It is impossible to state to what extent the funds of all the forty or more railway loans were wisely and honestly

[22] Information on German portion of the Hukuang bonds from letter of Mr. T. S. Lamont, of J. P. Morgan & Co., July 30, 1926.

expended. Of these loans two were redeemed by another
issue, two were repaid, one was converted into a larger issue. One also is now in default. The total in secured
railway obligations outstanding, (1926) is £49,632,884,
or (at 9.5 $ Mex equals 1 £) $471,512,700 (silver).

Of this list of railway loans it is not possible to state
definitely the amount of each loan which was payable to
the Chinese government. It is possible, however, to do
this for all except the shorter term loans of the Peking-
Mukden, the Ssu-Tao Railway, the Lung-Hai Railway
and the Treasury Notes for railway material all made in
the years 1918 to 1923. These particular loans, in contrast to almost all the other loans, bear higher rates of
interest 7, 8, 9, and 9½ percent, which may indicate that
the proceeds were delivered to China at par, as with a number of other Japanese loans of that period, or at a small
discount;—or which may indicate a higher element of risk,
in the judgment of the lender. The characteristic rate
for railroad loans had been 5 per cent in the period up to
the Revolution. Disregarding these items for which the
" price to bankers " was unavailable, and considering the
balance of the obligations reviewed one finds that of a
total principal amount of all secured railway loans, contracted between 1898 and 1918, of £40,963,113, the
amount of the loan funds placed supposedly to China's
credit totals £37,656,978, or 92 per cent of the principal
sum. This is using the " price to the bankers " in each
case, and deducting from that any commission received
for floating or underwriting the loan where this is stated
as a lump sum. But China did not receive that sum of
£37 million, as available for construction or for incorpora-
tion in material productive assets. This figure can be reduced by deducting lump sum commissions for construction

on two railways of £35,000 each, making £37,586,978, or less than 92 per cent; and, if the 5 per cent commission on materials for acting as purchasing agent found in many railway loan contracts, and possibly charged in some other cases where not found, could be deducted, as well as the ¼ or 1 per cent commission on annual loan service throughout the life of the loan, found in half of the contracts, it would be clear that China's use of foreign capital has been costly. The bankers which have underwritten or sold China's railway bonds have on the average disposed of them at 98 per cent of par, making an average gross margin of 5 per cent to 6 per cent on the transactions. Furthermore, the figure available for construction could be reduced by deducting interest on the loan during the period of construction. Often delay in construction has been more common than speed and in several cases further loans were necessary or are necessary now to complete the work undertaken. Some delay in construction, of course, has been unavoidable. The Revolution, the European war, the unsettled post-war situation both at home and abroad have contributed.

The foreign banks, operating in these foreign loans for railway construction have gained in other ways than those mentioned just above. They have often been closely allied with the contracting firms which have carried forward the actual work, as the Hongkong and Shanghai bank with the British and Chinese Corporation. The agents of these banks or foreign firms, or foreigners appointed by them who have supervised construction or purchasing materials, who have acted as advisers or accountants or auditors, who have composed the administrative staff, outnumbering Chinese members in some cases in the earlier contracts, or, where Chinese members have outnumbered foreigners, the latter placed in such positions of influence as to play a part in controlling expenditure;—all these officials of bank or company have received salaries and this has contributed to the cost of construction.

It is not good, however, to gain the impression that all of the means employed by foreign capital to control operations have been aggressive or unnecessary interferences with China's internal life. The funds employed through foreign capital flotations did not come solely from the underwriting banks or agencies. Bonds of the Chinese Government were sold to the public in foreign countries and these investors would normally be interested, to some extent at least, in the provisions for assuring that sufficient property of income-bearing possibilities would result from the expenditure of the loan funds, that the mortgaged property would be a sufficient security. The bond buyer alone is ignorant and powerless as concerns far away matters. He looks to the underwriter for protection. In the case of a railway mortgage bond, it is more important to the investor that the railway be made an income-yielding asset, with income more than sufficient to cover fixed charges, than it is that so many miles of track and ties or embankments are ready for use. In other words, successful operation of the road completed is as important as construction. For this reason, it would seem, continued participation of foreign interests in railway administration, after construction has ceased, has been contracted for, in some cases, even for the life of the bond issue.

It will be recalled that in discussing the Tientsin-Pukow Railway terms, and later the Hukuang Railway terms, which are similar to the former, mention was made that these terms were more liberal than those formerly given to China. China demanded these more liberal terms. The

" Young China " movement was growing in the years before 1911.   The provincial authorities were bidding for popular support and for capital in attempts to obtain railway privileges which, begun perhaps by private companies, could be completed by proceeds of foreign loans made to them, the provincial authorities, and not the Central Government at Peking.   As one writer has phrased it,[23] a " monopoly of peculation for metropolitan mandarins " was desired.   The Central Government perceived that some greater degree of centralization was wanted and further, that China's own prestige should be strengthened.   She undoubtedly hoped for the unconditional loan of funds, a policy prevalent with most other nations where political insecurity or low national revenues are not complicating factors.   As it was, in the use of the funds, on contracts similar to Tientsin-Pukow terms, in which auditors could not stop withdrawal of funds, China has been accused of peculation, and if so, this means that the cost of construction has exceeded estimates, and the loan service will constitute a heavy charge on the revenues of the lines in question.   In the later contracts, then, " control " by the foreign capital agencies was not as complete as in earlier contracts, but it is to be recalled that many of the earlier contracts have not yet expired.

Most of the railway contracts have called for a virtual quasi-monopoly for the foreign agencies in the supply of materials for construction and operation, both as to the country of origin of goods and the firm supplying the goods.   This serves as an opportunity for profit.   Much as this phase of international capital loans has been deplored by economists, it has been a characteristic feature of all loan contracts and a demand on the part of all for-

[23] W. Straight, *Chinese Loan Negotiations*, p. 15.

eign lenders. The Hukuang negotiations revealed the importance attached to this phase of railway loan operations. In the earlier contracts it was a characteristic provision for the foreign company to receive 20 per cent of the net profits of the line in addition to 5 per cent on costs of materials, as the profit element in promotion. In a few of the later contracts this profit privilege was redeemed by an outright payment to the company concerned of a lump sum as mentioned in the Tientsin-Pukow terms—but the sharing of foreign concerns in the profits (net after operating expenses, as well as interest and loan service deductions) is yet a factor reducing the revenue to the Central Government from many Chinese Government Railways.

A word as to the relative advantages and disadvantages might not be out of place. Could China have built her own railways there would have been many advantages now enjoyed by others, which would have been hers to enjoy. But she could not. There are some who would center every evil in connection with foreign capital in China in the problem of foreign investment in Chinese railroads. True, in the early days of loans to China, the apparent persistence of foreign nations in obtaining railway concessions, undoubtedly led to much internal interference in China, and this is now deplored. " Spheres of interest " and other " trappings " of economic imperialism have now come into disrepute. True, it brought on opposition by the Chinese public. But when private companies attempted railways they quite generally failed. Furthermore, the Treasury has characteristically been empty or embarrassed, and foreign money could be obtained about as cheaply as Chinese capital could be obtained by domestic loan issues.

It is not proposed to dwell on the advantages of these railways to China. Some would argue them worth the

price, even though costs may have been quite high.   Suffice
it to say that the price and conditions might have been
less had Chinese internal structure been different, or had,
in some cases, the interest of foreign governments not been
mingled with that of individuals.   The disadvantages of
a lack of a system of roads and a lack of uniformity resulting from the separate activities of many national
groups, without sufficient attention to the greatest needs of
China, are also technical factors which have weight, and
which are to be regretted.

The worst feature of China's foreign relations in the
years from 1898 to 1912 was the rivalry between foreign
nations and groups of foreign nations for railway concessions and loan contracts.   Not only the bankers, but also
the diplomats of each nation were active.   One country
might strive for more careful control of funds destined to
productive economic use, while a competing country might
offer easier terms.   The one might truly have been working
in China's interest; the latter might have been working
against China's interest.   Finally, however, the beginnings
of internationalization of Chinese railways came with the
formation of the four-power group: the first consortium.
The period prior to 1910 was a period of international
competition for Chinese loan business.   The period since
1910 has seen a certain growth cf cooperation in Chinese
loan operations, which has been an improvement over the
earlier period in removing some of the international friction
concerning Chinese governmental finance.   Various attempts have been made in this direction which will be mentioned in other connections.   Statements of advances to
railway projects will be discussed under unsecured loans
and the relation of Chinese railway concessions granted but
not yet used, will be reserved until the Second Consortium
has been treated.

Underwriting Country	Title	Interest Rate	Date of Issue	Maturity	Price to Public	Price to Bankers	Other
1. Belgian Company	Loan for Lukowkiao Railway	5	1898	1928	96½	90	
2. Belgian Company	Peking-Hankow Supplementary Loan	5	1905	1928	96½	90	
3. Anglo-French syndicate	Peking-Hankow Redemption Loan	5	1908	1938	98	94	Interest
4. "Birchal" loans, British	National Redemption Loan for Peking-Hankow Railway	7	1910 1912	1920	108 100	97½ 100 93	£ 3,750 bond
5. British syndicate	Imperial Rys. of N. China (Peking-Mukden)	5	1899	1944	97	90	
6. British syndicate	Hsinmintung-Mukden Advance	5	1907	1927	[1]	93	
7. British syndicate	Peking-Mukden Ry.—Double Track Loan	8	1921	1926–7			
8. British syndicate	Peking-Mukden Ry.—Double Track Loan	8	1921	1926–7			
9. British	Hongkong Government Loan for Redemption of Canton-Hankow Contract	4½	1906	1915	100	100	
10. Franco-Russian syndicate	Cheng-Tai (Shansi) Ry. Loan	5	1902	1932	96	90	¼% on servi
11. Franco-Belgian syndicate	Kaifeng-Honan (Pienlo) Ry. Loan	5	1903	1934	96½	90	¼% on servi
12. Franco-Belgian syndicate	Kaifeng-Honan (Pienlo) Ry. Loan	5	1907	1934	98	90	¼% on servi
13. British syndicate	Shanghai-Nanking Ry. Loan	5	1904	1953	97½	90	5% on
14. British syndicate	Shanghai-Nanking Ry. Loan	5	1907	1953	95½ [5]	90	¼% deb
15. British syndicate	Shanghai-Nanking Land Loan	6	1913	1923			
16. British syndicate	Honan Ry. (Taokow-Chinghua)	5	1905	1935	87½ [7]	90	¼% on servi
17. British syndicate	Taokow-Chinghua Ry. Loan	8	1918	1923			
18. British syndicate	Taokow-Chinghua Ry. Loan	7½	1919	1929			
19. British syndicate	Canton-Kowloon Ry. Loan	5	1907	1937	100	94	£ 35,(str £ 100 for
20. Anglo-German syndicate	Tientsin-Pukow Ry. Loan—First	5	1908	1938	98¾	93	£ 2 wai pro
21. Anglo-German syndicate	Tientsin-Pukow Ry. Loan—Second	5	1909	1938	100	93	5% o
22. Anglo-German syndicate	Tientsin-Pukow Ry. Loan—Third	5	1910	1940	100½	95	¼% deb
23. Anglo-German syndicate	Tientsin-Pukow Ry. Loan—Fourth Advance on Unissued Thirds	5 7	1910 1912				
24. British syndicate	Shanghai-Hangchow-Ningpo Ry. Loan	5	1908	1938	99	93	£ 35, fee ¼% deb
25. British syndicate	Shanghai-Fengchien Mtge. Redemption Loan	6	1914	1934		91	¼% deb
26. Japanese	Kirin-Changchun Ry. Loan	5	1908	1934		93	
27. Japanese	Kirin-Changchun Ry. Loan (Revised)	5	1917	1947	[1]	91½	Nomi pal yei
28. Japanese	Chinese Imperial Government Railway Loan (Yuchuanpu)	5	1911	1936	97½	95	
29. Four-Power-Consortium	Hukuang Rys. Loan	5	1911	1951	99	95	5% o ¼% ser
30. Belgian	Lung-Hai Ry. Loan (Republican Gov.)	5	1913	1952	91	85	¼% ser
31. Belgian	Lung-Hai Ry. Short Term Loan	7	1919	1924			
32. Belgian	Lung-Hai Ry. Treasury Notes of 1920 Lung-Hai Ry. Treasury Notes of 1920	8 8	1920–21–23 1920–21–23	1933 1933			
33. Japanese	Ssupingkai-Chengchiatun Ry. Loan	5	1915	1955	100	94½	¼% deb
34. Japanese	Ssupingkai-Chengchiatun Ry. Loan	9	1918	1919	100		
35. Japanese	Ssupingkai-Taonanfu Ry. Loan	9½	1922	1923			
36. Japanese	Ssupingkai-Taonanfu (Tseng-Tac section)	9½	1922	1923			
37. Japanese	Nanchang-Kiukiang Ry. Loan [10]	6½	1912	1931	99	95	
38. Japanese	Nanchang-Kiukiang Ry. Second Loan [10]	6½	1914	1933			
39. Japanese	Nanchang-Kiukiang Ry. Third Loan [10]	6½	1914	1941			
40. Japanese	Nanchang-Kiukiang Ry. Fourth Loan [10]	7½	1922	1937			
41. Belgian	Treasury Notes for Railway Material	8	1922–23	1932	87		
42. Japanese	Treasury Notes for Tsingtao-Tsinanfu Railway Purchase	6	1922	1928			
	Total Secured Railway Loans, Original Principal in £ Sterling						
	Total loans on which "Amount Available" not known						
	Total of Loans on which "Amount Available" is known						
	Total "Amount Available" on these loans, 91.9%						
	Total Outstanding in £ Sterling						

[1] Not offered to public.
[2] Probably repaid.
[3] Assuming 3 years paid at £10,000 (interest and amortization). Interest not over $120,000 for 3 years.
[4] Probably less since some amortization has been paid, but no payment for 1925 mentioned in J. R. Baylin, op. cit., pp. 90 ff. Report of Minis
[5] Baylin states par—Ferrin states 95½.
[6] Taking 95% yield arbitrarily.
[7] Sold 1914 by Lloyds, Ltd. for the Peking syndicate.
[8] Deducting £200,000 stipulated in contract for waiver of net profits participation.
[9] Minister of Communications report, January 1922 gives £ 600,000 outstanding on Deutsche Asiatische advance of £900,424. I add £ 300,000
[10] This railway is under Chinese Government Railway administration, though the railway was a provincial private company. Proper to in

inal Principal	Original Principal in £ Sterling	Rate of Conversion	Amount Available to Chinese Gov. or Agencies	Outstanding	Date	Outstanding in £ Sterling	Remarks: Security
0,000 francs	180,000	25 fr. = 1 £	162,000	Repaid	1909		The railway and new lines
0,000 francs	500,000	25 fr. = 1 £	450,000	Repaid	1909		
0,000 £	5,000,000		4,700,000	3,250,000	Oct., 1925	3,250,000	Certain provincial revenues
0,000 £	220,000		214,500				Probably included in No. 3
0,000 £	450,000		450,000	Not given			
0,000 £	150,000		135,750				
0,000 £	2,300,000		2,070,000	1,092,500	Aug., 1925	1,092,500	The railway and extensions
0,000 yen	32,000	10 yen = 1 £	29,760	35,555 yen	Sept., 1925	3,555 ?	
0,000 £	500,000			240,000	Aug., 1925	240,000 ³	Railway
0,000 $ Mex.	222,222	$ 9 Mex. = 1£		1,700,000 $ Mex.	Sept., 1923	178,900 ⁴	Railway
0,000 £	1,000,000		1,000,000	Repaid			Opium revenues of Hupeh, Honan, Kwangtung Railway
0,000 francs	1,600,000	25 fr. = 1 £	1,440,000	18,572,000 francs	Sept., 1925	742,900	Railway
0,000 francs	1,000,000	25 fr. = 1 £	900,000	31,000,000 francs	Dec., 1923	1,240,000	Railway
0,000 francs	640,000	25 fr. = 1 £	576,000				
0,000 £	2,250,000		2,025,000	2,250,000		2,250,000	Amortization begins 1929
0,000 £	650,000		576,000	650,000		650,000	Railway-security
0,000 £	150,000		142,500 ⁶	Repaid			Land
0,000 £	800,000		720,000	495,700 £	Jan., 1926	495,700	Railway
0,000 $ G	60,000	5 $ G = 1 £		120,000 $ G	Jan., 1922	24,000	Railway
,838 £	126,838			63,419 £	Dec., 1925	63,419	Railway
,000 £	1,500,000		1,410,000	1,143,000 £ 5,500 £ overdue interest	June, 1925	1,148,500	Railway
,000 £	3,000,000		2,590,000 ⁵	3,250,000 £	Oct., 1925	3,250,000	Provincial Revenues
,000 £	2,000,000		1,860,000				
,000 £	3,000,000		2,850,000	2,250,000 £	Nov., 1925	2,250,000	Provincial Revenues
,424 £	1,200,424			900,000 £	Jan., 1922	900,000 ⁸	Provincial Revenues
,000 £	1,500,000		1,395,000	975,000 £	Dec., 1925	975,000	Surplus Revenues of Peking-Mukden Ry.
,000 £	375,000		341,250	337,500 £	Aug., 1925	337,500	Surplus Revenues of Peking-Mukden Ry.
,000 yen	215,000	10 yen = 1 £	199,950	Converted and refunded into new loan—1917			
,250 yen	451,113	10 yen = 1 £	412,768	6,500,000 yen less unredeemed portion of old issue 6,500,000 yen	Jan., 1926	650,000	Railway Peking-Hankow Ry.
,000 yen	1,000,000	10 yen = 1 £	950,000	12,350,000 yen in default	June, 1925	1,235,000	Revenues. Other revenues
,000 £	6,000,000		5,700,000	5,610,800 £	Dec., 1925	5,610,800	Hupeh and Hunan Salt and likin Taxes
,000 francs	4,000,000	25 fr. = 1 £	3,400,000	4,000,000 £	July, 1925	4,000,000	Railway
,000 francs	800,000	25 fr. = 1 £		20,000,000 francs		800,000	Exchanged for new 10 yr. bonds, due 1935
,000 B. francs	5,509,720	25 fr. = 1 £				5,509,720	Amortization begins 1926
,000 florins	2,105,290	12.1 fls. = 1 £				2,105,290	
,000 yen	500,000	10 yen = 1 £	472,500	5,000,000 yen Amortization begins	1926 1927	500,000	Railway Property
,000 yen	260,000	10 yen = 1 £		1,600,000 yen	1923	160,000	
,000 yen	1,370,000	10 yen = 1 £		13,700,000 yen	1925	1,370,000	Railway
,000 yen	300,000	10 yen = 1 £		3,000,000 yen	1923	300,000	Railway
,000 yen	500,000	10 yen = 1 £	475,000	5,000,000 yen	1926	500,000	Amortization begins 1927—Railway
,000 yen	50,000	10 yen = 1 £		500,000 yen	1926	50,000	Amortization begins 1929—Railway
,000 yen	200,000	10 yen = 1 £		2,000,000 yen	1926	200,000	1937—Railway
,000 yen	250,000	10 yen = 1 £		2,500,000 yen	1926	250,000	1932—Railway
,000 B. francs	3,300,000	60 B. fr. = 1 £		198,000,000 B. francs	1926	3,300,000	1928—Railway
,000 yen	4,000,000	10 yen = 1 £		40,000,000 yen	1926	4,000,000	
	61,217,607						
	20,254,494						
	40,963,113						
			37,656,978				
						49,632,884	

25 as of Sept., 1923, shows $1,700,000 outstanding, Chinese Economic Monthly, Nov., 1925, p. 43.

t.

CHAPTER III

In addition to the railway loans which have been treated, there are several industrial loans which have been made. The first of these dates from 1900. Though the number of these loans is not as great as in other classifications, they have been made for needed productive purposes, for telegraph, cable and wireless development. The most of the foreign capital in industry in China, in other than railroads, is in the form of private investment.

The Anglo-Danish Telegraph Loans

In 1900, it was projected to lay a cable from Tientsir. to Shanghai (Taku-Chefoo-Shanghai). A loan was negotiated with the Eastern Extension Telegraph Company of Denmark, for £210,000 at 5 per cent for thirty years. Subsequently another supplementary loan of £48,000 was made on the same conditions and due in 1930. The cable was made security for the loans.[1] These loans have been in default since September 30, 1922,[2] thus giving an amount outstanding of £109,279 (1926).

In 1911, these same companies loaned to the Chinese Government £500,000 more, for the development and improvement of telegraph and telephone service in China. The loan bore 5 per cent interest. Security for this latter

[1] MacMurray, p. 269, No. 1901/1. The British Government had an active part in the negotiations.

[2] J. R. Baylin, *op. cit.*, p.88. However, in Lee, *op. cit.*, p. 188, the amount outstanding is given as £79,640.

loan was given in the form of telegraph receipts to be obtained.[3]   Under the agreement China cannot allow any other land telegraph stations to communicate telegraphically with Europe or America.   The foreign companies make half-yearly payments to the Chinese Telegraph Administration of a percentage of their revenues from foreign telegrams to China and are expected to do so for the first 18 years of the loan period.   These payments constitute the basis for the security of the loan.   This loan also has been in default since September 30, 1922, with £ 288,220 outstanding (1926).[4]

The Banque Industrielle Loan

In 1913 the Government of the Republic of China contracted for a loan of 150,000,000 francs from the French bank, Banque Industrielle de Chine, this loan to be issued in 1914, under the title of the Five Percent Industrial Gold Loan of 1914.[5]   The contract stated that this loan was to be employed solely for the establishment of national industries and for the construction of public works, of which the first would be the construction of the port of Pukow.   Of this sum but 100,000,000 francs was actually loaned.   By annexes to the original contract [6] it was stated that any unused balance beyond that needed for the port of Pukow would be devoted to the establishment of industries and the execution of certain public works in the city of Peking, such as tramways, electric light and water works, improvements, sewers, buildings, etc.   These all were to be the guarantee of interest and principal on the loan

3 *China Year Book,* 1921–22, pp. 489–490.

4 J. R. Baylin, *op. cit.,* p. 88.   F. E. Lee gives £ 215,160 as outstanding on this loan.

5 MacMurray, p. 1055, No. 1913/10.

6 *Ibid.,* pp. 1062–1066, and annexes.

and this guarantee constituted a " first lien upon the said industries, material, appurtenances and revenues " (Annex 1). In addition the alcohol imposts in all provinces north of the Yangtze River were named as security (Annex 2). Thus this loan was secured by municipal taxes of Peking, revenues from works at Pukow, and the alcohol tax.

The flotation of this loan brought certain opposition from Great Britain in that the work at Pukow particularly and other operations planned were in her " sphere of interest." It was also called an unwise loan. But the French supported it and the loan was made to the extent of 100 million. It sold at $94\frac{1}{4}$ per cent of par.

The financial aspects of this loan bear attention. With interest at 5 per cent, the price of issue to the bank at 84 per cent of par, with the cost of engraving and printing the bonds at the expense of China, with the bank receiving the usual $\frac{1}{4}$ of 1 per cent on the annual loan service on the bonds, and with the bank retaining on deposit in Europe, out of the proceeds of the loan sufficient to assure the full payment of the first half year's interest and its $\frac{1}{4}$ per cent commission on the same, the amount available to China for productive use was 81,493,750 francs, not deducting the expenses mentioned for printing and engraving. China was to receive 3 per cent, however, upon all balances left with the Bank. Further, one article set forth that " insofar as it may be necessary to buy abroad, the choice will be given to French products. The bank will exert itself to the utmost in order that they may be obtained of the best quality and at the lowest price possible. But if any article should be obtainable in any country other than France, there would be allowed to the Bank a commission of 5 per cent of the purchase price of that article." [7]

[7] MacMurray, p. 1060.

A Chinese Director General and a European Auditor
General and a European Engineer in Chief were to be the
leading officials of each enterprise, these latter officials to
be agreed upon between the Director General and the Bank,
but the Chinese Government alone was to be in control of
the Port of Pukow and of the operation and management
of the industries and public works.   This latter statement,
however, did not preclude the condition that as regarded
loan funds all orders for payment were to be signed by
the Director General and the Engineer in Chief, jointly,
and further that these two would have the " most absolute
control over all expenditures and receipts of the port." [8]

Of this loan, 100,000,000 francs yet remain outstanding,
the amortization not beginning until the year 1930, and
the loan period being a total of fifty years.   This loan is
one of the obligations of China to the Banque Industrielle
and through it to the French citizens who had bought the
bonds, which has now been made a charge on the French
portion of the Boxer Indemnity and is therefore now a
charge on the Maritime Customs revenue.[9]   The Chinese
Government had subscribed 50,000,000 francs or one third
of the original capital of this bank in 1913.   It now holds
a share in the new managing company, the Société de
Gerance, which is rearranging the affairs of the bank.
Other loans falling in this latter arrangement will be mentioned in Part II under Unsecured Loans.   They are now
really secured loans.

The Telegraph Improvement Loan of 1918

On April 30, 1918, the Chinese Government signed, with
the Exchange Bank of China acting for and with the

[8] *Ibid.*, p. 1063.
[9] Cf. above, p. 20.

Japanese Banking Syndicate, an agreement for a loan of 20,000,000 yen for five years at 8 per cent, delivered at par to China, the latter agreeing to keep constantly on hand with the Exchange Bank a reserve fund equal to six months' interest. As security for this loan " all the property and revenue of the telegraph lines throughout the Republic of China" were hypothecated, with cognizance being taken, however, of the Anglo-Danish contracts outstanding, which were mentioned at the first of this chapter.[10] By a supplement to the contract it was agreed that Japanese experts were to be engaged if foreign experts were employed, and that preference should be given to Japanese goods.[11] This loan also is now in default, 20,-800,000 yen being outstanding.

Like many other loans negotiated during the year 1918 there was a diversion of funds to other purposes than those stated. In connection with this loan, the following statement of Mr. Kao-En-hung, Minister of Communications in 1922, referring not only to this loan but to three others as well (mentioned later under unsecured loans), is quite significant:

" All the properties and revenues of the telegraph, (and telephone) administration have been pledged as security with practically nothing left. If these loans were made use of for the increase of the capital investment and for the extension of the system, then the business of the telegraph (and telephone) administration would be much more developed. But the majority of these loans was either borrowed by the Ministry of Finance or spent by the Railway Administration. All spent by the telegraph administration was less than 15 per cent."

10 MacMurray, p. 1424, No. 1918/7.
11 *Ibid.*, p. 1428.

Thus not all loans which appear on the surface as productive loans are such. The Ministry of Finance received 16,973,333 yen, the Railway Administration 2,070,496 yen, this going almost entirely for principal and interest on certain loans, while the Ministry of Communications received 685,328 yen after 282,191 yen had been paid in interest on the telegraph loan in question.[12] Thus only 3½ per cent of the loan funds was available for productive use.

Summary

The secured loans for industrial purposes, other than railroads, are with the exception of the Telegraph Improvement Loan, to be classed as productive in the sense that material assets, productive of revenue or income, or potentially so, resulted from the use of the funds, at least somewhat proportionate to the amount received by China. It is to be noted that no loans for private enterprise have been included, only those which were contracted by the Central Government of China. Industrial development in China has been largely going forward through private channels, foreign and domestic.

The contracts are varied as to purpose as well as to financial details and it is only fair to say that, considering the different characteristics of, say, telegraph and port improvements, generalization is difficult as to whether the purposes were wise, or whether the cost to China was commensurate with the economic results achieved. The loans were designed to promote the public welfare in varied ways.

The amount which China received out of these borrowings cannot be definitely stated. However, the Govern-

12 This statement of expenditure and the quotation are found in Lee, *op. cit.*, pp. 210, 212, as translated from the *Chinese Government Gazette*, August 16 and 17, 1922.

TABLE C. FOREIGN SECURED

Title	Interest Rate	Date	Maturity	Price to Public	Price to Bankers	Original Principal
1. Anglo-Danish Telegraph Loan...........	5	1900	1930			210,000 £
2. Supplementary Taku-Chefoo Cable Loan...	5	1901	1930			48,000 £
3. Advance on Anglo-Danish Cable Loan.....	5	1911	1930			500,000 £
4. Banque Industrielle Loan..............	5	1914	1960	94½	84	100,000,000 francs
5. Telegraph Improvement Loan...........	8	1918	1923		100	20,000,000 yen
Total secured Industrial Loans........... Total principal on which "Amount Available" is not known...................						
Total Amount Available on No. 4 and No. 5.						
Total Outstanding on industrial loans....						

Conversion	Amount Available to Chinese Gov.	Outstanding	Date	Outstanding in £ Sterling	Remarks
		88,699 £		88,699	Principal and overdue interest in default since Sept. 1922
		20,580 £		20,580	Principal and overdue interest in default since Sept. 1922
		288,220 £		288,220	Principal and overdue interest in default since Sept. 1922
fr. = 1 £	3,260,000	100,000,000 francs	1925	4,000,000	Now secured by French portion of Boxer indemnity—i.e. by customs revenue
yen = 1 £	2,000,000	20,800,000 yen	1925	2,080,000	Security—Telegraph lines in China—in default
	5,260,000	or 87.66%			
				6,477,499	

ment contracted for loans of this group to the amount of £6,758,000 since 1900, and of these there were outstanding in 1926, £6,477,500. The "amount available" on the Banque Industrielle loan shows that China suffered a discount of about 19 per cent when all deductions are considered. Though the Telegraph Loan was delivered at par, the interest burden is at 8 per cent, and the loan in addition was unproductive. On these two loans only is the price to the bankers known.

There are other industrial loans to the Central Government of China which because of the doubtful character of their security are not here considered under secured loans but are treated in Part II. The distinction it is true is in part arbitrary, especially in view of the fact that the telegraph loans treated in this chapter are now (1926) in default.[13]

[13] The basis of distinction between the loans considered under the classification "secured" and those under the classification "unsecured" has been largely that of Dr. F. E. Lee, *op. cit.* His lists have been followed.

CHAPTER IV

ADMINISTRATIVE AND GENERAL LOANS

The loans obtained by China in the early period before 1894 had been largely for administrative purposes; those from 1894 to 1898 largely for war and indemnity purposes; while those from 1898 to 1912 were largely for economic purposes. The period since 1912 has included, together with the railway and industrial loans, already treated, several administrative loans. These loans are not strictly productive (in the sense that the funds were planned to be incorporated in material assets, potentially income-yielding), yet in a sense they could be so regarded since funds spent in reorganizing an administration or in reform of currency can so affect the economic life of a people as to improve materially their productive capacity, or to economize or increase the revenues of the Government. This chapter will provide opportunity further to consider the activities of the first Consortium of foreign bankers in China.

Before the formation of the Republic there had been floated several loans which are best treated under a general classification. Such were loans to viceroys of the Central Government, or to Provinces, which bore the guarantee of the Central Government. There were three of these totalling 4,500,000 taels and all have been repaid. One of these, the Hupeh Provincial Silver Loan, in 1911, was made for 2,000,000 taels, for 10 years, secured by the salt revenues, bearing 7 per cent. This loan was made to the Viceroy of Hukuang by the four-Power group, including

Great Britain, France, Germany and the United States.[1]

Other loans to Viceroys and Provinces were made by different agencies but for many of these definite information is not available.[2]

The Proposed Currency Reform and Manchurian Development Loan

Another loan contracted for before the establishment of the Republic was the Currency Reform Loan with the four-Power group, the final contract being signed April 25, 1911, the United States having signed the preliminary agreement in 1910. This loan was to be for £10,000,000 and was to include £3,000,000 for use in industrial development in Manchuria. China was to be assisted in reforming her currency by a representative of the banks. According to the contract the loan was to net 95 per cent to the Chinese Government, and to bear interest at 5 per cent; and have as security the wine and tobacco production and consumption taxes in Manchuria, and a new salt tax in Manchuria and the whole of China. The loan was never issued because of the Revolution, although an advance of £400,000 was made which was later repaid. This advance was planned to assist the abatement of plague in Manchuria and to cover other expenses. Although the contract is now cancelled the American Government has held that the United States continues to possess such an interest in the project that in the future it is entitled to consideration in reference to any action towards currency reform in China. This is largely because of the activity of the Commission headed by Dr. Jeremiah W. Jenks in 1903 and 1904, appointed by authority of Congress, which

[1] MacMurray, p. 902, No. 1911/8.

[2] Cf. MacMurray, p. 1030, No. 1913/5; also p. 906, No. 1911/9.

5

resulted from the appeal addressed by the Chinese Government to the American Government in reference to currency reform; and because in 1910 the Chinese Government addressed the request for the loan for currency reform directly to the American Government, and not to private individuals.[3] The contract had granted an option of preference in issuing any other loan for further industrial development in Manchuria. This, it would seem, expired with the contract, but any loan for this purpose or for currency reform would probably now come through the present Consortium. The Currency Reform and Manchurian Development contract is listed among those pooled in the Second Consortium.[4]

The Reorganization Loan of 1913 and the Consortium

When the Republic of China was organized in February, 1912, one of the most involved and difficult problems facing the new government was the question of finance. The Revolution had upset administrative machinery and the organization of tax collection. This financial disorganization can be traced back to the unsound financial system of the Manchu dynasty, which made the Central Government helpless and dependent upon the Provinces. The Central Government was not supposed to have any revenue of its own, depending entirely upon contributions from the Provinces levied in proportion to the latter's revenue. The National Treasury was empty and many governmental debts pressed for liquidation. The Imperial Government had striven hard to carry on its part in the Revolution but had exhausted its resources. The Revo-

[3] Cf. Note from American Legation, Peking, to China, MacMurray, p. 852, No. 1912/2, note.

[4] Cf. below, Chapter XIV.

lutionary leaders as well had been unable to procure money.
The new Republican groups were compelled to resort to
foreign loans. The old interdependent system of finance
yielded revenue until the Provinces withheld their contributions.[5] It was part of the policy of foreign governments
not to lend their support to loans to either faction and
to maintain neutrality.

When, however, the Manchus abdicated on February 12,
1912, and when it seemed very probable that a responsible
provisional Republican Government would be organized the
attitude of the Powers became one of interest in the problems of finance. The agents of the four Power Consortium
in Peking were approached by the Acting Minister of Finance, Mr. Chou-Tsu-chi for advances for the monthly
needs of the Peking Government, stating that 6,400,000
taels would be needed monthly by that government, and
further, that 7,000,000 taels would be needed immediately
by the Nanking Government.

The four power group advanced 2,000,000 taels on February 28th for the Nanking Government and on March
9th another advance of 1,100,000 taels for the Peking
Government. Of that date, March 9, 1912, Yuan Shi Kai,
Provisional President, addressed to the representatives of
the Consortium a letter which acknowledged the two advances mentioned, noted the sanctions of the respective
Powers to these advances, and further stated the grant of
an option to the banks not only for the provision of the
further monthly requirements of the Chinese Government
for the following four months, but also for the undertaking
of a comprehensive reorganization loan, providing that the
terms of the Consortium banks were as equally advantage-
ous as those otherwise obtainable, and instructed that ne-

[5] *Chinese Economic Monthly*, October, 1925, p. 6.

gotiations proceed. The security for the advances made was to be the revenue of the Salt Gabelle.[6]

It developed, however, that President Yuan did not mean all he had written. The Premier, Mr. Tong Shao Yi, proceeded shortly to obtain funds elsewhere. Other banking syndicates than the four Power Consortium were anxious to supply China with funds and the period from early 1912 until well into 1913 was one of intense rivalry among foreign financiers for opportunities of underwriting Chinese Government loans.

Meanwhile the ministers of Germany, France, United States and Great Britain in Peking refused to continue negotiations for the Consortium's reorganization loan and protested against the loan negotiations with other syndicates.[7] The Consortium Powers claimed China had been guilty of a clear breach of contract and determined to protect the advances made as well as the future rights of their nationals to whom had been pledged support. China at last admitted its breach of contract and good faith and negotiations were resumed with the Consortium.[8]

During the months of April and May, 12,000,000 taels, or £1,800,000, approximately, were advanced by the Consortium banks to the Republican Government.

For the Reorganization loan these groups demanded security as follows: that satisfactory purposes should be stated, that a system of audit should be created by China with foreigners as executives, that the salt taxes under pledge for the loan should be administered by the Maritime customs or some similar service under foreign direc-

---

[6] Cf. text of letter in *China Year Book,* 1913, p. 345; and *U. S. Foreign Relations,* 1912, pp. 113, 120.

[7] *U. S. Foreign Relations,* 1912, pp. 115, 122.

[8] *Ibid.,* pp. 124, 126.

tion,[9] since without such supervision the revenues would be insufficient.

To these demands China refused to assent,[10] and declared that since " reasonable " terms were not acceptable she would get the money from her own people. Efforts made in this direction were unsuccessful and China again sought foreign funds from agencies without the Consortium. There was strong popular feeling in China against a foreign financial monopoly. Thus the leaders of the Republican Government were hard pressed: a need of funds, little forthcoming within, foreign funds available only on conditions of supervision of expenditure and security, strong internal opposition to those conditions.

However, further advances were given by the banks, but only upon China's undertaking that it would not negotiate any further sums from independent foreign nationals. A foreign auditor was appointed on behalf of the bankers. But because of the deadlock on " supervision " in the final contract negotiations were suspended again. At this time the four Power Consortium became a Sextuple Group through the admission of Russian and Japanese financial interests upon invitation. An arrangement for equal participation was concluded and signed June 18, 1912, at a conference of the bankers in Paris.[11]

During the deadlock on " foreign supervision " in the final contract, China negotiated independently a loan for £10,000,000 with C. Birch Crisp & Company, a British concern.[12] Three months later £5,000,000 of the loan was floated despite the protests of the British Government.

[9] Willard Straight, *Chinese Loan Negotiations*, p. 27.

[10] *U. S. Foreign Relations*, 1912, pp. 133, 134.

[11] MacMurray, p. 1201, No. 1913/5.

[12] MacMurray, p. 967, No. 1912/9, or *China Year Book*, 1913, p. 360.

The latter was giving its support to the British banks which belonged to the Consortium and did not consider China free to borrow outside the Consortium since the latter in good faith had advanced £1,800,000 unsecured on the strength of China's pledge to deal only with the Consortium.[13]   The Crisp loan terms were notably more lenient.

Failing to prevent the issuance of the Crisp bonds negotiations were resumed by the Consortium.[14]   Argument continued over the interest rate, over indemnification for damages during the Revolution, over the number of foreign advisers for the Chinese Government and over the personnel itself, all of which brought impatience on both sides.   The sporadic and secret movements of the non-supported financiers, who continued to seek loan opportunities in China, threatened the dissolution of the Consortium and the demoralization of the Chinese.   Likewise the continued delay and inability of the Consortium financiers and their respective governments themselves to continue in common accord made it appear that the Consortium might end.

In the midst of this the sextuple group, fearful lest railway concessions, like the Lung-Hai Railway, which had just been given to Belgian interests,[15] should fall out of their grasp, decided to forsake the principle of internationalization as concerning industrial and railway loans and to lay down certain bases for competition in procuring such industrial loans, such as proper guarantees, control over expenditure, and approval by the Legation of the nationals concerned.

[13] *Correspondence re Chinese Loan negotiations*, China No. 2 (1912), p. 13.

[14] *U. S. Foreign Relations*, 1912, p. 153.

[15] Cf. above, p. 38.

The continued existence of the Consortium as a vital factor in Chinese finance was becoming dubious. On March 4, 1913, President Woodrow Wilson took office in Washington. The American policy took a complete reversal. In the place of the policy so strongly advocated during President Taft's regime of participation in such cooperative enterprises as the Consortium for the purpose, as stated, as much to safeguard the observance of the Open Door doctrine, and to prevent international friction concerning China, as to promote American financial interests, President Wilson's policy took the form of non-intervention lest through the administration, supervision or control of funds and revenues, the internal administrative independence of China should be assailed. " The responsibility of our Government implied in the encouragement of a loan thus secured and administered, is plain enough and is obnoxious to the principles upon which the government of our people rests. Our interests are those of the open door —a door of friendship and mutual advantage. This is the only door we care to enter." [16] In the light of this statement the American group withdrew from the Consortium, since the Department of State no longer desired participation.[17]

The Quintuple Consortium proceeded with its negotiations, but these were delayed mainly by the determination of the Powers to insist on nationality rather than efficiency as the determining factor in the choice of advisers. The Chinese Minister of Finance, March 11, 1913, called attention to the fact that the Powers were delaying progress

[16] *U. S. Foreign Relations*, 1913, p. 170, date of March 18, 1913; also in *New York Times*, March 19, 1913.

[17] This had been contemplated by the American group; cf. telegram Knox to American Minister. *Ibid.*, p. 163, February 20, 1913.

by their insistence on certain members of the personnel of the advisory staff and stated that he did not blame the bankers as much as the Powers themselves.[18] The French and Russian legations had objected to the appointment of a neutral and a German to certain posts, and wanted each an adviser of their respective nationalities. The American minister had not and the Japanese minister did not ask for any adviserships. The Russian Government claimed the right of advisership as a right already existing because of the stipulation in the Franco-Russian loan of 1895.[19] The matter of foreign advisers was finally arranged!

Then internal political difficulties in China delayed negotiations for a brief period until finally on April 26, 1913, the final contract was signed. There was far from a uniform popular approval of the loan. The purposes of the Reorganization Loan were set forth carefully in Article II and Annexes A-F inclusive, and included: payment of certain liabilities of the Chinese Government, many of them shortly maturing, the redemption in full of many outstanding provincial loans (practically speaking all foreign provincial debts owing to the Quintuple banks), disbandment of troops, current expenses of the administration, and reorganization of the salt administration. Over one half was to go for the repayment of debts. It would seem then that far less than half of the proceeds would go to productive purposes. A survey of the items suggests that not over $30,000,000 (Chinese) say roughly £3,000,000 was planned for productive purposes in the sense of some material or immaterial asset resulting, which might yield further income, such as a reorganized salt administration,

[18] *U. S. Foreign Relations*, 1913, p. 169.
[19] Cf. above, p. 7.

or buildings needed for governmental bureaus. From the viewpoint of the Central Government, the salt gabelle, hitherto a local tax, became a national tax, belonging to the Central Government. This was a helpful feature.

The agreement provided for a Chinese Chief Inspector and a Foreign Associate Chief Inspector for the Central Salt administration. The Salt Revenues were to be drawn upon only by the joint signatures of these two Chief Inspectors. In addition a foreign adviser was to be appointed. There were to be two foreign advisers in the Audit Bureau and one in the National Loans Department. The Chinese Government Salt Revenue Administration was not to be interfered with except in case of non-payment of interest or principal on the loan.[20]

The Second Reorganization Loan Advances

In 1917, before China became a participant in the European War, but when the operations of the Consortium were necessarily suspended, the government of China desired a loan of 10,000,000 yen, to be effected through the Yokohama-Specie Bank acting for the Japanese group, to be counted as an advance on a second reorganization loan which it proposed to negotiate with the Consortium. Treasury certificates were to be issued of one year's duration, to bear 7 per cent, and to be issued to the bankers at 93 per cent of par. The contract does not make it clear whether this discount is a year's interest or a commission. We will assume that this was interest. The proceeds would be further reduced by a banking commission of 1 per cent, making 92 per cent, and further by the expenses of printing the certificates, probably about

[20] The Reorganization and Crisp loans although secured primarily on the salt revenues have actually since 1918 been paid out of the customs revenue; cf. *Chinese Economic Monthly*, Oct., 1925, p. 8.

$3000 (Chinese). The certificates were to be secured on the salt revenue surplus. The purpose of the loan, as stated, was to apply the funds to administrative expenses of three months of that year.[21]

On January 6, 1918, another agreement for an advance of 10,000,000 yen was signed with the same agency, at same interest, but the agreement was more definite in regard to the original discount.[22] The first year's interest was to be discounted making 93 per cent turned over to China. If this was the meaning of the agreement for the first advance it was not so clearly stated. The bankers' commission in the second advance was likewise 1 per cent and expenses of printing were borne by China. Other details were similar to those of the first advance. The proceeds of the loan were to be devoted to reimbursement of certain loans previously made by the Bank of China to the Chinese Government,[23] and the Bank of China was to employ the money so received to restore the value of its notes. Both the Bank of China and the Bank of Communications had issued notes heavily, largely due to the government drawings from the banks, and were without adequate reserves. Portions of the ownership of both banks had been subscribed by the Chinese Government and at that time, 1918, the Chinese Government continued to hold part ownership in these banks.[24] Both of these advances on the second reorganization loan were later repaid.

[21] MacMurray, p. 1382, No. 1917/8.

[22] MacMurray, p. 1400, No. 1918/1. The *Far Eastern Review* for December, 1918, in a list of Japanese loans to China during 1916 to 1918, notes a third advance as of July, 1918, which it states was acknowledged by the Japanese Government. Dr. Lee does not list this alleged advance. Nothing further can be stated regarding it.

[23] MacMurray, p. 1404.

[24] Cf. balance sheets for 1917, 1918, 1919, in *China Year Book*, 1921–22, pp. 281–282, 284. The Bank of China has since been transferred to private ownership.

Miscellaneous Secured Loans

Several other secured loans were made by the Japanese banking interests, which were members of the Consortium during the years 1917 to 1918, which can be classified as miscellaneous secured loans and treated in this chapter. The Japanese financial interest established in China during these years when the other great financial powers were heavily engaged in the European War was very real. The entire list of Japanese loans is quite long and much more will be said of them in Part II since they were largely unsecured.[25]

The Japanese Share of the " 96 Million " Loan

The number of short term loans which were made in 1918, 1919, and 1920 at high interest rates was large and, after having them examined by a special commission appointed for the purpose, a number of them were consolidated and converted into the so-called 96 Million Loan. The regulations for this bond issue were promulgated by Presidential Mandate dated February 11, 1922. The bonds of this issue are known also as the Tenth Year 8 per cent Refunding bonds. Because many of the old loans were contracted in Japanese currency the new bonds were issued in two portions, 39,608,700 in yen, and 56,391,300 in Chinese silver dollars.[26] The Japanese share is secured and is a foreign loan. The Chinese share is of doubtful security and is an internal loan. The service of the former is entrusted to the Yokohama Specie Bank, which deducts the

[25] Such a list can be found in the *Far Eastern Review*, XIV, 421, for Dec., 1918; in F. H. Huang, *op. cit.*, pp. 51–55; and by reference to lists in Lee, *op. cit.*, pp. 191–198; or in *China Year Book*, 1923, pp. 721–22. Cf. below, pp. 132.

[26] Cf. J. R. Baylin, *op. cit.*, p. 23.

necessary amounts from the salt surplus deposited with it, while the latter, though equally secured on both the Customs surplus and the salt surplus has dropped considerably in market value because regular payments of principal and interest have not been carried out. The retention of the salt surplus by provincial authorities has been one reason for this.[27] In January, 1925 there remained outstanding 35,861,772 yen of the Japanese share,[28] while 12,700,000 yen represented the arrears in payments in June, 1925.[29]

Summary

In this chapter some fifteen loans or advances to the Chinese Government have been considered under the classification of " administrative and general Loans." The total of these loans, extending from 1907 to 1922 is the equivalent of £ 42,235,869 according to rates of conversion in Table D. Of this amount £ 34,333,245 was the amount outstanding in 1926. Information was not available on all these loans as to the amount of the proceeds payable to the Chinese Government or the agency of that Government for whom the loan was contracted and guaranteed. On all but six, however, some indication can be made, in almost every case the indication being dependable. The total of the principal of those loans whose yield to China is known is £ 34,716,666. The best indications are that China received £ 30,702,916, or 88.5 per cent of the principal sum to be repaid. Since the price of issue to the public of many of these loans is not known, it cannot be stated what the characteristic commission for underwriting happened to be. Clear it is, however, that in the loans of

[27] Cf. *Chinese Econ. Monthly,* October, 1925, p. 9. Also March, 1926, p. 101.

[28] Lee, *op. cit.,* p. 191.

[29] According to Baylin, p. 23.

later date made by Japanese interests the terms were very liberal. The reasons for this, however, may have been more than strictly financial. Japan has been accused of using, since 1915, when the Twenty-One Demands were forced upon China, this economic device of readily available funds for each and every purpose on easy terms, to ingratiate herself with the Chinese Government and people and obtain political influence.

China secured these 30 million pounds at an average rate of interest of $5\frac{1}{4}$ per cent [30] which partially explains the large initial discount noted above of 11.5 per cent. The large size of the Reorganization Loan of 1913 and its terms serves to overshadow the terms of other loans. Whether or not the terms of the Reorganization Loan were the most unfavorable among this group, as it would appear, is an argument that can only be answered by future events. In part it may be said that the reorganization of the salt administration has made possible an increase in the hypothecable revenues and has increased the security of those loans already secured thereon. Further, it is clear that, though the Reorganization Loan brought foreign participation in Chinese governmental administration, this is international in scope and is of the kind that is less apt to cloak individual nationalistic aggression, or undermining influences, or secret commitments, than is the policy of single national participation by financial groups closely allied with a particular government, and seeking economic and political advantage in the country with which it deals.

Summary of Secured Foreign Debt

In the preceding chapters attention has been given to most of the secured foreign debts of the Chinese Govern-

[30] A weighted average.

ment.   Summarizing, one discovers that throughout the
period of China's use of foreign funds the Central Government has contracted debts as follows, together with the
outstanding amounts as of January 1, 1926:

	Original Principal	Amount Outstanding
Early Period before 1890.....£	9,000,000	none
The Sino-Japanese Indemnity.	35,300,000	none
War, Military and Indemnity Loans....................	61,438,000	£ 22,671,530
Boxer Indemnity............	67,500,000	40,000,000 [31]
Railway Loans..............	61,217,600	49,632,884
General and Administrative Loans....................	42,235,870	34,333,245
Industrial Loans............	6,758,000	6,477,500
Total all foreign secured debt contracted since 1865..............	283,449,470	153,115,159
Deducting Indemnities...	102,800,000	40,000,000
Total Foreign Loans.....£	180,649,470	£ 113,115,159

Sixty-three percent of the total of foreign secured loans
contracted are outstanding.   Of that which has been repaid £ 16,555,000 represents over twenty obligations
which have been entirely redeemed.   In three of four cases
the bonds were redeemed out of the proceeds of new bond
issues included among those contracted.

Most of the outstanding secured loans have definite
plans of amortization as arranged in tables attached to
the loan agreements.[32]   The Chinese Bureau of Economic
Information [33] gives a list of payments which fell due in

[31] My estimate deducting German, Austrian and Russian portions.
[32] Some in MacMurray, others in Baylin.
[33] In Baylin, *op. cit.*, p. 90 ff.

1925,[34] and for which the necessary funds were raised, which totals as follows:

General and Administrative (including War Loans).£	5,463,394
Railway Loans.............................	3,857,164
	£ 9,320,558

These payments represent interest and amortization on most of the outstanding secured loans which have been treated above. To this total should be added £ 175,850 as interest only, on a number of loans, not in default, upon which amortization has not yet begun and which were not listed in the source referred to above.

Then, too, an addition should be made of £ 549,504 or even more, which represents what should have been paid in 1925 on the telegraph loans, and other originally secured loans, now in default, which have been considered in the preceding chapters. This is not inclusive, however, of annual charges due on loans of doubtful security or with no security at all, which are yet to be considered, even though these loans may have been provided with regular amortization plans.

The Chinese Government, therefore, is obligated annually to pay as an annual charge of interest and amortization on the foreign secured loans outstanding at least to the amount of £ 10,045,912. This figure compares favorably with the amount given for 1926 in the Chinese Economic Monthly,[35] which was £ 10,256,305, using the same rates for conversion as employed above.

[34] Conversion to £ sterling made at following rates: 1 £ equals 10 yen, 5 G $, 9.5 $ Mex, 25 gold francs, or 12.1 g. Florins.

[35] In March, 1926, p. 127 ff., " A list of Secured Loan Payments Falling Due in 1926."

Title	Interest Rate	Date	Maturity	Price to Public	Price to Bankers	Original Principal	in
1. Loan to Viceroy of Canton......	7	1907	1917			2,000,000 taels	
2. Loan to Viceroy of Hukuang.....	5	1909	1919			500,000 taels	
3. Loan to Viceroy of Hukuang.....	7	1911	1921	100	100	2,000,000 taels	
4. Crisp Loan (British)...........	5	1912	1952	95	89	5,000,000 £	
5. Anglo-Franco-Belgian Advances..	5	1912	1913	97		1,250,000 £	
6. Italo-Belgian Loan.............	8	1912	1913			625,000 £	
7. Italo-Belgian Loan.............	5	1914	1918			400,000 £	
8. Reorganization Loan...........	5	1913	1960	90	84	25,000,000 £	2
9. Japanese Advance on second Re-organization Loan...........	7	1917	1918		93	10,000,000 yen	
10. Second Reorganization Loan.....	7	1918	1919		99	10,000,000 yen	
11. Chihli Flood Relief Loan.......	7	1917	1918	.	98¾	5,000,000 yen	
12. Plague Suppression Loan	7	1918	1919		100	1,000,000 yen	
13. Japanese "Arms" Loan.........	7	1918			90	14,000,000 yen	
14. Treasury Notes for Compensation of Public Properties at Tsingtao.	6	1922	1938			14,000,000 yen	
15. Chinese Government Refunding Bonds—(Japanese portion of the "96 Million" Loan)........	8	1922	1929			39,608,700 yen	
Total Foreign Secured General Loans...................							
Total Principal of items for which "Amount Available" not known.							¥
Total Principal on which "Amount Available" is known..							
Total "Amount Available" to Chinese Government as shown..							3
Total Outstanding on all General Loans....................							

of sion	Amount Available to Chinese Gov.	Outstanding	Date	Outstanding in £ Sterling	Remarks
= 1 £		Repaid			
= 1 £		Repaid			
= 1 £		Repaid			
	4,450,000	4,762,752	Sept., 1925	4,762,752	Secured by Salt Revenues
	1,212,500	Repaid			
		Converted into No. 7			
		Repaid			
	21,000,000	24,495,780 £	Jan., 1926	24,495,780	Secured by Salt Revenues and customs surplus. Negotiated through consortium
1 £	930,000	Repaid			
1 £	990,000	Repaid			
1 £	493,750	Redeemed out of proceeds of No. 15			8% Bonds of 1922
1 £	100,000	Redeemed out of proceeds of No. 15			8% Bonds of 1922
1 £	1,260,000	Refunded by No. 14			
1 £		14,885,363 yen	June, 1925	1,488,536	Secured by surplus of Salt Revenues
1 £		35,861,772 yen	Jan., 1925	3,586,177	Secured by surplus of Salt Revenues
	30,702,916				
		or 88.5%			
				34,333,245	

PART II

UNSECURED LOANS

CHAPTER V

RAILWAY AND INDUSTRIAL LOANS

The loans treated in Part I have been those whose security is more or less assured. The loans treated in Part II are those loans whose security as originally given is doubtful or those loans for which no security was given at all. In the first place, it may be stated that these loans are of several classes not carefully distinguished: (a) short term loans, originally made for terms relatively short, usually bank loans; (b) loans made for periods of approximately one year or longer; (c) advances made to newly projected railways. In addition there is the floating debt contracted for purchase of foreign goods, whose terms are of the nature of a loan, involving interest and due date. The unsecured debt is one of the worst features of Chinese finance. Almost all of these obligations are overdue and definitely in default. Others have been partly met out of the proceeds of domestic loan issues. The Chinese Government appointed a Commission for the Redemption of Domestic and Foreign Short Term Debts, which has been working particularly on the short term loans. Many of the short term loans have been brought before this Commission. The lists of these loans as given in various publications do not distinguish between foreign and domestic loans.[1] It may be fairly stated that the majority of these short term obligations are domestic loans, or owed to foreign banks operating in China, and in terms of silver.

[1] In *China Year Book*, 1925, pp. 745–749; in F. E. Lee, *op. cit.*, pp. 199–203.

For these reasons they will not be discussed at this point but will be briefly summarized later.

Attention will then be directed to the other types of unsecured loans made in connection with railways and industries in China. This will include the railway advances.

Railway Advances

One finds in books on railways in China, and in MacMurray's *Treaties and Agreements,* mention and records of many railroads which have been projected, for which rights of construction and rights of financing have been contracted, which have never been or but partially been availed of by the foreign capital involved. The Chinese Revolution provided a slight setback but recovery was in swing when the European war prevented the completion of much financing. The conclusion of the war found former capital markets for China unable to lend support, and the uncertainty in the Chinese situation itself, brought delay in railway construction in China.

Several contracts were followed shortly after their signature by advances from the investment banking concerns, and should be considered. Some are partially secured, and doubtful, some not at all secured. This includes the " Nishihara " advances on railways. See Table E.

The Siems-Carey project, American, is one of interest, but space will scarcely allow full treatment here. In 1915, a St. Paul contracting firm, Siems-Carey & Co., became interested in China's possibilities. As a result of a survey and negotiations, a contract was signed May 17, 1916, providing for the construction of 1500 miles of railroads.[2] By a supplementary agreement this was later reduced to

[2] MacMurray, p. 1313, No. 1916-7, or *Foreign Relations, 1916,* pp. 183-188.

1100 miles. The firm was to sell $1,000,000 of gold bonds every year from the signing of the contract to the time of completion of the construction work. Other details were 5 per cent interest, 5 per cent commission or discount for selling the bonds, a first trust mortgage on the railways to be built, a 5 per cent commission on materials cost which were purchased, 8 per cent on all other monies expended for construction, 25 per cent of net profits from operation until all bonds outstanding were met. The 25 per cent was later reduced to 20 per cent.

Protest came from Russia to the construction of the line proposed from Fengchen to Ningshia claiming violation of promises of China in 1910 in regard to Russian priority in new railways north of Peking. China would not agree to the Russian position, nor would the United States. The American International Corporation, and the Siems-Carey Railway and Canal Company, refused to proceed with this particular project until the issue was settled. Hence this was postponed and a road from Chuchow to Chincow was decided upon, a distance of 700 miles.[3]

The war with Germany, however, came upon America to prevent the flotation of this loan and only $1,150,000 Gold was advanced against Chinese Treasury bills for three years. Interest was at 7 per cent and a discount of 9 per cent, making the amount China received $1,046,500 Gold. There is no security for this loan and $1,150,000 is still outstanding (January, 1925).

Japanese Railway Loans

One of the features of the unsecured debt problem is that of the so-called " Nishihara " loans, loans made by Japan through its banks operating in China, namely the

[3] Cf. *Foreign Relations*, 1916, p. 189 *et seq.*

Industrial Bank of Japan, the Bank of Taiwan, and the Bank of Chosen. These loans were made principally in the year 1918 and the principal sum of all of these loans is yet a matter of doubt. A few of them were secured and were treated in Chapter IV.[4]

A number of these loans took the form of an " advance " of substantial size on railway contracts signed in preliminary form by China, but not stipulating very much in definitive form as to the important financial elements to feature in the bond issue itself when made. These railway contracts covered wide areas in Shantung, Manchuria and Mongolia, and, considering the argument of priority of interest, seemed to assure to Japan a future opportunity for capital investment when the European war should have closed. Mention only of these railways will be made as follows:

> the Jehol-Toanon Railway, and to the sea,
> the Changchun-Taonon Railway, and
> the Kirin-Kaiyan Railway,

with these involving an advance of 20,000,000 yen;

> the Kirin-Huening Railway with an advance of 10,000,000 yen
> the Tsinan-Shunteh Railway, and
> the Kaomi-Hsuchow Railway,

these involving an advance of 20,000,000 yen. Thus 50,-000,000 yen or £5,000,000 were advanced by Japan with no pledged security other than Chinese Government Treasury bills and the assurance that the advance was to be paid back from the proceeds of an issue of a government public loan.

[4] Cf. p. 63.

In regard to the security and use of funds, the preliminary agreements [5] pledged the revenues of the roads and the railways themselves, when built, but since these have not been built it is apparent that the security is quite doubtful. In fact these funds, together with the advances on the Cheng-Yu, the Tung-Chen and the Shanghai-Hangchow railways, to a total of $87,200,000 (Mex.) were used originally by the Ministry of Finance and not by the Ministry of Communications.[6] All of these railway loan advances of the " Nishihara " group are in default with over 54,000,000 yen outstanding (1925).[7] These advances, however, created an interest burden of 3,950,000 yen per annum, since interest on the loans was at 7½ and 8 per cent.

There are listed among the unsecured debts certain railway loans and other debts contracted for short terms.[8] On the Peking Suiyuan Railway for example there were contracted the following:

			Per Cent.
Loan	1918	3,000,000 yen	10.8
Loan	1921	3,000,000 yen	10.8
Account	1921	2,953,000 yen	8.
"	1919	746,000 yen	10.
"	1918	39,000 Gold	10.
"	1919	1,140,000 yen	12.
"	1920	289,000 $ Mex.	12.

All but the first three have no security whatever. The amounts outstanding on these debts just enumerated (June 30, 1925) are 11,102,721 yen, $51,445 Gold, and $277,139

5 MacMurray, No. 1918/9, No. 1918/15, No. 1918/16.

6 Cf. Report of Minister of Communications in *Chinese Economic Monthly*, Nov., 1925, p. 42.

7 F. E. Lee, *op. cit.*, p. 192.

8 F. E. Lee, *op. cit.*, pp. 191–208.

silver.   Unsecured debts on the Tientsin-Pukow railway to the amount of about $5,000,000 were contracted and are outstanding, and on the Peking-Hankow to the amount of about $950,000.

The foreign unsecured or doubtfully secured railway obligations of the Chinese Government, insofar as they have been presented, and are now outstanding, total £10,-308,960 (at 1925 information and at rates of conversion appearing in Table E), or roughly £10,000,000.   This of course is not the entire unsecured railway debt since no domestic obligations are included.   The secured railway foreign debt, it will be recalled from Table B was given as £49,632,884, which added to the above leaves a total of foreign railway indebtedness of the government of £59,632,884.[9]

The total debt of the Ministry of Communications on September 30, 1923, has been given by the Minister as $707,300,000.[10]   In the same report an itemized list of obligations appears, the foreign railway loans appearing to total $581,007,405, as of September 30, 1923.   This includes principal outstanding as of that date and interest unpaid of matured liability.[11]   The figure of £59,632,884 of total foreign railway indebtedness, given above, if converted to silver at $10 (the same rate used by the Minister) compares favorably and makes allowance for an in-

[9] Cf. statement of Foreign Debts of Chinese Government Railways, issued by Chinese Government, Bureau of Economic Information in Jan., 1922 as copied in Lee, *op. cit.*, p. 139, April, 1922, $54,826,000.

[10] Cf. Report of Minister of Communications on " Development of Communications in China " in *Chinese Economic Monthly*, Nov., 1925, pp. 31, 34, 42 ff.   His conversion to silver at rough rates of $10 Mex.—£1 $1 Mex.—$2G.

[11] This is not completely accurate since several items cannot be segregated as to foreign and domestic, but is sufficiently indicative.

crease in the unsecured debt and for unpaid interest on obligations in default.[12]

Industrial Loans

Most of the foreign unsecured loans for industrial purposes were made in good faith but with some of them there is room for doubt as to purpose. Statements of purpose or the title given may be misleading.

The Grand Canal Loan

American and Japanese capital participated in advances to the amount of $938,983 (G) made in 1917 on a $6,-000,000 (G) contract for conservancy work along the Grand Canal and the Huai River.[13] This now has outstanding $515,778. Japan insisted on participation in this loan which was originally an American contract, on the claim of Japanese inheritance of all German rights in Shantung provinces among which was an option on all public works involving the use of foreign capital. Although America had never recognized this monopoly claim Japanese participation was accepted to silence objection.

The Wireless Loans of 1918 and 1919

In 1918, the Mutsui Bussen Kaisha, a Japanese concern, obtained a contract for the erection of a wireless station, which agreement had first been concluded with a Danish firm. The sum estimated for construction of the radio telegraphic station in question was £536,267 and the contracting firm was to raise this sum on behalf of China and pay the annual interest and installments on the loan. Interest was put at 8 per cent. The contractors however

12 F. E. Lee, *op. cit.*, p. 138.
13 MacMurray, No. 1916/5 and No. 1916/6.

were to have charge of operations and were to pay China 10 per cent of the gross receipts upon messages. China reserved the right to liquidate by paying the unpaid portion at any time.[14] This appears to be a private investment, yet the Chinese government is involved in redemption. Furthermore, the Minister of the Navy signed for China. It signifies a Japanese wireless station on Chinese soil under Japanese control.

Another loan of 5,000,000 yen, of 1918, through this same firm, at 7½ per cent is recorded.

The Marconi Wireless Loans

In August, 1918, the Marconi Wireless Telegraph Company, an English Company, made a loan to the Chinese Government of £600,000 at 8 per cent, of which one-half was to be used for the purchase of two hundred wireless telephone sets, and the other half was to be transferred to the government without discount.[15]

In October of the same year the amount was increased by £200,000 for the purpose of erecting three wireless stations to cost £66,000, f.o.b. British port, the balance of £134,000 being available for transportation, erection, etc.[16] Of this only £170,376 was actually paid.[17] Further the Chinese Government agreed to pay the salary of $800 a month and expenses of an engineer to supervise the erection, to be sent out from London by the company. The use of the funds of this second Marconi loan is given in a statement from the Minister of Communications, in 1922,

14 MacMurray, p. 1519, App. F.
15 MacMurray, p. 1440, No. 1918/12.
16 *Ibid.*, p. 1452, No. 1918/17.
17 J. R. Baylin, *op. cit.*, p. 78.

which accounts for £ 149,319 drawn by the Ministry at various times.[18]   This can briefly be summarized as follows:

Expenditure not known	£ 67,000
Company advances, salary, expenses of engineers, materials	3,319
Machinery purchased	66,000
Interest	5,604
Other drawings	7,395
	£ 149,319

The item of other drawings was converted into silver making $57,431 and spent as follows:

Engineer and expenses	$ 9,000
Expenses	86,323
	$95,323
Deficit	37,892
	$57,431

The deficit was made up from other sources than the loan funds. However, in Lee, the original sum is given as £ 170,376, and the amount outstanding in default as £ 222,859, as of June 30, 1925.

From this accounting the use of 45 per cent of the loan funds is unknown, and of the balance not all was used productively.

Of the £ 600,000 loan, the balance is now £ 874,000 and in default.   Both loans bore 8 per cent interest.   In 1919, £ 100,000, at 8 per cent were further loaned, like the first loan for 10 years, through the Marconi Company, and this loan is now in default for non-payment of interest, the amout outstanding being £ 145,839.   The three Marconi loans outstanding total at least £ 1,242,700.

[18] F. E. Lee, *op. cit.*, p. 215,—figures cited from *Chinese Government Gazette* of August 16 and 17, 1922.

One feature of the contract for the first of these loans is found in clause 12 of the agreement, whereby the Chinese Government promised in the event it desired to erect a factory for maintenance or manufacture of wireless installations, the Government would open negotiations with the company. It is understood, states MacMurray, that in pursuance of this clause an agreement was signed in May, 1919,[19] providing for a Chinese National Wireless Telegraph Company, with joint Government and Marconi Company ownership, the latter sharing 2/3 in profits, the former 1/3, the latter having a controlling voice on the board, the Government having a right to buy out the Marconi Company, but only after 20 years, and to equalize profits only on payment of £300,000 to the Marconi Company. Further, the Chinese company was granted an almost exclusive monopoly on repair and maintenance of all wireless telegraph and telephone apparatus in China. The Chinese company was to have Marconi patent rights exclusively in China, during the continuance of Marconi Company ownership and control in the same. Thus China has through these foreign loans become bound in other ways than the loans, particularly in the granting of such special privilege and monopoly to particular interests.

The Chiujitzu Telephone Agreement

In October, 1918, the Chinese Government contracted a loan for 10,000,000 yen, with the China-Japan Industrial Development Company, bearing 8 per cent interest, to run for three years. This contract called the Chiujitzu Telephone Loan Agreement of 1919,[20] stated at the outset

[19] Cf. MacMurray, p. 1442, No. 1918/12, note.
[20] Cf. F. E. Lee, *op. cit.*. Appendix E, p. 216, obtained from publication by Ministry of Communications in China.

that it was for the purpose of extending the 1916 short-term loan (the terms of which were not made public) and of effecting extensions and improvements to the telephone business which required the investment of capital. The loan was to net 97.7 to the Chinese Government.

Certain commitments of this agreement are of more than passing interest. "Within seven years from the date of the signature of this agreement (N. B. extending beyond the period of the agreement), whenever China desires to extend or establish any telephone exchange, Party 'B' (the Japanese Co.) shall supply the necessary materials in the following manner": [21] In order to ascertain the market value of materials, China might take out 50 per cent at any time and invite tenders of other merchants, but foi same quality and price it was to go by preference to Party " B." The balance of 50 per cent would then be supplied at the prices thus established. But note this qualifying clause: " If the prices in the tenders of other companies are quoted purely for competition, without taking into consideration the cost comprising the raw materials, labor, and expenses, then the above provision does not hold good." This "above provision" implies that then Party " B " would be responsible for everything. Is it not possible and highly probable that these clauses could be so interpreted as to give a Japanese monopoly on the extension or establishment of "any telephone exchange"? As a further inducement, in case China did not call for competing tenders she might treat payment for the goods ordered as a loan; if otherwise, however, then " cash without delay."

Another commitment is very important. In Article 4, clause (a), security for the loan is stated in part, as " all

[21] Article 1, part quoted, part summarized.

the properties and revenues, *with operating rights*, of the various telephone exchanges and long distance telephones under the administration of Party ' A ' (i.e., China) existing at present or *developed in future*." Dr. Lee states, " This clearly violates certain other contracts of the Ministry of Communications." This clause, together with the other relative to purchase of materials, have bound China in this field and appear as a monopoly granted to a foreign company, and in violation of the spirit of the " open door." The agreement was not signed by any representative of the Japanese Government.

The Ministry of Communications has published the expenditures made out of the proceeds of this loan,[22] which are not detailed, but quite indicative. China received 9,-770,000 yen plus 313,828 yen as interest on funds left on deposit, making 10,083,828 yen. These were divided as follows:

Expenditures by the telegraph administration for materials	yen 1,229,322
Expenditures by the railway administration for principal and interest payments on certain loans	4,227,700
Expenditures by the Ministry of Finance	1,400,000
Expenditures by the Ministry of Communications, for interest and capital charges on other loans	1,228,286
Interest on the present loan	1,893,698

In other words, the telegraph administration received and spent in some way about 12 to 13 per cent of the funds. Certainly not more than that could be called productive and probably not all of that. In 1923, unpaid interest to the amount of 2,183,711 yen was arranged as a loan at 9 per cent for three years. Of this 2,281,978 yen is

22 Copied in F. E. Lee, *op. cit.*, p. 218.

unpaid, and of the main obligation 11,211,765 yen is un-paid and in default.[23]

Telegraph Improvement Advance of 1920

Another loan to the amount of 10,220,000 yen at 9 per cent, for 13 years, was obtained by China through the Eastern Asia Industrial Development Company (Japanese), for the purpose of improving telegraph lines, the loan being based on the telegraph installations to be made. The contract for the advance signed February 10, 1920, however, does state (Article 4) " On the above advance, Party ' A ' shall pledge all the properties and revenues of the wire telegraphs as security." [24] How inclusive this article should be interpreted is questionable. Certainly if referable to all China it violates the telegraph loan contract of April 30, 1918 mentioned under secured loans, even though both companies concerned are Japanese.[25]

Another feature of this loan agreement of 1920 is in regard to purchase of materials. Article 8 states: " As to materials, machine, etc., which should be purchased from foreign countries, when the quality and price are not much different from those of Party ' B ' (i.e., the Japanese), then the same shall be purchased from Party ' B ' (i.e., the Japanese)." This clause is confusing. Read one way, when the quality and price of the Japanese goods are not much different from the quality and price of the Japanese goods, all goods which should be purchased in

[23] According to F. E. Lee, *op. cit.*, p. 192. The *China Year Book*, 1923, p. 448, gives 6,030,000 yen received but 15,000,000 yen outstanding in June, 1922. In App. E, p. 200, Lee gives report of Minister of Communications showing 6,030,000 yen received.

[24] This agreement is in F. E. Lee, *op. cit.*, App. E, p. 219.

[25] Above, p. 48. The contract of April 30, 1918, is MacMurray, No. 1918/7.

foreign countries should be purchased from the Japanese, giving a monopoly. Read another way, the meaning of the clause depends on the meaning of " should be purchased." If this signifies necessity then all goods for the work must be purchased in foreign countries, and also, unless the price of these goods are much different from those of Japanese, that the goods should be purchased from the Japanese.

Of the proceeds of this loan, 2,730,000 yen at least went for military purposes and 810,000 for interest on the loan.[26] On June 30, 1925, 11,154,310 yen was the amount outstanding.[27] In practice, interest on this loan has partially been met out of the Chinese share of telegraph revenues from the Chefoo-Dairen cable and the South Manchurian lines.[28]

The Federal Wireless Loans

In 1921, the American Federal Wireless Telephone and Telegraph Co. signed with the Ministry of Communications for a loan to the latter of $4,620,000 (G) to erect certain wireless stations in China. There developed opposition to this on the part of the British and Japanese, the protest claiming that certain rights of their nationals under existing contracts had been violated. The American Government, however, supported the agreement on the grounds of the American-Chinese Treaty of 1858, of which Article 30 states that any right, privilege, or favor, granted to any other nation by China, shall " at once freely inure to the benefit of the United States, its public officers,

---

26 Cf. statement of Minister of Communications copied in F. F. Lee, *op. cit.*, App. E, p. 220.

27 F. E. Lee, *op. cit.*, p. 192.

28 J. R. Baylin, *op. cit.*, p. 80.

merchants and citizens." The loan was made for $6,500,-
000 (G) to bear 8 per cent on unpaid portions, with
price of issue at 93. The wireless stations to be erected
were to be security, together with revenues therefrom.
Th contractor was to have full supervision of construction
for 10 years, but during that period was to pay the Government 10 per cent of the gross receipts of each station.
The management of the stations was to be joint Chinese
and American. This issue, known as the Twenty Year
8 per cent China Federal Radio Administration Sinking
Fund Gold Loan of 1921, eventually will be secured by
the wireless telegraph revenues as will also the Mitsui Wireless Loan.[29]

Other Loans

Two other industrial loans may be mentioned. The
Mining and Forestry Loan, a " Nishihara " loan, was negotiated in 1918, secretly, by the Ministers of Commerce
and Agriculture, and of Finance, through a Japanese
banking syndicate. The loan was for 30,000,000 yen, for
10 years, at $7\frac{1}{2}$ per cent interest, with delivery of the
proceeds without discount to China. It was to be secured
by the gold mines of Kirin and Heilungkiang and by governmental revenues from gold mines and national forests.[30]
The loan was made for the purpose of mining and forestry
development in those areas. It is very doubtful if much
or any of the proceeds went to these purposes. These
elements of security as they stand are insufficient. The
outstanding amount of the loan was 31,125,000 yen and
was in default in January, 1925.

The other loan is that of the Vickers Company aeroplane

[29] J. R. Baylin, pp. 82, 83, 89.
[30] MacMurray, p. 1434, No. 1918/11; also J. R. Baylin, p. 84.

7

loan of 1919, made with this company by the Ministry
of Communications. China agreed to buy 100 aeroplanes,
Viney Commercial type, to be delivered by the close of
1920. The total cost was to be £1,803,200, represented
by Treasury notes, and was to bear 8 per cent, due 1929.
The debt in 1922 amounted to £2,235,968.[31] No security
at all was pledged but provision was made for five amortization payments. In the absence of specific revenue security,
it is doubtful if the Chinese Government has been able to
carry this out.

Summary

In this treatment of the unsecured and doubtfully secured railway and industrial loans to China, it has not
been possible to summarize the amount available out of
these loan operations to the Chinese Government. In the
case of most of these loans such has not been known. For
most of them original contracts were available, but not all
conditions of the loan or advance were disclosed therein.
Clear, it is, however, that the interest burden has been
quite high, those loans with no security at all having the
highest rates generally; except the " Nishihara " loans,
from Japanese sources, which, as stated elsewhere, having
relatively lower rates, and either small or no discounts, in
comparison with other loans of similar status, may reflect
other than purely investment interest. The fact that so
much of the funds, particularly of these " Nishihara "
loans, never reached the purposes for which they were
contracted, that other departments of the Government of
China spent them, and that many of the facts in regard
to these loans are singularly unavailable, reveal the lack

[31] Cf. F. E. Lee, *op. cit.*, p. 192; J. R. Baylin, p. 26; also *Far
Eastern Review*, Dec., 1919, p. 771.

Title	Interest Rate	Year	Amount of Original Contract	A
1. Tatung-Chengtu Ry.[1]		1913	10,000,000 £	770,
2. Pukow-Sinyang Ry.[2]			3,000,000 £	5,798,
3. Nanking-Hunan Ry.[3]	6	1914		207,
				2,000,0
				486,00
4. Ching-Yu Ry.[4]	5	1914	600,000,000 francs	32,115,
5. Siems-Carey Projects[5]	7	1916	{ 1,000,000 G $ Every year until projects completed }	1,150,
6. Pin-Hei Ry.[6]	8½	1916	50,000,000 R.	1,500,
7. Taokow-Chinghua[7]	7½	1920		45,
8. Nishihara Advances[8]			50,000,000 yen	50,000,
Total Advances on Railways				
Total Outstanding on Railway Advances				

[1] MacMurray, p. 1042, No. 1913/8.
[2] Ibid, p. 1068, No. 1913/12.
[3] Ibid, p. 1113, No. 1914/4.
[4] Ibid, p. 1099, No. 1914/2.   J. R. Baylin gives this advance as 100,000,000 francs.
[5] Ibid, p. 1313, No. 1916/7 and U. S. Foreign Relations. 1916, p. 183.
[6] Cf. U. S. Foreign Relations, 1916, p. 210.
[7] F. E. Lee, op. cit. p. 205.
[8] MacMurray, No. 1918/9, No. 1918/15, No. 1918/16.

nt of ce in ling	Rate of Conversion	Security (Doubtful)	Nationality of Concessionaire	Outstanding in £ Sterling	Date
217 40	25 fr. = 1 £	{ ⅔ Profits of Shansi Ry.	Franco-Belgian Co.	1,000,317	Sept., 1922
56 66	7.5 taels = 1 £	Surplus Profits of Peking-Mukden Ry.	British British	219,775 331,466	June, 1925 Jan., 1925
20	25 fr. = 1 £	Railway	Franco-Belgian	1,284,620	Sept., 1922
00	85 G = 1 £	None	American	230,000	Jan., 1925
54 43 00	10 yen = 1 £		Russian British Japanese	54,054 45,743 5,400,000	Amount doubtful 1926
96 £					
				8,565,975	

of careful finance and the sinister influences at work in the Chinese Government during the period, particularly, of 1917 and 1918. It is impossible to state to what extent all the loans considered in this chapter were productive. They were so planned, if their titles are significant, but further than that information is virtually non-existent, except as in some cases mentioned where information was definitely disclosed.

CHAPTER VI

OTHER UNSECURED LOANS

Among the problems facing China during the period of the European War, when the nations which had formerly loaned to her were busily engaged, was the problem of finding funds to meet obligations and even deficits in administrative expenditure. China, formerly, had met many of her maturing obligations by further borrowing. Before the period of extensive Japanese loaning to China in 1917 and 1918, which has already been mentioned, China turned to America.

American Loans

In April, 1916, Lee Higginson and Company and the Chinese Government entered into an agreement for the sale of $5,000,000 (G) in treasury notes of China, of three years duration, at 6 per cent. The company was to dispose of them at least for 97 per cent of their face value and the Chinese Government was to receive at least 93 per cent, allowing not more than 4 per cent commission to the company for underwriting.[1] The company made an advance of $1,000,000 but for some reason the notes were never issued.

Other negotiations followed with other American interests and finally in 1916 a loan of $5,000,000 (G) from the Continental and Commercial Trust and Savings Bank of Chicago was concluded, to be represented by Chinese Gov-

[1] MacMurray, p. 1279.

ernment Treasury notes, for three years, at 6 per cent.
These were offered for sale in November, 1916, and were
over-subscribed. The security pledged was the entire
amount of the wine and tobacco public sale tax, which was
declared to be free from all encumberances. The notes
were to yield at least 91 per cent to China and the sale
to the public was to be at not less than 97 per cent. If
at a higher figure the excess above 97 per cent was to
be divided between the Government and the bank. China
had rights of redemption at 101 for the first year and at
100½ thereafter.[2] By a supplementary agreement, the
goods tax, estimated to yield $4,490,383 (Mex.), of the
four provinces of Honan, Anhui, Fukien, and Shensi, was
pledged.[3] The loan was renewed in 1919 for $5,500,000
(G) and a new series of notes, due 1922, were issued.
When these fell due China did not have sufficient revenues
to redeem and hence defaulted on the payment. The default was serious, but not so much because of this one loan
as because others as well were in default. No interest had
been paid and the principal of $5,500,000 (G) was still
outstanding in 1926.[4] The wine and tobacco taxes are
capable of yielding revenue sufficient to meet this obligation, but, though the revenues have been collected, they
have been appropriated for provincial uses and each year
less than half has been forwarded to central authorities.
For the three years, 1919–1921, the average revenue collected each year was $14,664,000 (Mex.). Of this $1,-
938,000 went for administrative expenses in collection,
$6,690,000 was retained by provincial authorities, and
$6,036,000 went to Peking.[5]

[2] MacMurray, p. 1337.
[3] MacMurray, p. 1343.
[4] J. R. Baylin, *op. cit.*, p. 25.
[5] Y. H. Chang, *Financial Reconstruction of China*, p. 4.

Another American loan was made in December, 1919, by the Pacific Development Corporation through the Chase National Bank. This loan was for $5,500,000 (G) to be represented by 2 year treasury notes bearing 6 per cent, and to be secured by the surplus revenue of the wine and tobacco tax.[6] The entire revenues from this source were declared to exceed annually $20,000,000 (Mex.). When due this loan was compelled to go by default, for the same reason as in the Continental Bank loan above, and was then extended. The outstanding amount was $7,232,666 (G), principal and unpaid interest in 1925.[7] A condition of this loan was the appointment of an American adviser to the post of Associate Inspector General of the Wine and Tobacco Administration for a period of three years.

Japanese Loans

In addition to the American loans many unsecured loans came from Japanese financial institutions. Mention has been made of the large number of these loans in 1917, 1918, and 1919 in previous chapters. The total of these Japanese loans may never be completely known until some international commission is established to examine all of China's commitments, as was provided by a resolution of the Washington Conference. The details of many of these loans must also remain unknown. The totals continue to be a matter of dispute between China and Japan.

A summary of all the unsecured debts in the China Year Book [8] showing a statement as of 1922, indicates loans outstanding in yen to the amount of 162,406,102 yen. This refers only to loans expressed in yen and not to the total

[6] *New York Times*, Dec. 31, 1919.
[7] F. E. Lee, *op. cit.*, p. 191.
[8] 1925, p. 741.

of China's unsecured indebtedness. It does not even include all the Japanese loans in this category. The obligations made through Japanese banks and companies, which are unsecured or of doubtful security, as listed by Dr. F. E. Lee covering the period from 1916 to 1925, total over 265 million yen.[9] The amount outstanding on these same obligations at latest information in January, 1926 was 283,608,200 yen.[10] This does not purport to be complete and includes only items expressed in yen. There are several obligations, owed to Japanese bankers and companies, expressed in Chinese currencies, but these do not total much over $6 million (Mex.). Of the total in yen over 120,000,000 yen were the " Nishihara " loans. Two more Japanese loans will be mentioned specifically.

In 1917, the Bank of Communications of China, a quasi-governmental institution, signed an agreement with three Japanese banks, for a loan of 5,000,000 yen, to be secured by the deposit of securities of the Lung-Hai Railway and bonds of the Treasury of China. Interest was stated at $7\frac{1}{2}$ per cent and the whole amount of the proceeds was to be delivered to the Bank of Communications " without discount or commission." The purpose stated was that of " reorganizing the business " of the Bank.[11] On September 28, 1917, a supplementary loan of 20,000,000 yen was contracted, at $7\frac{1}{2}$ per cent, to be " paid at face value and no commission." This loan was also from the same three Japanese banks, for the equally indefinite purpose

[9] Includes only those expressed in yen. There are a few, not large, expressed in Chinese dollars, the three largest of which total only $7,850,000 (Mex.). One item of 32 million yen, probably a duplication, is omitted from this calculation.

[10] This excludes one item of large size about which there is question of duplication for 42,300,000 yen.

[11] MacMurray, p. 1345, No. 1917/1.

of "reorganizing its Affairs." There was no security other than a treasury certificate for $25,000,000 (Mex.). The second or supplementary loan is often called one of the "Nishihara" loans. The funds were probably used for redemption of the Bank of Communications' circulating notes. Both agreements are characteristically short and indefinite as to many features,[12] as are others of the Japanese loan agreements of that period. Though these two obligations were made by the Bank, they were secured by government securities and hence constitute government obligations.

Mention has now been made in several places of many of the so-called "Nishihara" loans, concluded by the Chinese Government with various Japanese banks in 1917 and 1918. These totalled 145,000,000 yen of which two, the Telegraph loan of 1918, and the Flood Relief loan were listed as secured. The latter for 5,000,000 yen was redeemed out of the " 96 Million " refunding issue of 1922, while the former for 20,000,000 yen is in default. There has been controversy over the total amount of these " Nishihara " loans. Of the total original principal (now outstanding) of 145,000,000 yen, 100,000,000 yen was underwritten by three Japanese banks—the Bank of Taiwan, the Industrial Bank of Japan, and the Bank of Chosen—working in close cooperation. The total amount of these " Nishihara " loans has been estimated by other than Chinese authorities at as high as 200 million yen. The character of these loans, as being prompted by the Japanese Government originally, as it has been alleged, is further supported by the fact that a bill, providing for government liquidation to bondholders of the " Nishihara " loans, was introduced early in 1926 into the Japanese Parliament by

12 *Ibid.*, p. 1387, No. 1917/9.

the government. This bill was to authorize the exchange of 143,000,000 yen in Japanese Government bonds for the " Nishihara " bonds. Thus the " Nishihara " loans would be assumed by the Japanese Government. The budget bill for 1926 also contained an item of 7 million yen for the payment of back interest on these obligations.

Loans for Military Purposes

Among the unsecured loans of the Chinese Government one finds over fifteen items whose titles clearly indicate a military character, or which are known to have been contracted for ammunition supplies and military purposes.[13] A summary would show that loans were contracted for these purposes to the amount of 50,483,072 yen, 2,002,083 pounds sterling, and 3,435,331 dollars (Mex.), making a total of about £ 7,000,000 and the three million and a half in Chinese currency. A number of other items for these purposes are in doubt. Some are probably duplicates of others already counted, but if these doubtful loans are added one has the equivalent of a total of £ 10,642,770 in foreign currencies as well as $5,173,750 in Chinese currency. On those not in doubt there is outstanding £ 8,- 750,575 and $2,004,157 (Mex.).[14] It would be a conservative statement indeed to say that at least $100,000,000 of the unsecured foreign indebtedness of the Chinese Government in 1926 represented debts contracted for military purposes. The present figure is undoubtedly much higher.

[13] Included in this treatment is the war participation loan by the Nishihara syndicate, for 20 million yen. Cf. MacMurray, p. 1446 and notes, No. 1918/14.

[14] According to lists given by F. E. Lee, *op. cit.*, pp. 193–198.

Total of Outstanding Unsecured Foreign Debts—1926

A complete scientifically compiled statement of the outstanding foreign unsecured and doubtfully secured debt of the Chinese Government is impossible. This must already have become apparent to the reader who has noted the lack of careful accounting and finance and the uncertainty surrounding many obligations. Any figures which we can give must necessarily be indicative only, and as a working basis for a further consideration of Chinese financial problems.

The amounts of unsecured foreign debt in various currencies are: [15]

in $ (G)	14,451,123 ÷ 5........	£ 2,890,224
in £	4,191,478............	4,191,478
in yen	325,955,865 ÷ 10........	32,595,586
in francs	164,996,324 ÷ 25........	6,599,853
Sub-total..................		£ 46,277,141
in taels (varied)	1,550,767 × 1.5............	$ 2,326,150
in $ (Mex.)	66,497,388..................	66,497,388
Sub-total............................		$68,823,538
Railway Advances [16]............	3,057,391	
Totals.....................	£ 49,334,532	$68,823,538

Converting the foreign currencies to £'s sterling at their gold value and the taels roughly to Chinese dollars, one arrives at a figure of over £ 49,334,532 and $68,823,538.

It will be recalled that, in discussing the Boxer indemnity

[15] This is a summary of the material itemized in F. E. Lee, *op. cit.*, pp. 191–198. Some of these items may represent floating debt. The majority are figures for 1925, the balance for 1924 or 1922. These have all been combined. A few of these are perhaps duplications, noted by Dr. Lee to the amount of £9,109,000.

[16] F. E. Lee, *op. cit.*, p. 205.

it was pointed out that certain unsecured obligations of the Chinese Government, principally to the Banque Industrielle de Chine, have been made secured on the customs revenue and converted into gold dollar obligations as a result of the French settlement. The amounts of these obligations in various currencies to be deducted then from the foregoing statement of unsecured indebtedness are:

£	72,967................................	£ 72,967
Francs 139,929,275 ÷ 25....................		5,597,171
	In Foreign Currencies....................	£ 5,670,138
and Taels	860,083 × 1.5....................	$1,290,124
$ Mex.	352,772........................	352,772
	In Chinese currencies....................	$1,642,896 (Mex.)

This reduces the unsecured debt given above by £ 5,670,138 and $1,642,896 (Mex.) making £ 43,664,394, plus $67,-180,642 (Mex.). The effect of this reduction upon the Boxer indemnity has been reviewed. The estimate in Table A of £ 40,000,000 as remaining on the Boxer indemnity is sufficiently conservative to include these obligations, and for that reason they have been deducted here.

The Commission on Redemption of Foreign and Domestic Short term loans has brought before it obligations to the amount of $58,607,670, has repaid $35,103,724 by means of the 8 per cent Tenth Year Domestic Bonds and thus shows remaining $25,503,945 (Mex.).[17] This item is not alone foreign. It is more largely domestic. It will not be included here in a statement of the outstanding foreign unsecured debt.

The doubtful items, that is, those about which there is some possibility of duplication, were given as £9,109,000, thus leaving as the lowest possible statement of the un-

17 Cf. F. E. Lee, *op. cit.*, pp. 199–203.

secured debt at £34,555,400 plus the $67,180,642 (Mex.).
To this must be added six years' interest upon the portion
of these figures which were included at their 1922 amounts,
which is estimated at £5,000,000. If this is added and
the foreign currencies converted to Chinese dollars at $9.5
to the £ sterling, and added to the silver obligations, the
lowest figure for unsecured indebtedness becomes $443,-
000,000.

This is a large sum to have contracted in such a short
period of time. The interest charges on these loans vary
from no interest at all to 14½ per cent, with 8, 10, and
12 as rates commonly found. The " Nishihara " loans are
notable in that they all bore 7½ per cent or 8 per cent
interest.

The unsecured debt problem is now receiving attention.
It becomes a real problem since with most of these loans
in default the credit of the Chinese Government is seriously
impaired. This phase of the fiscal problem was being
studied by the Peking Tariff Conference when it was forced
to suspend its meetings in 1926. Several proposals for
consolidation of this indebtedness have been drawn up.
This problem of consolidation as related to the financial
capacity of the Chinese Government is treated in Chapter
X.

At the Peking Conference various estimates of the unsecured debt were presented. As presented by the Commission on Redemption the unsecured and inadequately secured foreign debts of the Government of China were said
to be between $525,000,000 (Mex.) and $635,000,000
(Mex.), depending upon the rates of conversion to be employed; and as presented by the loan statements themselves
between $607,000,000 (Mex.) and $742,000,000 (Mex.),
again depending upon the rates of exchange employed.

In the China Year Book, 1925, and the monographs by M. Padoux and Mr. Chang statements are given as of 1922 or 1923 for the obligations of the Ministry of Finance only.[18] Variations are found in all statements, due to different rates of conversion used, or to differences in classifications as to secured and unsecured debt. An expert of the Financial Readjustment Commission reported as of June 30, 1924, the unsecured foreign debt of the Ministry of Finance computed in silver at $317,241,280;[19] while the Department of Loans, Ministry of Finance, reported as of November 30, 1925, a total of $354,018,612.[20] If the estimates given in Chapter V of unsecured railway obligations as totalling about £10,000,000, and of telegraph and telephone obligations of £6,000,000, are converted to silver at $10 = 1£ one would have $150,-000,000 (Mex.). If this is taken as the unsecured foreign debt of the Ministry of Communications and is added to the debt of the Ministry of Finance the total of foreign unsecured indebtedness of the Chinese Government becomes $504,018,612. The foreign unsecured indebtedness can therefore be roughly treated as at least $500,000,000 (Mex.).[21]

The annual interest burden upon such an indebtedness, if calculated at the rates of interest as called for by the loans themselves, to say nothing of the repayment provisions, would be between $40,000,000 and $45,000,000

---

[18] *China Year Book*, 1925, p. 741; G. Padoux, *Financial Reconstruction of China*, p. 5; Chang Ying-Hua, *Financial Reconstruction of China*, pp. 18–19, 24–25.

[19] In *Chinese Economic Monthly*, October, 1925, p. 12.

[20] In *Chinese Economic Bulletin*, February 27, 1926, p. 116.

[21] *The London Economist* of October 31, 1925, p. 695, gives the foreign unsecured estimate at $495,000,000 (Mex.).

(Mex.). No exact statement is possible. This, of course, is not now being paid, but is causing the unsecured debt to mount larger and larger. The annual interest burden upon the "doubtfully secured" loans, which have been included in the statement here given of unsecured indebtedness, would be £2,031,930, or at $9.5 to the £, $19,-000,000 (Mex.). The outstanding total of these "doubtfully secured" items is £22,000,000.[22]

---

[22] As found in items Nos. 93 to 115, inclusive, in Lee's lists, *op. cit.*, pp. 191–192.

PART III

CHINESE GOVERNMENT INDEBTEDNESS AND
FINANCIAL CAPACITY

CHAPTER VII

The Foreign Debt of the Chinese Government

At the close of the survey of each class of loans considered a summary of the outstanding amounts has been given. There have been imposed upon China two indemnities, in original amounts K. Taels 230,000,000 and Hk. Taels 450,000,000 totalling say £102,800,000. The Chinese Government has contracted foreign debt through foreign loans since 1865 to a principal amount of at least £325,000,000, which added to the indemnities makes £428,000,000. One of these indemnities has been paid, the other has been reduced. Some of the loans have been repaid although most are in part outstanding.

These outstanding amounts of the Chinese Government's foreign debt can be summarized as follows, as of most recent information at January 1, 1926:

A. Secured Loans:

War, Military and Indemnity Loans......£	22,671,530
Railway Loans........................	49,632,885
Industrial Loans......................	6,477,500
General and Administrative Loans........	34,333,245
Total Outstanding Secured Loans........£	113,115,160

B. Unsecured Loans and Debt:

Expressed in foreign currencies...........£	43,664,400
Expressed in $ silver reduced to £ sterling at 9.5, $68,880,642...................	6,061,540
Overdue interest on part................	2,500,000
Total unsecured foreign debt [1]............	52,225,940

C. The Boxer Indemnity: [2]......................£ 40,000,000

Grand Total A, B, and C................£ 205,341,100

[1] This probably does not include all the foreign floating debt, for which recent figures beyond 1922 are unavailable. In that year it was placed by the National Commission for the Study of Financial Problems (Jan., 1922) at a total, foreign and domestic, of $47,012,000 (Mex.). Part of this has undoubtedly been included but perhaps not all. The foreign portion is probably £3,500,000.

[2] This is probably conservative. *Chinese Economic Bulletin* places this at $396,518,786 as of Dec., 1925, Vol. VIII, No. 262, p. 116.

The approximate foreign debt of the Chinese Government is thus about £205,000,000, or expressed in Chinese currency $1,947,000,000.[3] This compares favorably with the following material found in " Currency, Banking and Finance in China," by Dr. F. E. Lee, based on 1922, largely:[4]

Secured General Obligations	$1,029,500,000 (Mex.)
Secured Railway Obligations	496,000,000
Secured Telegraph, etc. Obligations	45,297,000
Unsecured Debt	300,000,000
Floating Debt	35,000,000
	$1,905,797,000 (Mex.)

Not all however of this debt as given, of £205,000,000, is payable in foreign currencies. Deducting the item which was changed from silver to pounds the foreign debt can be expressed as £199,100,660 and $68,880,642 (Mex.).

It is interesting to note the differing statements of the foreign indebtedness of the Chinese Government as given by the writers or agencies at top of the opposite page. The variations as among these various estimates are to be accounted for in part by exchange rates used in computation. It is to be constantly remembered that China's currency is a silver currency and that the size of such reckonings in silver depends upon the rate of conversion employed. The Ministry of Finance estimates were reckoned at $8 (Mex.) to the £ sterling. This was too low says M. G. Padoux in January, 1923, the rate then being $9 (Mex.) equal to £1. The yen was also low at $.86 (Mex.)

[3] At $9.5 Mex. = £1.

[4] *Op. cit.*, ch. xiii, *passim*; drawn from various official reports with the possibility of duplication admitted. Dr. Lee himself makes a round estimate of $1,600,000,000 of total foreign debt.

Source	As of	Estimate in millions	Undivided items given	Estimate corrected
Dr. Chang Ying Hua.	1923	$1,923	82 [a]	$1,964
Preliminary Report,				
Fin. Readj. Comm..	1923	1,660	187 [b]	1,722
Chinese Econ. Monthly.	1923	1,340	666 [c]	1,784
Chinese Econ. Monthly.	1924	1,211	516 [c]	1,727
Revised Report, Fin.				
Readj. Comm......	Dec., 1924	1,153	707 [d]	1,733
Ministry of Finance				
(*Chin. Ec. Bull.*, F.				
1926)............	1925	1,164	707 [d]	1,744

[a] 82 million overdue interest on dom. and for. unsecured debts—take 1/2.

[b] 187 million "balance undistinguished"—take 1/3.

[c] "Floating debt"—take 2/3.

[d] Ministry of Communications debt—take 580 millions.

equal to 1 yen.   Dr. Chang [5] converted at $9 to the pound and at $.90 to the yen.   All the work on my estimates was at $9.50 equal to one pound and at $1 equal to 1 yen, these being representative rates as of the close of 1925 and the early part of 1926.

Furthermore all foreign currencies were treated in my estimates at their gold value, except where otherwise stated, being converted at normal gold rates to £ sterling, while some of these other estimates have made conversions at rates equal to the average depreciation of certain currencies for the year in question.   After all, statements in Chinese currency can be but " approximate figures, because the foreign loans are in all kinds of currencies which cannot be accurately converted into silver dollars or £ sterling " says

[5] Dr. Chang is sometime Minister of Finance, Director General, Bureau of Currency, and Chairman, National Commission for Study of Financial Problems.

the *Chinese Economic Monthly*. For all of these reasons the estimate of $1,947,000,000 seems to be fairly well supported. It is not claimed that this is absolutely dependable. It has been said that a complete and accurate statement of all the loans to the Government of China would be a practical impossibility, and that in view of the circumstances under which many of these loans were made it is doubtful whether such a list could be compiled by the Chinese Government itself.[6]

Information was obtained as to the amount available to China on loans to a principal amount of £146,000,000, of which about £132,000,000 or 90 per cent was received by the Chinese Government. Ten per cent represents the average discount below par at which loans to China were taken by the bankers. The price of issue to the public was generally sufficiently above 90 per cent to accord an underwriting profit of 4 to 5 per cent and often more.

An indication of the extent to which China's credit is now impaired can be obtained from the fact that of the loans treated as " secured " in this study £8,000,000 in outstanding amounts are in default, as well as the unsecured debt of £50,000,000 [7] (exclusive of railway advances but inclusive of overdue interest), making £58,000,000, or well over one fourth of the entire foreign debt.

These foreign debts, as observed, are in a very large measure gold debts. Even those which are expressed in silver are owed to interests which are outside of China and there is with them as well as with the debts expressed in foreign currencies the problem of obtaining exchange. But there is this difference, that in the case of those expressed in silver the creditors will be paid in silver and must

---

[6] W. W. Willoughby, *Foreign Rights and Interests.*

[7] If not in default as to principal, at least as to interest.

themselves convert their silver dollars into foreign units, while in the case of the gold debt the Chinese Government has the task of obtaining exchange with which to meet interest and amortization charges. China's currency is on a silver basis and therefore any decline in the price of silver in London or other foreign country where the debt is to be paid, and where silver is regarded as a commodity, would increase the cost of paying the debts in gold, for China would have to deliver more silver to secure exchange. The amount of her debts can therefore be said to fluctuate with the price of silver. Further, the problem of securing such gold balances abroad as may be needed falls back in part upon the commercial operations of China as a country and these are affected by the price of silver. A decline in the price of silver, though possibly temporarily serving to stimulate export trade, by making China a good market for foreigners to buy in, will ultimately be reflected in higher price levels which might bring difficulties in selling goods for export.

Many of the debt contracts call for payment to foreign banks in Peking, Shanghai or other Chinese centers with exchange rates to be arranged for on or near the day of payment. When a large payment of interest or amortization is to be made the demand for sterling exchange becomes strong and more silver must be given for the pound sterling than might otherwise be true. Further, banks have been known to change their rates arbitrarily on a day when a large payment was to be made. Let us say the rate on London in Shanghai in telegraphic transfers were to change from 3/5–3/8 to 3/5–1/4, i.e., whereas for one Shanghai tael the bank would sell 3 s. 5–3/8 d. in London it will sell only 3 s. 5¼ d., thus requiring that more silver be given to obtain a pound. " A drop of a farthing in the sterling rate has caused the Chinese Government at times to pay ½ of 1 per cent more silver than it would have had to pay under (otherwise) current market rates for gold exchange." [8] This is not to say anything of the difficulties incident to domestic exchange.

The amount which China must annually pay in interest and amortization is as important as the amount of the debts outstanding. Any discussion of capacity to repay must center around the burden which annually falls upon the Chinese Government and China. Our problem is not that of ascertaining if China can or cannot repay all her Central Government debt next year. It is not only not expected, it is impossible. So many and varied are the terms of the loans that only a general answer can be given as to the total annual requirements. The total of secured loan payments for 1926 was not exactly the same as that for 1925. Further, so long as the interest on the unsecured debt remains unpaid the amount upon which interest might be reckoned is increasing. No regular plan exists for the repayment of most of these unsecured debts, hence no accurate statement as to annual charge now existing can be made. As far as the secured debt is concerned, since regular plans of amortization exist, the charge for any one year can be stated. In general, however, the requirements for the next few years can be given within certain limits.

The total of secured loan payments for 1925 was given in a previous chapter as £ 10,045,912 [9] and the interest only on the unsecured foreign debt as £ 3,685,000, making £ 13,728,912.

[8] Lee, *op. cit.,* p. 51.
[9] Total of list in *Chinese Economic Monthly,* plus other items; cf. ch. V.

Other estimates of the requirements of annual debt service are given below:

Source	As of	Payable in £ sterling	Payable in other currencies	Total [a]
Chinese Econ. Monthly, Jan., 1925	1923	£ 5.3 (Millions) £2 .2		£ 7.5 [b]
Chinese Econ. Monthly, Nov., 1925	1924 (Mex.)	$ 79.2	$29.2	$108.5 [b]
		Secured	Unsecured	Total
G. Padoux	1923 (Mex.)	$ 95. [c]	$45. [c]	$140.
Chinese Econ. Monthly for Oct., 1925 (by Expert of Financial Readj. Comm.)	1925 (Mex.)	$123. [c]	$50. [c]	$173.
F. E. Lee	1925			(Mex.) $120. [d]

[a] Converted to £ at gold value by myself.
[b] "As far as can be ascertained."
[c] Both foreign and domestic, but including no Ministry of Communications debt charge.
[d] Foreign only.

Since the foreign debt constitutes about 75 per cent of China's total debt, 75 per cent of $173,000,000, the estimate of the debt charge by the expert of the Financial Readjustment Commission, would be $130,000,000. The figure of £13,728,000 above made no inclusion of Boxer indemnity payment. In Chapter I the present status of the Boxer indemnity was reviewed. It was stated that the Chinese Government would have to pay annually 12 million taels, or (at 6.5 taels to the £) about £1,846,000 to the foreign governments or their agencies. This would bring the annual foreign debt charge to about £15,575,000.

However it was assumed that scarcely two thirds the indemnity, or 7,835,000 taels would have to be paid abroad and thus there would be added about £ 1,205,000 to the figure of £ 13,728,000 making £ 14,933,000 as the amount supposed to be paid abroad during the year 1925. If the secured payments supposed to be paid during 1926, of £ 10,256,305, be taken as a base and the same additions made as were made to the 1925 figure, the foreign debt charge becomes £ 15,787,000 and the amount of this probably to be paid abroad £ 15,146,000.

From the viewpoint of governmental expenditure to cover the interest and repayment of the secured debt as called for, and for payment of interest only on the unsecured debt, the Government of China should have had in 1925 a surplus above the other necessary expenditures of at least $150,000,000. As far as 1926 is concerned, this figure would be larger, not only because the figure above in pounds sterling was given as larger but also because the price of silver had fallen so that in November, 1926, the rate of exchange was more nearly $11.50 to the £ sterling. If conversion for 1926 be taken at an average of $10.50 to the £, the debt charge becomes, for 1926, $165,763,000. With a greater drop in the price of silver so that the rate becomes $12 to the £, this annual foreign debt charge would mount to about $190,000,000. Thus is illustrated the uncertain character of the amount of debt charges which would have to be included in a budget of the Chinese Government, and the very heavy burden which such foreign debts are apt to impose upon the resources of the Government. Of course as certain secured loans are paid off this would tend to fall, but in these calculations none of the burden of repayment of the foreign unsecured indebtedness is included. Further, interest was calculated at existing rates.   Some further provision for both repayment of principal and interest on the unsecured indebtedness will be necessary.   If some scheme for consolidation of the unsecured indebtedness is arranged, the interest will probably be made the same on the entire principal and provisions adopted for repayment of principal.   If the principal is left intact, and if the interest plus annual amortization is not placed below 8 per cent the total annual foreign debt charge is not apt to be less than $160,000,000 for a number of years.   Then, too, the Boxer indemnity payments are due to increase it in 1937.   It is, because of the possibility of the continuance of the present lower price of silver, apt to be more than this figure.   Can the Chinese Government meet these charges?

CHAPTER VIII

The Internal Indebtedness of the Chinese Central Government

The fiscal problem of paying interest on the foreign debt of the Central Government of China, as well as the problem of repayment, is bound up with the problem of internal indebtedness. Certain of the domestic loans to the Chinese Government are definitely secured, and revenues which are thus pledged cannot be looked to as a source of funds for foreign debt service until after such domestic loans are cared for. Furthermore, certain of the internal loans are secured upon revenues which used to be applied to the payment of foreign indebtedness.

The internal loans of the Chinese Government may be classified as secured and unsecured, though as will later be evident they could be classified as consolidated and non-consolidated. These internal debts have arisen out of the sale of bonds, the issuance of treasury notes or the borrowing through short term loans from banks. There is in addition indebtedness, generally unsecured, which has arisen out of the purchase of materials on terms, which terms have not been met; and also the accumulated arrears of administrative and other expenses.

As reported by the Department of Loans, of the Ministry of Finance, up to December 31, 1925, the outstanding amounts of the internal loan debt are as follows: [1]

[1] *Chinese Economic Bulletin,* Feb. 27, 1926, p. 116.

Secured Loans:
    Domestic bonds...........................$242,510,333
    Treasury notes...........................   24,082,500
Unsecured Loans:
    Domestic bonds...........................   19,196,468
    Treasury notes...........................   42,209,095
    Salt Surplus Loans.......................   45,688,332
    Loans from Chinese Banks...............   42,167,934
    Advances from banks   34,901,989

    Total.............................$450,756,651

One difficulty in stating the internal indebtedness is found in the fact that loans classified as " secured " in one instance or source will be called " inadequately secured " or " unsecured " in another source.   The Commission for the Readjustment of Finance [2] states that as of December 31, 1925, the inadequately secured domestic obligations totalled $260,253,280 (Mex.) but this statement included one bond issue of $71,715,026 which was not included in the " unsecured " statement of the Ministry of Finance.   The total amounts of the inadequately secured domestic obligations of the Ministry of Finance as prepared by the above Commission are as follows:

Eight per cent Bonds (Silver Portion).......$ 71,715,026
First Year Consolidated and Eighth Year Con-
    solidated Bonds........................   16,073,800
Salt Surplus Loans........................   44,112,388
Short Term Loans.........................   38,904,282
Advances by Banks.......................   30,333,399
Treasury Notes...........................   59,114,384

    Total.............................$260,253,280 (Mex.)

To this figure could be added the statement of the internal secured loans outstanding as of July 1, 1925, as given by the Chinese Government Bureau of Economic In-

[2] In *Tables of Inadequately Secured Loans of the Ministry of Finance.* Peking, November, 1925.

formation in data on loans issued. Excluding the Eight
Per Cent Bonds enumerated above, the secured loans
amounted to $178,470,016,[3] which added to the total of
inadequately secured loans above, given by the Commission,
makes $438,723,296. Hence, though classifications differ,
the resulting totals approach each other.

The Commission for the Readjustment of Finance in its
preliminary statements gave the internal indebtedness of
the Chinese Government as $461,000,000 with an unsecured
item undistinguished as to foreign or domestic of $187,-
000,000, and without adding items for salaries, etc. in arrears. If two thirds of this undivided item be taken, the
total internal indebtedness would appear as $585,000,000.
Revised figures of the Commission as of December, 1924,
show for the Ministry of Finance loan indebtedness of
$481,245,492 on internal obligations.[4] The Ministry of
Communications debt is not included in this total. The
Ministry of Communications debt was given as a total of
both foreign and domestic indebtedness of $707,300,000
as of February, 1925, the nearest comparable date. Of
this the domestic debt has been estimated as being at least
$75,000,000,[5] which would bring the figure to $556,-
000,000. Thus in 1924, the total internal loan indebtedness of the Chinese Government was between 555 and 585
million dollars of Chinese currency. No more recent statement of the internal indebtedness of the Ministry of Com-

[3] This figure does not include any secured treasury notes. Includes
fourteenth year loan. Cf. Baylin, *op. cit.*, appendix.

[4] Compare with *Chinese Economic Monthly*, Jan., 1925, calculation
from which as of 1923 shows internal debt $484,360,000; and *ibid.*
for Nov., 1925, calculation from which as of 1924 would show
$471,316,600.

[5] My calculation from lists in *Chinese Economic Monthly*, Nov.,
1925, pp. 43–46, is $81,577,000.

munications has been available. Hence attention will be largely confined to the indebtedness of the Ministry of Finance. Taking, however, the estimate of $75,000,000 of internal indebtedness of the Ministry of Communications as conservative and adding it to the figure of $450 millions of dollars given by the Ministry of Finance as of December 31, 1925, one may place the internal indebtedness of the Chinese Government as of January, 1926, at least $525,-000,000 (Mex.), as far as loans are concerned, but not including any accumulated arrears in military or administrative salaries or other expenses. This latter item alone was estimated in 1923, by Mr. Chang Ying Hua,[6] to be $198,643,000, which if added would bring the indebtedness close to $725,000,000. It is probably all of that amount.

Subsequent to January, 1926, the writer has been informed, Chinese Government internal indebtedness has increased over $300,000,000 through loans contracted.

The service of these internal debts will require in interest alone $30,000,000 at least annually, the interest on the inadequately secured portion being over twenty millions and on the secured portion over ten millions of dollars.[7] Of the total of inadequately secured obligations about $15,-000,000 outstanding call for no interest at all. Interest rates on the balance of this total vary from 5 per cent to 24 per cent, with the majority of this interest-bearing unsecured debt having rates in excess of 8 per cent and over 80 millions having rates in excess of 12 per cent.

The National Consolidated Loan Service

Up to the spring of 1921, ten series of domestic loan bonds had been issued by the Central Government of the

[6] In *Financial Reconstruction of China*, pp. 12–15, Table IX.
[7] My calculation: *Tables of Inadequately Secured Loans, cit. supra.*

Republic of China.[8] This includes one issued by the Imperial Government in its last days. These bond issues were: the Patriotic Loan, the 8 per cent Military Loan, the 1st Year, the 3d Year, the 4th Year, the 5th Year, the 7th Year Short Term, the 7th Year Long Term, the 8th Year, and the 9th Year Currency Reorganization Loans. In 1921 the total amount of these outstanding was approximately $315,000,000.[9] Of these only the 3d Year, the 4th Year, and the 7th Year Short Term loans were definitely and reliably secured. The first two of these three had been secured by the pledge of native customs, the cancelled German and Austrian portions of the Boxer Indemnity, and, though later, the two-thirds portion of the deferred Russian indemnity. The 7th Year Short Term loan was secured on the deferred indemnities to the allies.[10] The remainder of the domestic loans mentioned had not been well taken care of. Some of these bonds were being quoted on the market at only twenty per cent of their face value.

Further, in 1921, several of these loans had called for redemption prior to that time, which had not been accomplished since the Government had defaulted several times. The Government's credit had been seriously weakened. In addition to this many of the bonds had been issued far below face value and since the market quotations were quite low it seemed to the Government unwise to redeem at 100 per cent. Those who had bought these bonds in the open market would experience no injustice through

[8] This is clearly exclusive of early domestic issues such as the Merchant's Loan of 1894 and the Trust Loan of 1896. Cf. Huang, *op. cit.*, pp. 14–16.

[9] *Chinese Economic Monthly*, October, 1925, pp. 9–11.

[10] The Boxer Indemnity was reviewed in Chapter I above.

redemption at a discount, and they probably did not expect full or immediate repayment.[11]

For all of these reasons, by Presidential Mandate in March, 1921, there was established the National Consolidated Loan Service to cover China's Domestic loan bonds other than the 3d, 4th and 7th Year (Short Term) bond issues. The sinking fund of this service was to provide, as far as possible, for principal and interest and was to be controlled by the Inspector General of Customs. It was to be built up from the following revenues appropriated for that purpose: the surplus of the maritime and native customs revenues after all foreign obligations secured thereon and the 3d, 4th and 7th (Short Term) internal bonds had been met,[12] the surplus revenue of the salt ga-belle, but not exceeding $14,000,000 per annum, and the wine and tobacco revenues, not exceeding $10,000,000. If the wine and tobacco revenues proved insufficient to provide this sum the Ministry of Communications was to make up the shortage out of its surplus revenues. In fact the Ministry was asked to advance a monthly sum of $500,000 for the service of the consolidated loans, until the wine and tobacco revenues were able to meet the charge imposed.

In 1921, the 6 per cent and 7 per cent Consolidated Bonds were issued in exchange for the 1st and 8th Year Bonds, exchanging $100 face value of the 1st Year Bonds for $40 of the 6 per cent Consols and the same amount of the 8th Year Bonds for $40 of the 7 per cent Consols. The statement of the Service for the year ending March 31, 1922, the first year, showed liabilities to be met of $25,-000,000 and funds received to meet these as follows: Salt Revenue, 9.5 millions, Ministry of Communications, 3.5

[11] Cf. F. E. Lee, *op. cit.*, p. 149 ff.
[12] Customs surplus added by Presidential Mandate in 1923.

millions, and 1921 customs' surplus 12 millions.[13]   The
Patriotic Loan has been entirely retired, and the Military
Loan has been almost redeemed.   The statement of the
National Consolidated Loan Service for 1925 showed that
the redemption and interest payments were, according to
the Loan Schedule which was worked out, one full year in
arrears.[14]   Receipts as found in the cash statement for
1925 were $25,920,257 as received from the Inspector Gen-
eral of Customs.[15]

The internal secured indebtedness of at least $178,000,-
000 takes priority as regards annual debt charge, not
only over possible application of surpluses of customs
revenue and salt revenue to the unsecured foreign debt but
also over several foreign issues, classed as secured, which
have been definitely imposed upon these revenues.   The annual debt charge upon such internal indebtedness must then
be added to that of the foreign secured debt before ascertaining any surpluses in revenue which might accrue for
the service of either the foreign or domestic unsecured
debt.   The amount of the interest alone upon these secured
internal issues amounts to $10,700,000.   The Consolidated
Loan Service takes $24,000,000 annually and the addition
of interest and amortization charges on those domestic
bonds not in the Consolidated Service to the amount of
$12,342,985, which was the amount of payments falling
due July, 1925–June, 1926, makes the annual total of
payments on the internal secured indebtedness at least
$36,000,000 Mex.[16]

[13] Supplement No. 22, *Chinese Economic Monthly*.

[14] Supplement No. 27, *Chinese Economic Monthly*.

[15] Of this $9,631,962 was from the 1924 customs surplus.

[16] *Chinese Economic Monthly* of Nov., 1925, gives annual debt
charges payable in Chinese currency as $29,252,696. This is not suf-
ficiently inclusive.

The unsecured internal indebtedness of the Chinese Government, except those portions which could be better styled "inadequately secured," such as the silver portion of the "96 Million" 8 per cent Refunding bonds, which are imposed upon the salt revenue surplus, and the other salt surplus loans, does not enjoy any such priority over foreign debts.   In regard to the unsecured domestic debt, a large part of the principal has already matured.   Interest is also in arrears.   M. G. Padoux, adviser to the Chinese Government, wrote, in 1923, " there is no hope of finding sufficient money to satisfy the creditors according to the original contracts.   It might even prove impossible to pay them were time only granted, because part of the money has been borrowed at such high rates that the accumulated interest would exceed the future available resources of the Government." [17]   The Chinese Government has had a Commission for the Redemption of Foreign and Domestic Short Term Debts at work on the problem since 1922.   At that time the amount of these advances was placed at $58,-607,670, of which $35,103,724 was redeemed out of the proceeds of the "96 Million" salt-surplus loan, leaving $23,503,945 outstanding at the end of September, 1922. The figures of the other Commission (for the Readjustment of Finance) given above indicate that this figure is now much larger.

The internal indebtedness of the Chinese Government has been almost entirely acquired since the formation of the Republic.   Domestic bonds found greater favor with the people than before the Revolution.   Altogether 18 issues of domestic bonds have been placed upon the market by the Ministry of Finance during the Republican period. Not all of these however remain.   Two were for the re-

[17] *Op. cit.,* p. 6.

9

demption of former issues and should not therefore be considered as additions; two were authorized but were not successfully issued. The more recent issues include the Thirteenth Year Treasury Note Issue of $4,200,000, the Fourteenth Year Loan of $15,000,000 and the Spring Festival Loan of the Fifteenth Year of the Republic for $8,000,000. The total of principal on all these issues during the Republican period is $356,480,788 of which $277,261,316 are outstanding thus evidencing that $79,219,472 have been retired. In addition there have been certain minor issues, not from the Ministry of Finance, which must be included to make the list complete. These are: the famine relief bonds of the Ministry of the Interior to the amount of $4,000,000, at 7 per cent, which have been partly repaid, there being outstanding July 1, 1925, $1,595,900; the industrial premium bonds of the Ministry of Agriculture and Commerce which were to raise capital for the Agriculture and Commerce Bank and for developing various industries, of which only a small portion were issued (the original authorization being $20,000,000); and the railway car bonds of the Ministry of Communications, bearing 8 per cent and secured by the surplus earnings of certain railways.[18]

The Total Indebtedness of the Chinese Government

The total indebtedness of the Chinese Government, both external and internal, can be summarized as follows:

External Debt:
Secured Loans............£ 113,115,160
Boxer Indemnity..........   40,000,000

[18] A good summary of history of internal loans has been given by D. K. Lieu of the Chinese Government Bureau of Economic Information, transcribed by F. E. Lee, *op. cit.*, p. 143 ff., from which some of this material is drawn.

```
Unsecured Loans and Debt
   and Overdue Interest
   on part:
   Expressed   in   foreign
      currencies . . . . . . . . .    46,164,400
      Expressed in Chinese currencies . . . . . . . $ 68,880,642
Internal Debt:
   Secured Loans . . . . . . . . . . . . . . . . . . . . . . . . .   178,470,016
   Unsecured Loans and Debts . . . . . . . . . . . . . .   260,253,280
   Ministry of Communications (Estimate) . . . .    75,000,000
   Arrears in Expenses (Estimate) . . . . . . . . . . .   200,000,000
                                                    _____

   Total Foreign and Domestic . . . . . £ 199,279,560   $782,603,938
```

If the figures in £ sterling are converted to Chinese dollars at the rate of $9.50 to the £, the resulting figure is $1,893,-155,720. Adding this figure to the other figure expressed in Chinese currency the resulting approximate total of Chinese Government indebtedness is $2,675,760,000.

It is interesting, however, to note the extent of the indebtedness which is definitely and adequately secured and that portion which is not. Reclassifying the following result is obtained:

```
Secured Debt:
   External . . . . . . . . . . . . . . . . £ 153,115,160
   Internal . . . . . . . . . . . . . . . . . . . . . . . . . . . . . . $178,470,016
                                          _____

Unsecured Debt:
   External . . . . . . . . . . . . . . . . £  46,164,400   $ 68,880,642
   Internal . . . . . . . . . . . . . . . . . . . . . . . . . . . . .   260,253,280
   Min. of Commun. . . . . . . . . . . . . . . . . . . . . .    75,000,000
   Arrears . . . . . . . . . . . . . . . . . . . . . . . . . . . . . .   200,000,000
                                          _____

   Total Unsecured Indebtedness . . . £  46,164,400   $604,133,922
```

If the figures in £ sterling are converted to Chinese
   dollars at the same rate as above the secured
   indebtedness is $1,633,064,036
While the unsecured indebtedness comes to 1,042,695,722
                                                         _____

Making a total approximately of $2,675,760,000

The figure of $2,675,760,000 can be compared with other statements of the total indebtedness of the Chinese Government. The preliminary report of the Commission for the Readjustment of Finance gave as of 1922, $2,308,-000,000, and adding the arrears item one would have $2,506,650,000. This Commission gave figures of December, 1924 as $1,634,000,000 for the Ministry of Finance, to which one must add the Ministry of Communications debt as of February, 1925 of $707,000,000 and the item of arrears, making $2,541,416,000.[19] The Ministry of Finance itself published figures as of December, 1925 of $1,615,256,069.[20] The same additions would make $2,-522,256,000. This item of arrears included is probably much larger than $200,000,000. This figure is based on Mr. Chang's estimate, as of 1923, and is the latest information available on this point. M. Padoux in 1923 stated that the total indebtedness of the Chinese Government, exclusive of the railway obligations was not over $1,900,-000,000.[21] The addition of the railway obligations of 700 millions and of arrears of 200 millions would make $2,600,000,000. Comparison with these various other estimates and statements is of course no more than indicative. Various bases of conversion have probably been employed. Then too time is in favor of the larger figure since, as will be evident later in discussing revenues and expenditures, the Government has been running behind during recent years. Because of the many problems involved which have been mentioned elsewhere " a statement of the national debt of China is at any time only tentative and cannot lay claim to full comprehensiveness or complete accuracy." [22]

19 Cf. F. E. Lee, *op. cit.*, pp. 159–160. *Trade Information Bulletin* No. 299, U. S. Department of Commerce, gives estimate of $2,500,-000,000, of which $723,000,000 probably unsecured.

20 *Chinese Economic Bulletin*, February 27, 1926, p. 116.

21 *Op. cit.*, p. 4.

22 F. E. Lee, *op. cit.*, p. 136.

CHAPTER IX

The Present Financial Incapacity of the Chinese Government

The repayment of principal, according to regular annual requirements, on the foreign secured debt, and the payment of interest on all the foreign debt, together demanding a total of $150,000,000 in 1925, and of at least $165,000,000 in 1926, requires that China shall find, over and above the necessary and ordinary expenditures of the Central Government an amount for the next few years of at least $165,000,000.[1] But this is not all. The internal secured debt charge for 1926 was stated as $36,000,000, which would take priority over the claims of the foreign unsecured debt. Thus the order of annual debt claims against the revenues of the Chinese Government is:

Foreign Secured Debts (1926 figure).........$126,060,000 [2]
Domestic Secured Debts (1926 figure)......... 36,000,000
Foreign Unsecured Debt (Interest Only)....... 38,690,000 [3]

Chinese Government revenues must exceed expenditures for other than debt charges by this amount if China's credit abroad is to be restored and kept unimpaired. The amount required for the domestic unsecured debt has not been included in this figure of $200,000,000. Certainly if a complete restoration of credit and confidence is to be attained by the Chinese Government the internal debt must all be cared for in a satisfactory fashion. It is, however, the

---

[1] If the price of silver does not show a rising tendency.

[2] £ 10,256,305 at $10.50 to the £ sterling, plus $18,370,000 of Boxer indemnity.

[3] Estimate only; this was not paid; it may be more than this.

121

purpose of this paper to consider the foreign debt, and hence the debt charges on the domestic unsecured debt are not to be considered " necessary expenditures " in a calculation of what revenues might be available for foreign debt reduction.   Does the Central Government now have such a surplus of revenue for meeting the annual requirements set forth?   It did not in 1925 or 1926 for the requirements of neither of those years were fully paid.   The extent of the indebtedness in default is testimony.   In 1925 only the foreign secured indebtedness to the amount of £ 10,045,912 was cared for, i.e. about $95,500,000, and the internal secured indebtedness to the amount of about $35,000,000, making a total of debt payments which were made of $130,500,000.

What are the amounts of revenue which the Central Government [4] has been receiving?   A statement of the revenues of the Central Government has been prepared by the Commission for the Readjustment of Finance at Peking under date of October, 1925.   This statement discloses the following amounts of revenue collected in China during 1922, 1923, and 1924.   To this has been added the less complete statement of Mr. Chang for 1919, 1920, and 1921 [5] which is tabulated on the opposite page.   Thus in the latter years mentioned an average of over 235 million dollars (Mex.) was collected throughout the Republic from these sources of Central Government revenue. This is not complete for there are other sundry taxes levied not included in this report.   A writer in the *Chinese Economic Monthly* [6] estimates present total revenues which

[4] The statistics given in this chapter refer to the old Peking Government, no longer existing. The Nationalist Government at Nanking is now the Central Government of China.

[5] In *Financial Reconstruction of China, passim.*

[6] *Chinese Economic Monthly*, October, 1925, p. 11.

Revenues Collected in China (1919–1924) (000 omitted)

	1919	1920	1921	1922	1923	1924
Maritime Customs...........	$ 73,760	$ 78,820	$ 93,140	$ 89,038	$ 95,256	$104,392
Native Customs (under Maritime Customs)				6,543	6,735	6,377
Inland Native Customs........				8,307 a	8,307 a	8,307
Salt Revenue Collections.......	80,820	79,290	78,220	85,789	79,545	70,554
Wine & Tobacco Tax & Fees.....	14,381	14,950	14,660	15,069	15,837	15,837 b
Stamp Revenue.............	2,727	2,995	3,114	3,382	3,004	3,047
Peking Octroi..............	1,615	1,889	1,993			
Postal Revenue Balance.				3,716	4,456	2,753
Year Surplus–Chin. Gov. Rys....				24,126	23,753	22,641 c
Total for year.............	$173,303	$177,944	$191,127	$235,944	$236,898	$233,862

Totals of first three years in table not comparable with last three.

a Assumed same as estimate for 1924 Nat. Cust. Inland.
b Assumed same as estimate for 1923.
c Figures for 1924 stated to be only approximate figures.

should go to the Central Government at $280,000,000 (Mex.). Further there are taxes which are not customarily going, or have not customarily gone to the Central Government. The land tax, which in former years was collected to the amount of from 75 to 100 million dollars is not mentioned since it is not now available to the Central Government and is going into provincial uses. The other important tax levied in China is likin, which is not a revenue of the Central Government but is collected by the provincial authorities rightly for their own uses.

It must not, however, be assumed that the Central Government in Peking had available during any one of these years 235 million dollars. The actual amounts remitted to Peking by the collecting authorities was as follows for several of these revenues during 1922, 1923 and 1924:[7]

	1922	1923	1924
Salt Revenue	$47,193,233	$41,543,563	$31,256,934
Wine & Tobacco Tax and Fees.	1,449,848	889,269	
Stamp Revenue	340,000	340,000 [a]	

[a] Average for 1919–1921 given; actual remittances not known; this item is exclusive of expense of administration of collecting the revenue.

The other revenues which were tabulated above are not affected since the maritime customs and the native customs within the 50-li limit are under foreign control, and the inland native customs figures are unavailable.[8] One notes then that of the salt revenues for 1924, 41.4 per cent was "appropriated by provincial authorities and military commanders" without consent, and altogether 47.2 per cent

[7] "Revenues of Central Government"—Financial Readjustment Commission, Oct., 1925.

[8] The Chinese Native Customs System has to do with Chinese goods moving in and out of non-treaty ports, and land frontier trade.

was not available to the Central Government since the balance (between 41.4 and 47.2 per cent) was "retained by local authorities with consent of the Central Government." [9] For 1922, 36.7 per cent and for 1923, 37.8 per cent of this same revenue was not remitted to Peking. For the wine and tobacco taxes and license fees for the years 1921–1923 inclusive only 18.5 per cent of the total collections was received in Peking. This presents what probably can be called the outstanding problem in the fiscal relations in China. The Government of China cannot collect its own revenues. "The Central Government has little authority outside the walls of Peking," as one writer phrased it in 1926.

The actual receipts of the Chinese Government are given in the following table of the actual receipts of the Central Government. In the case of the maritime customs the total collection is noted and not the surplus after debt charges (which surplus is really the only amount turned over to Chinese authorities by the Inspector General of Customs) because the debt service which is cared for out of the maritime customs is included in the statement of annual loan burden which has been made. [10]

The revenues from the railways, which are under the Government Railway Administration of the Ministry of Communications, are pledged, as already noted earlier, for many foreign loans. Statements of foreign loans on the Chinese Government Railways have usually been rendered separate from those of the Ministry of Finance. The Ministry of Communications cares for the payments to

[9] *The London Economist*, Oct. 31, 1925, p. 615, speaks of 1924 salt revenue as $99,644,000, of which $29,300,000 or 1/3 was appropriated by provincial authorities, etc.

[10] Press reports have indicated in Dec., 1926, that certain of the maritime customs-houses in the south had been seized so that not all of these collections were available in 1927.

ACTUAL RECEIPTS OF THE CENTRAL GOVERNMENT. (000 OMITTED)

	1922	1923	1924
Maritime Customs...............	$ 89,038	$ 95,256	$104,392
Native Customs (50-li)...........	6,543	6,735	6,376
Inland Native Customs..........	8,307	8,307	8,307 *
Salt Revenue...................	47,193	41,543	31,256
Wine & Tobacco, etc.............	1,449	889	889
Stamp Revenue.................	340	340	340
Postal Revenue..............	3,716	4,456	2,753
Railway Surplus................	24,126	23,753	22,641 *
Totals...................	$180,712	$181,279	$176,954

* Positive information could not be ascertained as to actual amount turned over to Peking; since no misappropriations known, benefit of doubt given to China.

be made upon all the railway, as well as the telephone and telegraph obligations.   Since these obligations' debt service was included in the total of annual debt service for which the Chinese Government is responsible the surplus from the Chinese Government Railways should be included in a statement of receipts.   The annual loan charge upon all the secured railway loans is, however, deducted before the railway revenue surplus is ascertained, but not all the railway obligations, such as the unsecured debt, have been so deducted.   The extent to which secured railway loan debt charges have been met can be roughly guaged from the " income debits " items of the Chinese Government Railways for 1922, 1923 and 1924.   This item was $18,-561,000 in 1922, $32,488,000 in 1923, and $29,622,000 in 1924.[11]   The secured railway loan charge on foreign

[11] From " Revenues of Central Government "—report of Financial Readjustment Commission, Oct., 1925, (already referred to above), p. 11.

obligations for 1925 was £3,857,164 which at $9.50 to the £ is $36,643,000.[12]

There is reason to believe that the Central Government has been experiencing some difficulty not only in obtaining the surplus on railway account which is supposed to be existing annually so as to apply it to other than railway uses, but also to obtain from the railways income sufficient to meet all the railway debt charges. The Minister of Communications of China has written as follows: ". . . the revenues from Communications during the last 13 years have been diverted to other purposes. . . . In more recent years, the revenues of the railways have become a source of income to the militarists, who appropriate them directly. The Kin-Han Railway alone supplies more than $10,-000,000 annually to military requirements. The funds that have been seized from other railways and telegraph offices are enormous. It is estimated that up to the end of the 13th year of the Republic no less than $180,000,000 have been appropriated in one way or another by different forces. The funds of the railways are exhausted and debts are piling up."[13] Then too there were interruptions in the service of a number of railways during 1924 and 1925 largely because of military operations. The retention of part of the railway revenues by local officials is responsible for the inclusion of a total of $175,000,000 of railway obligations in the list of unsecured debts. The same Minister of Communications quoted above stated in the report quoted that there were $219,887,711 in obligations of the Ministry of Communications, mostly railway obligations, which must be cared for by some program of general financial readjust-

[12] Compiled from J. R. Baylin, *op. cit.*, pp. 90 ff.

[13] Report of the Minister of Communications to Provisional Chief Executive for attention of Reorganization conference, *Chinese Economic Monthly*, Nov., 1925, pp. 31, 39, 41.

ment on the part of the Ministry of Finance since " it is beyond the resources of the Ministry (of Communications) to do anything for these loans." [14]   Hence, for all the reasons which have been given the railway surplus cannot be counted upon to help bear governmental burdens in other directions since if it were all applied to railway and other Ministry of Communications debts there would remain a large amount of indebtedness of that Ministry uncared for. The fact that the telephone and telegraph obligations are in default is evidence that, although there was a surplus of operating revenue over operating expenses of $4,000,000 in 1923, shown by the telegraph administration, no present help in debt reduction can be expected from this source. It will be a sufficient task for the Ministry to meet the obligations specifically imposed upon these revenues.

At most the actual receipts of the Chinese Government for several years have not exceeded $180,000,000, which, if no other governmental expenses were paid, would be but little more than enough to meet the interest and repayment charges on the foreign indebtedness in any one year. Though it would have been sufficient to cover the secured indebtedness charge for 1926 of $162,000,000 it would have left a balance of but $18,000,000, far less than sufficient to cover the bare administrative and essential military expenditure of the Central Government,[15] to say nothing of the foreign and internal unsecured debt charge for interest only, or the item of accumulated arrears to be reduced.

" The financial situation of China has reached a very critical stage."   Present financial incapacity to pay either

[14] *Ibid.*, pp. 45–6. Of this figure £ 17,375,000 are in foreign currencies.

[15] G. Padoux estimated, 1925, that the government could be operated on $48,000,000 a year; cf. below.

interest or amortization on the entire secured indebtedness, to say nothing of the tremendous unsecured debt, is evident, not only in the amount of loans in default, but also in the extent of the uncontrolled expenditures, which, rightly or wrongly, are taking precedence over both regular administrative expenses and over interest on the public debt. The total annual military expenditure already stands at $274,862,000.[16]

Dr. Lo Wen Kan, in reporting to the Financial Readjustment Commission in 1922 on the Twelfth Year Budget (1922–3) pointed out an estimated deficit of over 8 million dollars a month or $103,560,000 for the year, without even considering the amounts needed for loan services. This budget did not cover the entire country completely.[17] It is also concerned only with the actual receipts and disbursements of the Central Government. This budget includes an estimated expenditure for military purposes of $5,885,000 per month, and administrative expenditures exclusive of loan services of $3,120,000 per month, which with other items, makes a total of $9,200,000 per month or $110,400,000 for the year. Turning to receipts he notes the taxes received by the Central Government (not including revenues which are allocated to loan services) as of the year of 1921–22 as follows:

Mining tax................$ 191,875	
Stamp tax................. 570,336	(out of $ 3,000,000 collected)
Wine & Tobacco............ 1,312,102	(out of $13,012,000 collected)
Government Property........ 2,478	
Income tax................. 10,301	
1921 Customs Surplus....... 4,752,000	

$6,839,092

16 *Chinese Economic Monthly*, October, 1925, p. 12.

17 There were no available figures for the revenue and expenditures of the southeastern provinces of Kwangtung, Szechuan, Yunnan, and Kweichow, on behalf of the Central Government, so the Eighth Year budget figures were used in compiling the estimate from these areas. Cf. *China Year Book*, 1925, p. 728.

With these figures adopted for the year of the budget he estimates a deficit of $103,560,000 exclusive of loan services.

The situation could then be summed up as follows: the retention upon the part of the provinces and military commanders of Central Government revenues to be devoted to their own uses, the continuance of expenditures on the part of the Central Government at a point larger than revenues, resulting in the existence of increasing annual deficits, augmenting the total of indebtedness and augmenting the burden of expenditures for the future since both interest and principal charges thereon demand repayment.

The Chinese Government is not receiving its revenues, because though collected, they are being misappropriated. The fiscal relations between the provinces and the Central Government have never been clarified. M. Padoux, adviser to the Chinese Government writes, " The financial reconstruction of China is not primarily a financial problem. It is a constitutional and political question, the solution of which lies in the readjustment of the relations between the provinces and the Central Government." [18]   But if the Central Government had the degree of centralization and power which it had during the Presidency of Yuan Shih Kai it would be able not only to collect its revenues but also to prevent the tremendous outlay for military purposes, to opposing forces, which is going on. " It is in a state of precarious balance that China exists today. Over the vast area marked China on the map no government exists to keep its place among the nations of the world." [19]   " Viewed from the aspect of the two main

[18] In *op. cit.*, p. 1.
[19] Statement of Henry K. Norton, (before Institute of Politics, Williamstown, 1926), press release of Aug. 16.

functions of a government, the protection of life and property, and protection from outside aggression, the question of China's being a republic or not might be dismissed with the statement that China has no government." [20]   The London Economist of January 2, 1926 in regard to the then sitting Peking Tariff Conferences remarked, " Would any Central Government conceivably be able to prevent the provincial, military tyrants, the tuchuns, from continuing to collect likin on their own account, international commitments notwithstanding?   Would it be able to employ the increase of funds to come from the Maritime Customs to advantage? "

The material presented in this chapter has necessarily been drawn from statistics prior to 1927.   The situation since 1927 has improved somewhat under the administration of the Nationalist Government but the problems of huge military expenditures, of inadequate collection of revenues, of diversion of revenues away from the Central Government and of indefiniteness in the fiscal relations between the Provinces and Nanking have not been solved. The Nationalist Government has been forced to continue borrowing, mainly from internal sources, to cover budget deficits of 1927 and 1928.

But even if the Chinese Government were at this time able to collect all of the $235,000,000 of revenue it should receive as enumerated in the table above in this chapter, there would still be an insufficiency.   With expenditures running large, probably the military expenditures themselves as large as these revenues which the Government should have, there is little likelihood of payments being made upon debts, except where the debt service of certain

[20] Statement of Dean F. E. Lee (before Institute of Politics, Williamstown, 1926), press release of July 30.

loans is cared for out of specific revenues before the surplus from such revenues is turned over to the Chinese Government. Exclusive of the secured railway obligations, (which were met in 1925 to the amount of an annual charge of £3,800,000), the debt service for foreign and domestic secured debt and the interest on the foreign unsecured debt would be around $170,000,000 altogether. This leaves $65,000,000 from which would have to come all other governmental expenses, an impossibility at the present time.

Any hope of finding a revenue surplus capable of meeting all annual debt charges at the present time appears vain. But this is not to say that the Chinese Government can never secure the amounts needed at some time in the future. If the fiscal system is reorganized constitutionally giving to the Central Government superiority of position in certain revenues and power to collect them, much will be gained. This is the political problem and it is not the task of the economist to state the likelihood of political and governmental reconstruction. But, predicating the accomplishment of the unification of the country, the establishment of a strong Central Government and the solution of constitutional difficulties something can be said of the potential financial capacity of the Chinese Government.

The Nationalist Government in January, 1929, brought to China Dr. Edwin W. Kemmerer with a staff of American financial experts to investigate government finances and the currency, and to recommend measures of financial reconstruction and reform.

CHAPTER X

THE POTENTIAL FINANCIAL CAPACITY OF THE CHINESE GOVERNMENT

Financial capacity rests upon increased revenues and decreased expenditures. It is therefore necessary to make a survey of the revenue system of China to ascertain the possibilities of increased revenue, and to discover wherein expenditures can be reduced.

A survey of the budgets of the Government of China, in so far as such are available, from 1911 to 1920, including two Imperial Budgets, reveal that anticipated revenues for these various years were as follows: [21]

COMPARISON OF REVENUE IN CHINESE GOVERNMENT BUDGETS * IN MEX. $ THOUSANDS

	Ordinary	Extraordinary	Total
Imperial Budget—1911			$447,525
Imperial Budget—1912			370,273
Republican 1913–1914	317,901	15,760	333,661
Third Year 1915–1916	351,064	6,354	357,419
Old Fifth Year 1916 [b]	426,237	25,709	451,946
Fifth Year 1916–1917	388,009	44,350	432,359
Eighth Year 1919–1920	409,838	29,633	439,471

* Including the land tax and other sources of government revenue not enumerated in previous chapter; excluding receipts from public loans, so far as known.

[b] Budget as of January to December, made necessary by change in fiscal year instituted by Yuan Shih Kai.

[21] Cf. various issues of *China Year Book,* also A. W. Ferrin, *op. cit.,* p. 36, and F. E. Lee, *op. cit.,* p. 134.

10

The majority of these budgets have estimated the revenue possibilities of the Central Government under normal conditions as between $350,000,000 and $450,000,000. The budget for the Eighth Year is the budget considered most representative by the Commission for the Readjustment of Finance and is the situation to which the Commission would like to see the country and government revert. This budget estimates the ordinary revenue at $409,838,000 derived from the following sources:

ORDINARY REVENUE ANTICIPATED EIGHTH YEAR BUDGET JULY, 1919–JUNE, 1920.   (000 OMITTED)

Land Tax	$ 86,845
Customs Revenue	93,268
Salt Revenue	98,815
Tax on commodities, including likin	39,224
Regular and Miscellaneous taxes	29,182
Regular and Miscellaneous duties	4,332
Income from Government Investment	2,416
Miscellaneous Income from Provinces	5,579
Income of central administration	3,105
Income directly received by Central Government	47,072
	$409,838

The statement is made by Mr. James A. DeForce, Special Agent of the Finance and Investment Division of the U. S. Department of Commerce that this budget " would be able to meet the requirements of the Government were the total amount of revenue collected remitted to the Central Government." [22]

An expert of the Financial Readjustment Commission has estimated the revenue as amounting to $459,960,134, including both that receivable by the Central Government and that by the Provinces, as follows: [23]

[22] *Trade Information Bulletin*, No. 299, Dec. 1924, p. 11.

[23] *Chinese Economic Monthly*, October, 1925, p. 11–12, article on " China's Finances under the Republican Régime." The Provisional

1. Central Government Revenue:
   Customs and salt revenues, wine and tobacco fees,
   stamp duties, revenue from Government property,
   and receipts of Central Government offices........$280,437,696

2. National revenue disposable in the provinces:
   Land tax, likin, miscellaneous taxes and assessments,
   revenue from Government industries in provinces,
   etc.. 179,522,438

   Total.................................$459,960,134

The budgets which were given above represented national
revenues irrespective of whether they were collected by
the Central or provincial authorities. One difficulty has
always been that neither regular nor accurate reports from
the Provinces as to total collections have been received.
The statement from the expert of the Commission shows
certain revenue, included in the budget as Central Government revenue, such as the land tax, and certain commodity taxes, placed under a title "national revenue disposable in the Provinces." These revenues, though temporarily disposed by the Provinces, are revenues of the
Central Government, which financial readjustment might
allocate to the Central Government. Clear cut demarca-
tion of revenues as between the different grades of government is important as a condition of unquestioned future
financial capacity.

It is impossible to obtain the actual expenditures of the
Chinese Government. The condition of internal affairs
since the formation of the Republic, and more particularly
in the last few years has made unsettled and uncertain the
actual needs of the various departments of the Government.
Reference to the budgets of the Central Government since

National Budget for 1925 compiled by the Commission for the Readjustment of Finance showed Central Government revenue of
$284,308,280. Cf. *China Year Book*, 1928–29, p. 551.

1911 reveals the following data as far as estimated expenditures are concerned:

COMPARISON OF EXPENDITURES IN CHINESE GOVERNMENT BUDGETS
IN MEX. $ THOUSANDS

	Ordinary	Extra ordinary	Total	Deficit
Imp. Budget—1911..			447,672	147
Imp. Budget—1912..			402,466	32,193
1913–1914.........	423,684	218,553	642,237	308,575
1914–1915.........	254,923	102,101	357,024	6,385 plus *
1916 "Old Fifth"...	285,942	185,577	471,519	19,573
1916–1917.........	291,803	181,035	472,838	40,478
1919–1920.........	271,289	224,473	495,762	56,291

* Figures are incomplete. Budget however calls for receipts from loans to amount of $25,082,398, hence no surplus was really anticipated

The actual amount of the deficits annually developing in the last ten years has even been larger than as indicated in this table drawn from budget sources. The report of the Financial Readjustment Commission in February, 1925,[24] states " Since the Fifth Year of the Republic, the Government has found itself unable to meet the deficit except by contracting loans to effect temporary relief " which has been the cause for the rapid increase in the national indebtedness during these latter years. The report continues " the total annual expenditure amounts to about $566,000,000 while the total annual revenue is only $460,-000,000 " even if all the revenues were remitted to Peking.[25]

[24] " General Report of Commission on Readjustment of Finance," Feb. 1925, in *China Year Book*, 1925, p. 709.

[25] The Provisional Budget for 1925 prepared by the Financial Readjustment Commission showed Central Government expenditure of $309,658,486 including $166,466,939 on public debt services, plus $70,925,394 for the special budget of the Ministry of Communications

These revenues are not being so remitted but are being withheld, hence the annual deficit in recent years has been far above $106,000,000.

The expenditures are probably above $566,000,000. " The total amount ascertainable is $616,496,260, which does not include payments to certain military divisions not reported to the Central Government. Even without them the total military expenditure already stands at $274,-862,058, which is about 45 per cent of the total." [26] If the potential revenue is taken to be $460,000,000 this item of military expenditures is 60 per cent of revenues. Military expenditures take up too large a share of the national revenue. But even if military expenditures were reduced by one half the budget would not be in balance. A figure of $173,000,000 was given as the amount necessary to meet all the loan services upon all the foreign and domestic debt, exclusive of the Ministry of Communications' debt.[27] This figure constitutes about 30 per cent of total expenditure, or 40 per cent of total potential revenue. But this figure provides nothing for the amortization of the foreign and domestic unsecured debt. The administrative expenses have been given as $168,359,865, or 27 per cent of the total expenditure given.[28]

which included a capital account item of $48,249,241. Cf. *China Year Book*, 1928–29, p. 552

[26] Statement of expert of this Commission in *Chinese Economic Monthly*, Oct. 1925.

[27] Given as $173,274,337 by expert quoted. I figure $200,000,000 as debt charge;—secured debt charge; $120,600,000; unsecured, $79,-400,000, but with no provision for repayment of unsecured debt. Cf. below.

[28] By the same expert quoted.

The Consolidation of China's Unsecured Indebtedness

No further statement of the necessary expenditures of the Chinese Government can be made until first of all the requirements of the unsecured indebtedness be ascertained. The settlement of this indebtedness has been called " the first step in financial reconstruction." The estimates for interest only on the foreign or domestic unsecured debt given above were based on an assumed rate of interest of 8 per cent. A more satisfactory statement is necessary. The unsecured debt has been mounting rapidly for several years. Interest is in arrears. Practically all is in default. Failure to provide any definite plan, in fact inability, to meet such indebtedness has affected China's credit seriously both at home and abroad. Nearly all the Chinese banks are on the list of creditors under the domestic unsecured debt. There is no present chance of meeting these debts as they now stand and considering the financial condition of the Central Government. To meet all these obligations, and pay off principals and interests overdue and as they fall due is now admittedly impossible. The compounding of heavy interest would be an unbearable drain on the national treasury. With these obligations unadjusted the nation faces a budget which can in no way be balanced. Granted that increased revenues might be obtained so that something would be available for this indebtedness how would the Government proceed? Who would be first to receive interest or principal and how much? China's numerous unsecured or inadequately secured obligations, if met without causing serious international friction, must be dealt with as a whole by a comprehensive funding scheme to which all creditors would be likely to agree. Further, this indebtedness is now for varying terms, at varying rates, in different currencies, with varying original discounts.

Consolidation is necessary—replacing the existing debts with an issue of new bonds, generally uniform in character, imposed upon substantial security.

The suggestion for such consolidation is based on the following principles:

1. An extension of time for short term debts.

2. A reduction of interest in every case where excessive rates have been charged. A large part of the debt bears interest at rates well over 8 per cent because of the risk which was involved at the time of contracting the debt. The imposition of the new bonds upon ample security would make interest reduction imperative.

3. A reduction of principal in accordance with the amount actually received by the treasury. The ruinous discounts given on many of these loans [29] suggest that such reduction would be possible and plausible. On some of this indebtedness the holders never expected to be redeemed in full.[30] Further, the Chinese themselves who hold such obligations should be sufficiently interested in financial readjustment to recognize some such lowering of principal amounts.

The granting of adequate security would be the compensation for asking such extension of time and reduction of interest.

This consolidation might be handled in two parts, with two different sets of guiding principles, i.e. foreign, and domestic; or it might be handled as a single scheme. Considering the future best interest of the country as well as

[29] Especially on domestic loans. Note the 15th Year Spring Festival Loan: issue price, 82; advance payment of 2 yrs.' interest brings discount down to 66; other deductions, not all explained satisfactorily, net proceeds at 47½ of face value. *China Weekly Review* for March 13, 1926; also *Chinese Economic Bulletin*, Feb. 27, 1926.

[30] Padoux gives $33,700,000 in this class.

the interests of the foreign creditors it would be best to treat all the unsecured indebtedness in a single scheme. It might be found that some reduction of the principal, particularly on internal obligations, would be necessary, but if consideration is given to the amounts which the Chinese Government itself originally received this might not be unfair.   China's credit should be restored upon all Government obligations.   However, since the Railway surplus which was approximately $22,000,000 in 1924 could, by reorganization, be made available the internal unsecured indebtedness of the Ministry of Communications might be left to this Ministry to care for and the foreign unsecured debt only of this Ministry included in the consolidation.

With this in mind the amount of the unsecured debt to be covered by consolidation would be as follows:

Foreign unsecured (cf. Ch. 7) [a]	£ 34,555,400	$ 67,180,642
Interest overdue on part (cf. Ch. 7)	2,500,000	
Overdue Austrian Loans (cf. Ch. 1)	5,200,000	
Defaulted Min. of Communications "secured" debt to be taken over [b]	3,315,000	
Internal unsecured (Ministry of Finance) [c] . .		260,253,280
	£ 45,570,400	$327,433,922

[a] This item includes foreign unsecured railway and telegraph obligations.   These figures seemed the lowest possible statement which could be made.

[b] This includes the Railway Loan of 1911, long in default, and the Telegraph Imp. Loan of 1918, which was largely spent by the Ministry of Finance. Other "secured" telegraph loans, now in default, have been omitted since these by reorganization of telegraph administration can be adequately served.

[c] Internal unsecured debts of Ministry of Communications has been omitted since Railway and other Communications' surpluses should be adequate for these.

Thus an unsecured indebtedness expressed in foreign currencies, converted to pounds sterling at gold value, of

£ 45,570,400, and in Chinese currency of $402,434,000 would be consolidated. If the foreign currency debt be converted to silver at 10, this consolidated debt would be $723,134,000, but if a rate of conversion of say 11 were used the debt would be $828,704,000. This conversion is here made, however, for convenience in discussion and comparison only. It would not be wise to convert the foreign debt into new bonds expressed in Chinese currency. The creditors would ask for too large a margin as protection against the risk involved in movements of the market for silver. The new bonds could very well be expressed in as many currencies as are now found in the loan agreements. It will be recalled that in a previous chapter various estimates of the foreign unsecured indebtedness were given. Making the same additions as were made above these amounts would vary between 800 and 900 millions dollars. It would seem that a funding scheme which would net $900,000,000 would be sufficient to cover the unsecured indebtedness at this time. Ample provision could be made if a bond issue for $1,000,000,000 were authorized and substituted for these obligations. These bonds might bear 7 per cent.[31] A very large portion of the total debt now calls for 8 per cent or over. For those debts now bearing above 8 per cent a redemption premium of 12 per cent at the most ought to be agreeable. The amount of this premium could be a matter of adjustment. A well secured bond bearing 7 per cent issued at 88 per cent but redeemable at 100 ought to be acceptable for the higher interest bearing obligations such as 12 per cent or above, while those bearing 8 per cent could be funded at an issue price

---

[31] M. Padoux's plan called for 625 million of 7 per cent bonds, now inadequate. The material in Padoux's plan has been quite helpful in preparation of this section. Cf. *op. cit.*

on the bonds of 94 or 95, and those bearing 7 per cent at par.   Some of the unsecured debt has already been contracted for at rates lower than 7 per cent.   In such cases the bonds could bear lower rates of 6 per cent and 5 per cent and be exchanged at par.

If this consolidation could be effected it would probably be found that there would remain a substantial portion of the authorization which would not be needed.   At least an average of 90 per cent would be net to the Chinese Government and any balance of unissued bonds might be sold and the proceeds used to reduce the Government's accumulated arrears of administrative and military expenses.   In fact Mr. Chang Ying-Hua [32] suggests that, if provision is not further made for the unification of the country, the disbandment of troops as well as the accumulated arrears of expenses, no fundamental readjustment can be expected. He recommended a loan for $1,200,000,000, almost half of which should be applied to these latter purposes.   With an issue of $1,000,000,000 the balance of the internal financial indebtedness and other requirements would have to come from some other source subsequent to general financial reorganization.   The possibilities of increased revenue will be reviewed shortly.

What security could be pledged for these consolidated bonds?   The best security is the revenue of the maritime and native customs under the control of the Inspector General.   There is a greater possibility of increasing the charges here than in the case of any other tax.   It is to the interest of China to offer the best security obtainable.

A review of the customs relations of China will make clear some of the important features of this source of revenue.   The collection of duties on maritime trade was

[32] Elsewhere quoted as authority on Chinese finance.   Cf. *op. cit.*

carried on in a loose manner until 1854 when it was placed under a board of foreign inspectors numbering three, which were then British, American and French. The whole system of collection has since been made quite efficient. In 1898 an agreement was reached whereby the Chief Inspector of the Maritime Customs Administration should be British so long as the British trade in China predominates. It will be recalled how, for the Sino-Japanese war loans, the indemnity loans, the Boxer indemnity and other obligations the maritime customs revenue was pledged as security. Its efficient administration in foreign hands made it a quite acceptable security.

By the Treaty of Nanking of 1842, concluding the Opium War with Great Britain, it was agreed that a " fair and regular tariff of export and import customs and other dues " [33] was to be established at the treaty ports, which had been opened to residence and trade. In 1843 regulations for trade and a tariff were drawn up and issued. This tariff was based on a 5 per cent ad valorem rate for both exports and imports, many of the rates being made specific on this basis. By the Treaty of Tientsin, closing the Second Chinese War, the tariff was to be revised. Such revision resulted in a new tariff schedule based on the 5 per cent ad valorem, but calculated on then existing prices so as to make a schedule of specific rates. This tariff lasted for the next 44 years without change in such specific rates. In 1901, consequent to the Boxer indemnity, the import tariff was altered so as to constitute an " effective 5 per cent," the rates being based on the average prices of the three years ending 1899. But the ineffectiveness of these rates became increasingly evident. In 1914 it

[33] British Treaty of Nanking, 1842, article x.

was actually 3.96 per cent, in 1916, 3.13 per cent.[34]   Attempts by China to obtain revision met with failure until 1917, after China entered the European War, and a Commission worked on the task of revision in 1918, resulting in an effective 5 per cent.[35]

In recent years China has shown increased interest in tariff revision and particularly in tariff autonomy. The Washington Conference rejected the Chinese request for tariff autonomy but did agree to further immediate revision of the specific schedules to render the 5 per cent levy provided for in treaties " effective." The Conference further agreed to an additional levy, a surtax, of 2½ per cent, and a special surtax on luxuries of not over 5 per cent. A commission was to be entrusted with the duty of establishing this new schedule of rates, but such increased rates from surtaxes were to apply only on the condition that likin charges on foreign goods be abolished. Leaving out of consideration here the feasibility of abolishing these internal barrier taxes it can be considered how much revenue can be expected to come from these contemplated increases in the customs tariff. A special Conference was to be called to prepare the way for the abolition of likin and to prepare the 2½ per cent and other surtaxes to take effect when this should be accomplished. This special conference was convened in October, 1925, much later than anticipated due to delay in obtaining ratifications

[34] From a Chinese Government investigation referred to in Chong Su See, *The Foreign Trade of China*, pp. 361–2.

[35] In 1901 the native customhouses within 50 li (15 miles) of a treaty port were placed under the maritime customs administrations. The balance of the native customs has to do with Chinese junk traffic between non-treaty ports and across land frontiers, is under Chinese administration and should be distinguished from the maritime foreign customs.

of the Washington Treaties and Agreements.[36] This International Chinese Tariff Customs Conference was in session in Peking from October, 1925, until July, 1926, when it adjourned due to the fact that the Chinese members no longer attended the sessions on account of the breakdown of the government in Peking. The foreign members issued a statement expressing their unanimous desire to go on with the Conference when the Chinese delegates should again be able to be present. At the opening of this Conference a tentative agreement was reached to grant China complete control over its tariff on January 1, 1929, China promising on the same date to make a complete abolition of likin, the internal customs duties. No agreement, however, was reached upon the rates to be in force until January 1, 1929 nor upon the use to which any increased revenue would be devoted. No increase of any kind was provided, then, and even the provisional agreement for autonomy could have no force until a formal treaty had been concluded. China did, however, on October 24, 1925, promulgate the text of a new Tariff law to go into effect at the time agreed.[37] Before the Conference closed it appeared likely that China would be enabled to lay increased duties ranging from 5 per cent to 30 per cent in the interim but this did not materialize.

Without considering what have been the rates imposed by China now that tariff autonomy has been gained,[38] but

[36] The Gold Franc controversy, reviewed in Chap. I, was the chief element in this delay.

[37] Cf. *Chinese Economic Monthly*, November, 1925, p. 46.

[38] The new tariff law promulgated by China with its new rates was put into effect on February 1, 1929, but not until after considerable negotiation during 1928 and early 1929, during which new treaties were signed by the Nanking Government with at least thirteen powers, including the United States, Germany, Norway, Belgium, Italy, Denmark, Portugal, the Netherlands, Great Britain, Sweden, France, Spain and Japan.

noting the probable yield from the effective 5 per cent, the 2½ per cent surtax and the luxury surtaxes as were planned it is interesting to calculate what the Chinese Government might have received had the Conference been reopened and the new schedules imposed. These calculations will start from 1928 since, had a stable Government been restored in 1927, new schedules could not have been put into effect before that time. Several estimates of such increases of customs revenue have already been made. These are given in the accompanying table, with the various bases on which these estimates were made. The estimate made by the Chinese Government Bureau of Economic Information was based on an annual increase in revenue due to normal trade development of 8 per cent, because the average annual increase in the five years 1920 to 1924 was 8.6 per cent. In the table presented here the increase due to the surtax is omitted up to 1928. Their estimate proved to be too high for 1925 by $8,000,000. In computing the probable revenue, to ascertain if sufficient funds might be obtained for a consolidated issue, I have used the more conservative estimate of an annual increase of 4 per cent and an initial increment of revenue, to follow from a 2½ per cent surtax, of $30,000,000.

The service of interest alone on an issue of consolidated 7 per cent bonds of $1,000,000,000 would be about $70,-000,000 and if these bonds were made to run for a 20-year period with redemption spread over the last twelve years of such period, the interest and amortization during the last twelve years would be annually $124,502,400. Table H presents the probable revenue which would be obtained from such an increase in the import tariff of China, the present and future charges already imposed on the customs revenue and the surplus available for the service of a con-

TABLE F

THE MARITIME CUSTOMS REVENUE
PAST COLLECTIONS
(*In thousands of Hk. Taels*)

	Maritime	Native Customs under Maritime Administration	Total
1910....	35,571		
1911....	36,179	3,173	39,352
1912....	39,950	2,889	42,938
1913....	43,969	2,929	46,898
1914....	38,917	3,389	42,306
1915....	36,747	3,784	40,531
1916....	37,764	3,746	41,510
1917....	38,189	3,775	41,964
1918....	36,345	3,974	40,319
1919....	46,009	4,493	50,502
1920....	49,819	4,385	54,204
1921....	59,007	4,871	63,878
1922....	59,359	4,362	63,721
1923....	63,504.	4,490	67,994
1924....	69,595	4,251	73,846
1925....	69,865	4,746	74,611

Source: Table found in J. R. Baylin, *Foreign Loan Obligations of the Chinese Government*, published by the Chinese Government Bureau of Economic Information. 1925 figures in *Chinese Economic Monthly*, January 1926, p. 49. Taels can be converted to $ Mex. at 1.5.

solidated loan. There would be difficulty in meeting the interest charge upon such loan only in the first two years, yet if the surplus from the customs during the early years were reserved sufficient funds would be available. Throughout effort has been made to be conservative. There are variations of this proposed scheme which are possible. In the event that exchange should become more difficult due to a lower price of silver there is yet a margin of surplus revenue available. Further, if other revenues of the Government are reorganized some help might be obtained from them. However, the new tariff rates will probably increase the customs revenue sufficiently to cover adequately the needs of such a consolidated issue.

TABLE G

ESTIMATED FUTURE COLLECTIONS OF MARITIME CUSTOMS REVENUES

Based on Imposition of 2½ Per Cent. Surtax and Luxury Taxes (In Millions of $ Mex.)

Year	A Padoux	B Padoux Modified	C Delegation X	D Delegation Y a 2½% surtax	E Ch. Gov. Bur. of Ec. Inf.	F Delegation Y a 12½% tariff
1926....	99	110		99.3	121.8	160.2
1927....	102	113	110	103	131.5	167.2
1928....	132	147	117.2	107	181.8	173.9
1929....	134	149	124.4	146	195.2	215.6
1930....	136	151	132.1	151.9	210.8	224.2
1931....	138	153	140.8	158	227.6	233.2
1932....	up		149.5	164.2	245.6	242.5
1933....	to		158.2	·170.8		252.2
1934....	1950		166.9	177.7		262.3
1935....	when		175.6	184.8		272.8
1936....	equal		184.3			
1937....	to		190.6			
1945....			238.6			
1950....	150					

A. Padoux's estimate based upon 1922. He estimated total customs revenue (including native customs under Maritime administration) for 1923 at $88,000,000. It actually was 67,994,000 hk. taels or (at his rate of 73) $93,100,000. Likewise 1925 estimated at $96,-000,000 (due to natural increase only), and it actually was 74,611,000 taels (at 73) or $102,200,000. His assumed increase of $28,000,000 annually due to new taxes added 1928 on, in the above table, with normal increase of trade bringing $2,000,000 annual increase of revenue. Cf. G. Padoux, *The Financial Reconstruction of China and the Consolidation of the Unsecured Indebtedness.*

B. Taking 1925 base of $110,000,000 as same for 1926 and adding same increases for growth of trade and $32,000,000 per year as increase estimated to come from new surtax and luxury tax, added from 1928 on.

C. This is the estimate of Japanese delegation at Peking Conference constructed as follows:

Annual increase of import 5 per cent effective to 1928	$4,000,000
After 1929	3,000,000
After 1936 to 1945	2,000,000
Import surtax 2½ per cent, annual increase to 1928	2,000,000
After 1929	1,500,000
After 1936 to 1945	1,000,000
Luxury surtax, increase of	3,000,000 (constant)
Export duty, increase to 1935 of	1,200,000

D. This is estimate of American delegation on increase due to the 2½ per cent surtax. The interim 5 per cent tax, if imposed, it was estimated would increase annually by just twice the amounts by which the above estimate increases. If both the interim 5 per cent and the surtax of 2½ per cent were imposed, making a 12½ per cent tariff, estimate as in column F. Based on 1924 figures.

E. Chinese Government Bureau of Economic Information estimate, May, 1925, found in *Chinese Economic Bulletin,* May 23, 1925, p. 290. 8 per cent increase annually due to normal trade development assumed on 1924 base. This was not obtained in 1925. Increase from surtaxes also estimated to increase at 8 per cent annually. If native customs under maritime administration were added, $6,-400,000 annually not increasing could be added to each figure.

F. American delegation estimate of increase of revenue due to a 12½ per cent tariff. Cf. note D.

11

TABLE H

PROBABLE REVENUE FROM MARITIME CUSTOMS AND THE SERVICE OF
A CONSOLIDATED LOAN ISSUE

(Thousands omitted)

Year	Probable Revenue		Present Charges	Surplus Available		Consolidated Loan Service
	Maximum	Minimum		Maximum	Minimum	
1927....	$110,000	$110,000	$85,150	$24,850		
1928....	140,000	117,200	86,500	$ 53,500	$ 30,700	$ 70,000
1929....	146,000	124,400	82,100	64,900	42,300	70,000
1930....	152,000	132,100	78,000	74,900	54,100	70,000
1931....	159,000	140,800	67,000	92,000	73,800	70,000
1932....	165,000	149,500	66,000	99,000	83,500	70,000
1933....	171,000	158,200	56,500	114,500	101,700	70,000
1934....	177,000	166,900	56,500	120,500	110,400	70,000
1935....	185,000	175,600	56,000	129,000	119,600	70,000
1936....	192,000	184,300	56,000	136,000	128,300	124,502
1937....	199,000	190,600	55,500	144,500	135,100	124,502
1938....	208,000		50,500	157,500		124,502
1939....	216,000		50,000	166,000		124,502
1940....	225,000		50,000	175,000		124,502
1945....	234,000	238,600	33,500	200,500	205,100	124,502
1946....	243,000		15,000	228,000		124,502

Maximum probable revenue based on $30,000,000 initial increase of customs revenue, increasing conservatively at 4 per cent. for normal trade development. Minimum probable revenue is from column *C*, previous table. Present charges are from Padoux, *op. cit.* p. 15, plus $1,000,000 annually for payment on 14 million yen Treasury Notes of 1923 for Compensation of Public Properties and Salt Interests of Tsingtao, cf. Baylin, *op. cit.*, p. 27.

Other Expenditures

As far as figures have been ascertainable they have disclosed great wastefulness in public expenditures. Deficits have been characteristic of Chinese finance since before the formation of the Republic, and these deficits have formerly

been made up out of the receipts from public loans.   Until
China's credit is restored, further resort to public loans
for such purposes is inadvisable and at best it is advisable
only when the deficit represents improvements or productive
assets.   The deficits in recent years have been very large.
Expenditures must be curtailed.

Now the problem of reducing expenditures, as well as
the problem of collecting taxes, to say nothing of increasing them, is fundamentally a political problem.   It is not
exactly the restoration of a strong central Government, for
instability, unrest, agitation, ferment have been evident
since long before the establishment of the Republic.   It is
and often has been remarked " China-Chaos."   Yet a
strong central Government cannot be set up without money,
without expenditures.   As long as there are large military
groups unwilling to acknowledge Central Government authority and actually forcing the government to support
them little can be done.   This indeed is arguing in a circle
but it is to be hoped that the Central Government at Nanking which has emerged will prove strong enough to shake
off these shackles and proceed with all the work involved in
fiscal reorganization.

Monsieur G. Padoux, adviser to the Chinese Government, in a study made in September 1925 estimated that
the government could be operated on $48,000,000 a year,
$31,000,000 for administrative expenditure and $17,000,-
000 for military expenditure.   This estimate did not include the self-supporting ministries and bureaus, the expenses of which are deducted from receipts, nor, obviously
does it include amounts required for the service of the outstanding debt.[39]

The administrative expenses of the Government necessary

39 Information from *Trade Information Bulletin*, No. 400, p. 11.

are tabulated by the Financial Readjustment Commission as follows, being the expenditures, with modifications, found in the budget of 1919–1920 for the Eighth Fiscal Year: [40]

	Ordinary	Contingent	Total
Organizations under Central Government.......	$ 22,441,350	$ 2,748,192	$ 25,189,542
Foreign Affairs...........	4,048,428	1,140,106	5,178,534
Interior.................	3,446,932	2,282,466	5,729,398
Finance.................	29,519,302	6,878,455	36,397,757
Army...................	52,814,744	53,512,245	106,326,989
Navy...................	8,643,296	120,000	8,763,296
Judiciary...............	1,817,191		1,817,191
Education..............	3,255,270	301,740	3,557,010
Agriculture and Commerce.	1,541,800	410,447	1,952,247
Communications........	1,323,747	149,218	1,472,965
Mongolian and Tibetan Aff.	1,109,915	50,000	1,159,915
	$129,961,975	$67,582,869	$197,544,844

If this estimate rather than that of M. Padoux be taken and to it added the requirements of interest and amortization on all China's central Government indebtedness (including the service of a consolidated loan replacing the unsecured indebtedness as outlined above but not including Communications debt), the total necessary expenditures amount to $389,105,824. The debt charges can be summarized as follows:

Foreign secured debt, exclusive of Communications'
secured debt, annually about £ 6,399,140 for next few
years, at 10.5.....................................$ 67,190,980
Boxer Indemnity...................................... 18,370,000
Domestic secured..................................... 36,000,000
New Consolidated Issue.............................. 70,000,000

Total annual debt charge............................$191,560980·

[40] Copied from *Trade Information Bulletin*, U. S. Dept. of Commerce, No. 400, p. 11. Also found in F. E. Lee, *op. cit.*, p. 130.

Of course this statement of debt charge is apt to vary from year to year because of the possible lower price of silver, but then the annual charge on several of the domestic secured debts as well as on several of the foreign debts is due to end within a few years. It is not apt to be over 200 millions of dollars.

What are the possibilities in increased revenues to the Central Government with which to meet these needed expenditures?

The Revenue Possibilities of the Chinese Central Government

As was apparent in the preceding chapter the fiscal relations existing between the various grades of government in China lie at the basis of many of the difficulties of the Central Government in obtaining revenue and controlling expenditures. It is valuable to review these relationships.

China before 1912 was under the sovereignty of an Emperor who was conceived to be the owner of everything and every person in all the Empire, by right of conquest. Landowners were considered his tenants and hence were expected to pay a rent or tribute to him as landlord. Such was the basis of the land tax, the grain tribute and other tributary payments. In earlier times payment in kind was as common as payment in pure cash. Of later years payments in kind have been commuted into money payments.

There were furthermore provincial contributions: to the Imperial Household, to the Board of War for national defense, to the Board of Revenue, and also contributions specifically for central administration, for indemnity payments, and for Central Government foreign debt charges. Sometimes contributions to other needy Provinces were demanded, which were looked upon as going to the Central

Government as a contribution, and as coming from the Central Government as a subsidy to the Province in need.

Dr. Chuan Shih Li summarizes as follows in his book on " Central and Local Finance in China," [41]

" First, there was communism of finance between the different grades of government,
Second, there was the provincial contribution,
Third, there was the central subsidy,
Finally, there was communism of revenue between the different grades of government."

Then Mr. H. B. Morse states,[42] showing the contrast with Occidental practices of the " common purse," " In China, theory and practice are divergent; in theory, everything is subject to the Sovereign, land property, revenue; in practice, the revenue is assigned piecemeal from certain sources of collection to certain defined heads of Imperial expenditure and must be remitted independently for the purposes assigned." So great were these complexities that to prepare a national budget of revenue and expenditure would " puzzle the shrewdest firm of chartered accountants" [43]

The lack of a separation of revenue between the central, the provincial and the local governing bodies resulted in a " scramble for revenue." Suggestions have been made for the separation of national finances from provincial and local finances but this has never yet been realized completely. Social and political institutions are slow to change, particularly in China. In 1913, the Ministry of Finance drew up a bill providing for separation of revenues but this bill was never enacted by parliament. Many

[41] Pp. 55–58.

[42] In *Trade and Administration of China*, p. 95.

[43] Quoted by Morse, *op. cit.*, from E. H. Parker, *China, Past and Present*, 1903.

of its provisions, however, were later enforced through treasury rulings under the presidency of Yuan Shih Kai, as well as subsequently. "Concentration of political power in the hands of a highly centralized form of government under Yuan Shih Kai was responsible for the success of financial reorganization" in the years 1914 and 1915.[44] The customs revenue and salt revenue were already Central Government revenues.[45] In 1914 "strict supervision was exercised over the receipts and expenditures of the provinces" in the making of the budgets for that year. In 1915 Peking authorities specified the revenue from the Title Deeds Tax, the Stamp Tax, the Wine and Tobacco Tax and Fees and certain license receipts as belonging to the Central Government.[46] To these can be added the revenue from Government property and the receipts of Central Government offices of different kinds. The revenues disposable in the provinces included likin and numerous other taxes and assessments. The land tax is now spent by the Provinces but was recommended in 1913 as a revenue for national purposes,[47] though a surtax was recommended to be used for local purposes.

There is real need for a clarification of the fiscal relations with definite separation of existing revenues as between the provinces and the Central Government. The backwardness of China's political and fiscal arrangements, their decentralization, is an important cause of the poor financial standing of the Government of China. To quote

[44] *Chinese Economic Monthly*, Oct., 1925, p. 6. Article on "China's Finances under Republican Régime." Article further states at Yuan's death in 1916 "the process of decentralization began to operate once more." Soon Peking found itself as helpless as ever.

[45] Salt revenue as result of Reorganization loan of 1913.

[46] *Chinese Economic Monthly, cit.*, p. 7.

[47] Chuan Shih Li, *op. cit.*, p. 76–77.

again from M. Padoux, " The present condition of affairs cannot improve materially unless the nature of the relations between the Central Government and the provinces be clearly defined (which is the constitutional side of the problem), and unless the new distribution of power between the provinces and the Central Government is accepted by the provincial authorities or forced upon them (which is the political side of the problem)." [48]   If these problems are solved, and if all national revenues are consolidated in payments into a common treasury, if the system of collection is reorganized to insure the receipt of sums actually collected, if the retention of taxes by the provinces for their own uses, as described in the previous chapter, ceases, then there is the possibility that China's Central Government budget will not only be balanced but will be able to provide in the future for an expansion of administrative activities.

With these things in mind let us turn to a consideration of specific taxes and sources, of revenue.

The Land Tax was once the main dependence of the Imperial Treasury. Mr. Jamieson,[49] applying his studies of the Province of Honan to the whole of China, says, " I calculated (1897) there were 400,000,000 English acres (equal to 650,000 sq. miles) of cultivated land in China, or at 6 mow per acre, 2,400,000,000 mow. If the average which I consider good for Honan holds good generally for the Empire, the whole amount levied from the people as land tax would amount to Taels 451,000,000."   Morse remarks that this includes the commuted grain tribute and hence, the land tax alone would work out to taels 375,-000,000.   The probable actual collection says Morse, is

[48] *Op. cit.*, p. 2.

[49] Author of *Land Taxation in the Province of Honan*—quoted by Morse, *op. cit.*, p. 106.

Taels 102,000,000 or $153,000,000.[50] The budget for 1919–1920, however, called for an estimated ordinary revenue from this source for national purposes of $86,845,000 and in 1916 for $95,973,000. Mr. Chang Ying-hua states that the average collection for 1919–1921 was $80,-090,000, of which $16,990,000 was retained by the Southwestern Provinces. The balance however he says is not to be considered " available to the Central Government but can only be considered as an amount appropriated for provincial uses." [51]

In 1713, the rental value of land was fixed by the Emperor Kang-hsi, who declared that such should be unchangeable. The present tax of ¾ tael per mow is based on these valuations of 1713. At that time the area of cultivated land was probably less than 1/5 that of the land now under cultivation. There have been numerous authorized deductions and today much land is undervalued on the old basis. Other exactions added by provincial and local authorities have increased the irregularity of this tax throughout China. Morse states that the Republic has made no change in the method of assessing or collecting the land tax. One writer states, " A complete revaluation of all lands in China under existing conditions would undoubtedly result in a very material increase in the proceeds of the land tax." [52] The tax is levied only on agricultural land supposedly, except that land once agricultural and hence taxed, but now urban, due to the growth of cities, must continue to bear the tax. As now levied, however, in spite of lack of uniformity the land tax is " Not enough

---

[50] *Op. cit.,* p. 106.
[51] *Op cit.,* p. 6.
[52] A. W. Ferrin, *op. cit.,* p. 37.

to discourage agriculture " being " estimated as averaging for all China 1/20 to 1/30 of the gross produce." [53]

Considering, as Morse says, that it is entirely safe to estimate the amounts collected as at least three times the amounts actually returned to the Central Government,[54] and considering the possibilities of revaluation, proper administration and collection the land tax ought to yield to the Central Government at least $100,000,000. There is of course the possibility that in the reorganization of the fiscal relations between the various grades of government that the land tax will be allocated to the provinces. The assumption of $100,000,000 was based upon the idea that only about 1/3 of the actual collection would be remitted. It might be possible for a time to allocate one third to the Central Government with the proviso that upon the abolition of likin, if indeed that is accomplished, the land tax should become entirely a source of provincial revenue.

The Salt Taxes, as indicated in statements of Chinese Government revenue already given, form an important part of the revenue system. The salt trade has always been a Government monopoly in China. The salt monopoly and tax had not been administered, in the days of the Imperial Government, so as to yield the maximum return. The collection up to 1909 had been the duty of the provincial governments along lines set down by the Imperial Government. In 1910, a Central Salt Bureau was formed but this was scarcely established when the Revolution broke out and the salt administration was placed under the Ministry of Finance. In 1913, when the Reorganization Loan of 1913 was under consideration, the bankers demanded a reorganization of the Salt Administra-

53 E. T. Williams, *China, Yesterday and Today*, p. 94.
54 Morse, *op. cit.*, p. 104.

tion, since the salt revenues were offered as security for this loan, and since these as administered were insufficient. The most that had ever been received in Peking in any one year, according to investigations made before the loan was signed, was 13,000,000 taels. The administration was reorganized under the joint supervision of one Chinese and one foreign chief inspector.[55] The total collections, with administrative expenses deducted have increased under this administration from $60,409,000 in 1914 to $85,789,000 in 1922, but have fallen to $70,544,000 in 1924. The amounts however which have been available for the Central Government from this revenue have been regularly decreasing since 1921 because an increasingly large amount, as pointed out in the previous chapter, has been retained by provincial authorities.[56] The salt taxes, recognized as Central Government revenue, and regularly remitted to Peking, or even collected by Central authorities, ought to yield at least $90,000,000.

Other Taxes. " The reorganization of the Salt Gabelle points the way for reform." There should be a " reorganization of the existing system of internal taxation in order to produce the maximum of return." [57] The possibilities of increased revenue from the maritime customs and from the native customs under the maritime customs have already been reviewed in this chapter.

The Native Customs were a part of the original Chinese customs system, and together with the land tax and the salt tax formed the backbone of the old system of Chinese Imperial finance. The native custom houses within 15 miles

[55] Cf. discussion above, Chap. IV. Also cf. A. W. Ferrin, *op. cit.*, p. 42.

[56] Cf. *China Year Book*, 1924, pp. 792-793, also cf. F. E. Lee, *op. cit.*, p. 128.

[57] H. M. Vinacke, *Industrial Development in China*, p. 74-5.

of the treaty ports were placed in 1901 under the administration of the Maritime Customs Administration. In regard to these, but more particularly with regard to the customs houses inland and on the land frontiers, under Chinese direction, it can be said that no increase in revenue can be expected. The entire disappearance of the native customs in the not distant future is likely. Dr. Friedrich Otte, expert on the Chinese customs system, says, " No matter what reforms are effected, nothing can change the trend of economic events which foretells the disappearance of the Native Customs from a purely scientific point of view." [58] The return from the native customs under Chinese direction for 1912 to 1914, the most recent years available, was an annual amount of about $8,307,736.[59] In estimating future revenues a figure of ¾ of this amount, or $6,230,000 has been taken.

In the budgets of the Chinese Government there has appeared the item, " Regular and Miscellaneous Taxes " including the title deeds tax, the wine tax, the tobacco tax, cattle tax, tea tax, business tax, mining tax, shop tax, sugar tax, and numerous others. Then there have also been numerous duties. It has been said that the Chinese were the most miscellaneously taxed people in the world. There is need for revision. There is lack of system and this lack of system means an unnecessary expenditure for levying and collecting these taxes. In reforming the tax system greater place could be given to luxury taxes. Of the taxes mentioned above, the wine and tobacco taxes produce the largest amount of revenue and these could be extended. It will be recalled that these taxes were pledged

[58] *Chinese Economic Monthly*, February, 1926, article on " Chinese Native Customs System," pp. 61–69.

[59] From " Revenues of Central Government," Financial Readjustment Commission Report, Oct., 1925.

as security for the Continental and Commercial Bank Loan and the Pacific Development Company Loans, both of which are in default, but which would be released from these taxes if consolidated with the balance of the inadequately secured indebtedness as outlined above. Ferrin states that the income from the wine and tobacco taxes can be more than doubled.[60] Figures were presented at the time that the Continental loan was under consideration showing that the combined revenues of the wine and tobacco taxes and the Government tobacco monopoly could be made to exceed very easily $25,000,000 a year. Others have declared that a thorough reform of the wine and tobacco administration should result in a net revenue as great as that from salt, which exceeds $75,000,000 a year. In the table of estimated revenues below the revenue which could be obtained from wine and tobacco taxes has been placed at $25,000,000.

An income tax has been effective in China since 1921, with rates varying from ½ per cent on incomes of $501 to $2,000 to 5 per cent on incomes from $201,000 to $500,000, with ½ per cent additional on each $100,000 of income above $500,000. The basic income of $500 is exempt. Until now this tax has not brought in much revenue, that for 1921 being $10,311, but it contains possibilities for greatly increased revenue.

A corporation tax has been suggested since the corporate form of organization is just coming into use. As pointed out by Professor Vinacke this tax should be framed so as not to discourage the formation of corporations since to do so would retard industrial development.

The many other taxes mentioned above need not be specifically reviewed. Their possible revenue has been

60 *Op. cit.*, p. 45–6.

conservatively included in the accompanying table which summarizes the probable future revenue of the Central Government if the fiscal relations within China are clarified and if the taxation system is reformed as suggested. The revenue from the Stamp duty is included at its latest figure as also that of the Peking Octroi, the tax levied at the gates of Peking. The miscellaneous taxes, duties, fees, income from Government investments, and income received directly by the Central Government are included at $60,-000,000, being less by 20 per cent than the sum total of these items appearing in the budget of the Eighth Year, for 1919–1920.

TABLE OF PROBABLE FUTURE REVENUE OF THE CENTRAL GOVERNMENT
OF CHINA

	Ordinary
Maritime customs revenue (1927)	$115,000,000
Salt Revenues	90,000,000
Land Tax	100,000,000
Wine and Tobacco taxes	25,000,000
Native Customs	6,230,000
Stamp duty	3,286,000
Peking Octroi	2,680,000
Postal Revenue	3,000,000
Miscellaneous taxes, fees, income	60,000,000
	$405,196,000

If the customs surtax of 2½ per cent be considered, causing the customs to yield a total of $152,000,000 by 1930, and other luxury taxes which might yield $10,000,000 a year, this figure of probable revenue becomes $452,000,000.[61] This represents what might be expected to be the revenue of the Central Government of China within say five years

[61] In a United Press dispatch, Shanghai, Jan. 12, 1929, The Nationalist Government at Nanking estimates its 1929 revenue at $457,-000,000, according to T. V. Soong, Minister of Finance, of which 41 per cent will be spent on the national army.

if reorganization is effected.   As stated at the close of the last chapter this analysis was predicated on the accomplishment of unification, the establishment of a strong Central Government and the solution of constitutional difficulties. The immediate prospect in this, the political sphere, is becoming more hopeful, it is true, but from the economic standpoint the budget can in time be balanced.   The necessary expenditures were placed at $309,105,824 and there is the prospect of over $400,000,000 to be obtained in revenue if the proper agencies are but set to work.

China today shows many appearances of bankruptcy yet China's resources are vast and a very large increase of her ordinary revenues upon the return of peace is possible and feasible without adding materially to the burden of taxation borne by the people if the system of taxation be thoroughly reformed.   There seems little to do but wait for the solution of internal problems.   As the customs revenue shall be increased by the imposition of the new rates as indicated but without the necessary abolition of likin coming immediately because of the unavoidable internal difficulties, if China's unsecured indebtedness could be consolidated, performed, perhaps with assistance by some international board with representative Chinese participation, perhaps even the Maritime Customs Administration, much of the difficulties connected with China's public debt could be met even if the balance of her financial difficulties were required to wait for solution.   The chief difficulty connected with public debts which would then be unsolved would be the indebtedness of the Ministry of Communications.

There yet remain two problems connected with Chinese finance which have not been discussed.   The one of these is the abolition of likin and the other is the reform of the

currency. By the Mackay Treaty of 1902 Great Britain
consented to a 12½ per cent import tariff providing China
should undertake to abolish likin. By the Commercial
Treaty of 1902 with the United States the latter had
agreed to customs tariff revision upon the abolition of likin.
Writers upon Chinese finance have with but few exceptions
advocated the removal of these internal taxes upon goods
in transit in the interest of trade and internal economic
unity. The Washington Nine Power Treaty provided for
the Peking Tariff Conference to consider the raising of
the import tariff by 2½ per cent upon the abolition of
likin. The Nationalist Government has expressed its determination to abolish likin. Likin is collected by provincial authorities rightly for their own use. It would
seem that this is not the time to remove a tax as lucrative
as likin and one upon which the provinces have come to
place such dependence. The tax is recognized and accepted by those on whom it falls. The tax literally is
" a contribution of one-thousandth," i.e. " one-tenth of one
per cent," though as now collected there is wide irregularity. Foreign goods, in accordance with treaty provisions, have had an advantage over Chinese products in
that upon payment of a 2½ per cent ad valorem tax in
addition to the import tariff a transit pass is issued which
has freed the foreign goods of likin impositions. Sir
Francis Aglen, former Inspector General of Customs, suggested that the Maritime Customs should continue to issue
transit passes, that it should be given the duty of collecting transit dues, and that the dues so collected should be
definitely allocated to the provincial exchequers and dis-
tributed prorata. Thus the dues could be regularized.
Likin would not be abolished but would be organized and
standardized. This could apply to all goods both foreign

and Chinese and equitable rates be established. Until China is in a much stronger position it would be wise therefore not to eliminate this source of revenue but if anything to make it more uniform throughout the provinces and for the provincial authorities more assured.[62]

In regard to currency reform, Dr. Lee remarks, " it will be difficult to establish a real fiscal system until the currency of the country is reformed." " To be exact, there are no monetary systems in China." [63] By both the Mackay Treaty of 1902 and the American Commercial Treaty of the same year China agreed to take the necessary steps to provide a uniform national coinage. In 1903 China appealed directly to the United States Government for aid in the matter of monetary reform. A commission headed by Dr. J. W. Jenks was appointed by authority of Congress in 1903. This commission studied the problem and made its report and recommendations but nothing was done. It has already been shown that the Currency Reform Loan of 1911 was never floated. In January, 1929, Dr. E. W. Kemmerer went to China, at the request of the Nationalist Government, to study the possibility of currency reform accompanied by an American commission of financial experts, including Dr. Arthur N. Young and Dr. John Parke Young. The reform of Chinese currency is important but must be considered more as an element in a long run readjustment of Chinese finance rather than as an immediate step.

The fact remains, however, that the great complexity of media of exchange, of monies of account, of weights, and of coins is a very real problem, both in its relation to the

[62] Certain likin revenues are part security for foreign loans to Central Government also.

[63] F. E. Lee, *op. cit.*, p. 8, 124.

12

reorganization of internal government finance, and in its influence upon trade, both internal and foreign. China's currencies are silver currencies. The most difficult problem for the foreign business man is the handling of foreign exchange. Though domestic exchange is confusing to the Chinese themselves, they have become much more adept in the methods of exchange, through centuries of training and through the development of a " gambling instinct." With the foreigner there is always the necessity of considering the market price of silver, since this is a commodity in gold standard countries. The rate of exchange between these latter countries and China is after all the equation between the price of gold and silver. The former has a price which is legally fixed by the mint price of gold, as for example in the United States. The variable factor is the price of silver. Rates of exchange must then follow fluctuations in the market price of silver.[64]   Silver has fluctuated in price decidedly in recent years. In 1920 silver struck 89½ pence per ounce on the London market whereas on December 18, 1926 it sold at 24 11/16 pence per ounce. During 1927 and 1928 the silver market was fairly quiet. Prices moved within narrow limits, fluctuating between 55 and 60 cents per ounce in the United States.

The movements of silver then become a real factor in the financial capacity of the Chinese Government. The decline of over 20 per cent in the latter part of 1926 from the average price of 1925 increased the difficulty of debt payments and if these lower prices continue the burden of debts on China, as already noted elsewhere will be very much greater.

[64] Cf. W. F. Spaulding, *Eastern Exchange, Currency, and Finance*, pp. 311–312, and " Silver market in 1925," *Chinese Economic Monthly*, April, 1926, p. 148.

The Indian Currency Commission in its recent report (1926) recommended the complete adoption of gold as a standard for India's monetary system, retaining silver as a circulating medium on a gold basis. Its recommendations look to the closing of the mints to the further coinage of silver, the gradual reduction of the government's large silver reserves and the building up of a gold reserve. This was the reason for the decline in the price of silver in the months of September, October and November of 1926. The preponderance of the factors influencing the price of silver at this time June, 1929 seem to be bearish. Silver has long been India's standard of value as well as its currency. The people of that country have long been accustomed to accumulating stores of silver and silver ornaments. Owing to the favorable balance of trade which India has enjoyed for a long period of time that country has become the silver " sink " of the world. There is the possibility of Indian financiers becoming sellers of the metal, as press reports indicate Chinese speculators recently became, thus further depressing the value of silver. The Indian silver reserves will probably be reduced gradually through several years, as in 1928. The Indian Government has not been in the market for silver for coinage purposes for a number of years and it is questionable whether the Indian market will be missed as far as silver for coinage goes. But the Indian market will in part be missed as the people of India possibly come to lose faith in silver. As to production, while silver has increased, the production ratio with gold shows that in the last twenty-five years only about ten times as much silver (in fine ounces) has been produced as gold, whereas in years prior to this period the ratio tended to be much higher. In 1924, 239,068,295 fine ounces of silver were produced as against 18,826,086 fine ounces of gold, which is a ratio of 12.7 to 1.[65]   Two-thirds of the world's consumption of silver, which in 1928 amounted to approximately 308,000,000 ounces, was taken by China and India.

It would be difficult to predict the future course of the silver market.   The decline so far, if maintained, and certainly if increased, and indeed the present lower price, should affect price levels, moving them upward.   If wages be not increased in proportion this should accentuate the existing poverty in China.   While the drop in silver may temporarily make these countries good markets for foreigners to buy in, acting like any other decline in exchange it should also make it harder for Chinese to buy abroad. If the price levels in China move upward this will soon be balanced.   Nevertheless, movements of the price of silver constitute an element of instability in the development of Chinese industry and commerce and in the improvement of the economic position of the Chinese people, which things are after all fundamental considerations in the financial capacity of the Chinese Government.

The financial aspects of China's foreign government debt problem have been treated.   It is necessary for the Chinese Government so to reconstruct its fiscal system as to make possible the accumulation of a budget surplus equal annually to the sums to be paid abroad.   The government has the responsibility of collecting from the people the funds necessary for such payments, but, as already indicated, there are expenditures which are essential to the maintenance of the government and its services which contribute to the economic development and to political unity, and these, from a Chinese viewpoint at least, are primary

[65] Figures are those of Director of Mint at Washington. Cf. also *Commerce and Finance*, no. 40, 10/6/26, p. 2017-8.

considerations. It would be shortsighted policy which would attempt external debt payments at the expense of necessary domestic expenditures, continued budgetary deficits, and political instability. The Chinese Government in its present impotent condition cannot find the necessary budget surplus. It can, however, after political unity and constitutional readjustment have been effected, balance its budget through consolidation of its unsecured indebtedness based upon an increased tariff, reorganization of the fiscal system, and curtailment of military expenditures or any other unnecessary expenditures.

PART IV

TRADE AND INDUSTRIAL DEVELOPMENT

CHAPTER XI

The problem of paying the external debt is not alone fiscal and financial. It is also economic. China's net international income from trade and service operations must equal the payments to be made abroad. This is the problem of transferring the revenues set apart for debt service from funds collected in terms of Chinese currency—silver taels, dollars, " cash "—each of varied kinds—into foreign units which are gold currencies. This requires the purchase from banks of foreign bills of exchange, the supply of which comes from sellings goods or " services " to foreigners, or which in some other way becomes available. The Chinese Government cannot hope to pay by an export of silver the annual amounts required, even if sufficient silver were available, since the continued export of such quantities of silver would probably have a depressing effect upon the price of silver abroad and thus make more difficult debt payment. Silver is a commodity in the countries of China's creditors.

Many of the debt contracts call for payment in some Chinese center to foreign banks. These banks have the task of building up ·the balances in London, Paris, or America upon which they may draw bills to the order of bondholders and other creditors. This is done by purchasing foreign bills of exchange. The supply of these at any one time is largely limited and is the resultant of all the trade and other operations which are to the credit of China on international account. The Chinese Government (or these banks) in paying debts should obtain only the surplus of exchange—namely, that which is not necessary to pay for imports of goods and to provide for the conduct of private operations. If the Chinese Government, or indirectly these banks, attempted to secure more than such surplus there would be a marked decline in Chinese exchange, due to the fact that the banks would have the burden of making good abroad the bills which they had sold, largely by export of specie. In a sense, of course, the handling by these foreign banks in China, who act as agents of the bondholders or creditors, of some of the transfer operations makes such interest and amortization payments private operations, and just as " essential " perhaps as any other act of private interests. But in a larger sense it is a public activity. Certainly if the circumstances of China's international position are adverse such will be reflected already in the rates of exchange prevailing in the market when the Government approaches a foreign bank to arrange payment, and if it appears that rates shortly will be lower, or that the debt operations will force them lower, the bank will demand a lower rate of exchange thus increasing the burden upon the Chinese Government in terms of silver. Of course, even if the rates go lower than anticipated the Government will have to bear the burden since its obligations are ultimately in most cases to the bondholders themselves. Hence the Government is interested in the transfer problem. The problem of obtaining a surplus of exchange is unavoidable in the consideration of these public debts to private creditors as well as those owed to governments abroad. A persistent effort to pay foreign debts in the face of a continually adverse position in international accounts would operate to disrupt trade and perhaps to bankrupt the country.

In another sense this amounts to saying that if China does not send out more goods or services to foreigners than it receives from them its government cannot pay its debts abroad. A nation's exports of all items of value pay for its imports of value. A nation makes actual payments by disposing of goods or services or other items of value. The instruments of payment are the resultants of such operations.

Hence to consider the extent to which China as a nation can pay off the annual charges of interest and amortization of the national foreign public debt requires a study of China's international income accounts, and of the possibility of increasing, at present or in the future, the surplus of exchange available.

As far as the visible items of trade are concerned China has been characteristically an importing nation. China has not yet become an industrial nation. She has largely been a producer of agricultural and other raw materials, of foodstuffs, and of hand finished commodities. Her specific trade movements are being treated in the next chapter. Without going into the changes that are to be observed in the character of Chinese commerce, one can consider the aggregate movements of trade.

The discussion of the history of the Chinese loans has shown that China has been borrowing since the Sino-Japanese War. The effect of such continuous and increasing borrowing would normally be for a country such as China to increase the imports of commodities. Attempts at repayment would tend to increase the exports of commodities. During this period of indebtedness China has not been able to increase the exports of goods in such a measure as to pay for the imports of goods and services, for which she has also become increasingly indebted to

TABLE I
CHINA'S INTERNATIONAL MOVEMENTS
GOODS AND TREASURE [2]
BALANCE OF VISIBLE ITEMS
1912 TO 1923
(In Thousands of Haikwan taels)

Year	Silver				Gold		Total—Bullion and Specie [a]				Merchandise [b]		
	Im-ports	Ex-ports	Net Import	Net Export	Net Import	Net Export	Im-ports	Ex-ports	Net Import	Net Export	Imports	Ex-ports	Excess of Import
1912	45,098	25,850	19,248		7,458		54,394	27,688	26,706		473,097	370,520	102,577
1913	55,711	19,743	35,968			1,386	58,776	24,194	34,582		570,163	403,306	166,857
1914	16,499	30,122		13,623		13,001	17,360	43,984		26,624	569,241	356,227	213,014
1915	20,718	39,100		18,382		17,392	21,537	57,311		35,774	454,476	418,861	35,615
1916	37,088	65,766		28,678	11,801		56,991	73,868		16,877	516,407	481,797	34,610
1917	27,507	48,490		20,983	8,847		41,379	53,515		12,136	549,519	462,932	86,587
1918	36,124	12,629	23,495			1,054	37,352	14,911	22,441		554,893	485,883	69,010
1919	62,094	8,968	53,126		41,183		113,173	18,864	94,309		646,998	630,809	16,189
1920	126,354	33,715	92,639			17,502	177,321	102,184	75,137		762,250	541,631	220,619
1921	89,545	57,114	32,431			16,461	119,044	103,074	15,970		906,122	601,256	304,866
1922	75,687	36,114	39,573		4,123		85,495	41,799	43,696		945,049	654,892	290,157
1923	93,941	26,745	67,196			5,667	104,087	42,558	61,529		923,403	752,917	170,486
1924	49,529	23,745	26,002			9,735	51,576	35,309	16,267		1,018,211	771,784	246,427
1925	73,927	11,403	62,524			1,038	75,772	14,286	61,486		947,865	776,353	171,512

a There is apt to be a small unrecorded movement of specie, largely inward, as carried on persons of passengers.

b Figures for imports and exports of merchandise are the "net" figures, from which are excluded imports of foreign goods re-exported.

1 Figures for both goods and specie movements are from the Maritime Customs Trade Statistics, cf. China Year Book, 1923, p. 294, ibid, 1925, p. 993. This is not the total trade of China. Land frontier movements do not entirely enter Maritime Customs Statistics. Also not included is trade carried in vessels of the Chinese type, plying between foreign ports and non-treaty ports, which "junks" are unlicensed under the Treaty tariff and not regulated by the Maritime Customs. Goods carried coastwise are of course not included, but movements to and from Hong Kong are returned as "foreign." Cf. See, p. 392; cf. China Year Book, 1924, p. 677, ibid, 1925, p. 283.

PART B

TOTAL EXCESS MERCHANDISE AND SPECIE IMPORTS OVER LIKE EXPORTS

Converted to Gold Value

Year	In Hk. Taels (thousands)	Value of Hk. Tael in $ Gold, each year	in $ Gold
1912	129,283	.74 a	95,669
1913	201,439	.73	147,050
1914	186,390	.67	124,881
1915	159 b	.62	98 b
1916	17,733	.78	13,852
1917	74,452	1.08	80,407
1918	91,451	1.19	108,826
1919	110,498	1.35	149,172
1920	295,756	1.23	363,779
1921	320,836	.76	243,835
1922	333,853	.81	270,420
1923	232,015	.82	190,252
1924	262,694	.81	212,782
1925	232,998	.84	195,718

a Average gold value for each year, from Lee, op. cit., p. 51.

b Excess of exports.

foreign countries, as well as to cover interest and debt reduction charges on the foreign debt. The balance has had to be made up from other sources.

A century ago the exports of China greatly exceeded the imports, and the balance was generally paid by an importation of silver. But after the greater opening of China to foreign commerce the trade balance became adverse, and has been so since 1831, with the exception of a few years. The opening of five treaty ports by the Treaty of Nanking in 1842 was a turning point in Chinese trade.[1] In the years 1864 and 1872 to 1876 exports exceeded imports by small amounts, the greatest balance of exports being 10,500,000 Haikwan taels in 1876.

The accompanying Table I presents the visible elements in China's foreign trade during the years 1912 to 1923, inclusive. This table shows certain striking changes in the excess of imports of merchandise over exports of the same during the period of the European War, 1915 to 1919. The characteristically large excess of imports was reduced and this was due to a slightly reduced volume of goods imports in point of value and an increased amount of goods exports in point of value. The year 1918 saw a change in the flow of the precious metals, principally silver. Whereas China had been, since 1914, exporting silver she returned to an excess of imports of treasure over exports of the same, which had been the general situation prior to 1914. China was, then, importing silver in spite of an unfavorable balance in merchandise movements, evidencing that there must have been invisible items of credit to China which caused this flow of silver to China.

Considering both goods and treasure one sees a tem-

[1] Cf. Chapter IV on " The Turning Point of the Foreign Trade " in Chong Su See, *The Foreign Trade of China*, p. 114 ff.

porary condition in 1914 of a very small favorable balance of these visible items, and in the other years, 1916 to 1919, a condition less unfavorable than existed before the war or even after. The falling off of exports in 1920, however, and the increase in imports brought a continued and increased unfavorable condition in visible accounts for several years. The net unfavorable balance for the four years 1916 to 1919, inclusive, 304,133,000 Haikwan taels, was but slightly larger than the total for the year 1920 and not as great as that of 1921 or 1922. The total of the years 1920 to 1922, inclusive, was 950,445,000 taels unfavorable to China, or an average of 317,000,000 taels annually. The size of the unfavorable balance in terms of gold currency (U. S. $ gold) is shown in Part B of this table, showing that the value of silver is a significant factor in the amount of adverse balances.

From 1921 to 1925, inclusive, the net unfavorable balance of merchandise totalled 1,183,500,000 Haikwan taels. The net importation of treasure during this period was 198,900,000 taels, making a total of 1,382,400,000 taels of net unfavorable balance on visible accounts for these five years. This is an average of 276,480,000 taels per year. The total unfavorable balance is apparently increasing in recent years in terms of silver, though falling values for silver tend to reflect a falling figure. Such a large debit balance together with the annual requirements of foreign debts which have been met were met from other sources. As far as visible trade movements are concerned China shows a large unfavorable balance. What are the invisible items in China's accounts which make this possible?

The question of balancing China's international accounts has engaged the attention of economists both in China and elsewhere for a long time but " so far no satisfactory

answer has been worked out." [3]   The greatest difficulty lies
in securing statistics, or even reliable estimates about the
various items of the " invisible balance."   Several estimates
have been made in the past.   H. B. Morse, elsewhere
quoted, made an estimate in 1903 for the Maritime Customs,[4] and in 1910 Mr. Morse revised this estimate slightly.[5]
In 1909 the Maritime Customs published an estimate.[6]   S.
R. Wagel, a writer on Chinese finance, made an estimate
for 1912.[7]   In 1919, for the year 1913, Mr. See made
slight changes in his estimate.[8]   In 1925, Mr. John H.
Nelson made different estimates on certain items.[9]   In
1926, Dr. Charles F. Remer presented valuable data for
several periods of China's trade history.[10]

These statements of visible and estimated invisible items
have been brought together in Table J, with all figures
changed to Chinese dollars rather than taels, in which
some of the estimates were made.[11]   The estimate of the
writer for the period 1920 to 1923, inclusive, is also given
on an average annual basis.

The statistics for visible movements of goods and treasure come from the Maritime Customs Reports.   The bases

[3] Statement of Chinese Government Bureau of Economic Information in letter to writer, Aug. 27, 1926.

[4] " *An Inquiry into Commercial Liabilities and Assets of China in
International Trade;* cf. also *Returns of Trade and Trade Reports
of Maritime Customs*, 1904, p. 1, p. xvi; found also in H. B. Morse,
Trade and Administration of China, pp. 327–9.

[5] Cf. G. H. Blakeslee (Ed.) *China and the Far East*, p. 107.

[6] Cf. China: *Returns of Trade*, etc., 1919, p. 1, p. 52.

[7] Cf. S. R. Wagel, *Finance in China*, Shanghai, 1914, p. 473.

[8] Cf. Chong S. See, *The Foreign Trade of China* pp. 334–336.

[9] Cf. *Trade Information Bulletin* No. 312, pp. 5–6 (U. S. Dept.
of Com.).

[10] Cf. Charles F. Remer, *The Foreign Trade of China*, Chap. VII
on " Trade Balances and Specie Movements."

[11] Taels have been converted to $ Mex. at $1.50 equal to 1 tael.

TABLE J—COMPARATIVE INTERNATIONAL BALANCE SHEETS OF CHINA
(*In Thousands of $ Mex.*)

	H. B. Morse Estimate for 1903	S. R. Wagel Estimate for 1912	C. S. See Estimate for 1913	Average Annual Estimates for 1920–1923
Debits				
Imports, Merchandise...	$465,680	$709,645	$ 855,243	$1,326,000 [12]
Imports, Specie........	55,500	81,597	88,000	182,100 [13]
Foreign Loans, Interest and Amortization.....	66,315	76,500	87,000	90,150 [14]
Expenditures of Chinese Legations Abroad.....		2,250	3,000	2,700 [15]
Expenditures of Chinese tourists Abroad......	6,480	4,500	4,500	5,000 [16]
Remittances by foreigners in China........	34,125	30,000	30,000	45,000 [17]
Freight and Insurance Bought.............		15,000	15,000	
Munitions of War (Gov. Purchases)...........	7,500	5,250		4,500 [18]
Totals...........	$635,600	$924,742	$1,082,743	$1,655,450

[12] Imports and exports of merchandise, " net," i.e. " net " refers to gross imports less value of foreign goods re-exported during the year. Same for exports, hence " net " exports refers to exports of Chinese produce. Original data from *China Year Book*, 1925, p. 283, from Maritime Customs Statistics. Since 1904 goods have uniformly been valued at " moment of entering into China's international exchange " which has meant a c.i.f. basis for imports and an f.o.b. basis for exports. Hence, exports are somewhat undervalued as compared with imports. " Too much significance is not to be attached to the actual amount of the excess of imports "—C. F. Remer, *Quart. Jo. Econ.*, Aug., 1926, p. 623.

[13] Cf. China Year Book, 1925, p. 993.

[14] Average amount of annual payments made, not those supposed to be made,—about £9,490,000 at $9.50 to the £. This is not completely accurate. Cf. J. R. Baylin, " Foreign Loan Obligations of China," p. 90, and Chap. V, above. This is, I believe, representative.

[15] From Chinese Government budgets. Cf. *China Year Book*, 1921–22, p. 234, also 1923, p. 707, also 1925, p. 725.

[16] Estimate only, increasing previous figures slightly.

[17] Allowed to remain same as Wagel. Freight on imports already included in imports on c.i.f. basis. This item is probably larger. Some material on insurance sold in China in *China Year Book*, 1925, pp. 935–9.

[18] Reduced from previous estimates though possibly larger.

13

TABLE J—*Continued*

	H. B. Morse Estimate for 1903	S. R. Wagel Estimate for 1912	C. S. See Estimate for 1913	Average Annual Estimates for 1920–1923
Credits				
Exports, Merchandise...	$354,807	$555,780	$ 604,958	$ 956,400 [12]
Exports, Specie.........	49,570	41,544	36,297	108,400 [13]
Excess of exports in land frontier trade........	30,000	6,000	6,000	10,000 [19]
Legations of foreign nations in China........		10,500	10,500	15,000 [20]
Expenses of foreign Garrisons..............		13,500	13,500	18,000 [20]
Expenses of foreign Vessels of War.........	77,250	30,000	30,000	35,000 [20]

[19] Recorded land imports greater than recorded land exports 1909–1916, vice-versa, 1916 to 1923, with imports again exceeding in 1923. (Cf. *China Year Book*, 1919, pp. 140–143; also 1925.)   In 1906, when Morse estimated $30,000,000 unrecorded excess of exports, there was a recorded excess of exports of 2,565,000 taels in land frontier trade with Russian territory.   In 1912 when Wagel estimated an unrecorded excess of exports of $6,000,000 there was a recorded import surplus on land frontier trade with Russian territory of 8,-000,000 taels.   Recorded export trade to Russian territory of (all ports and land) 1921–1923 was 72 per cent of similar exports 1912–1914.   Recorded land trade with Russian territory showed excess of imports of 4,247,000 taels, in 1923.   Conditions of recording trade as far as can be ascertained, have not materially changed.   The Inspectorate General of Customs replies to my inquiry that a great part of the land frontier trade "would not come under our cognizance.   We have no available data from which the required estimates could be compiled."   Considering all of the facts available I estimate $10,000,000 as the average annual amount of this item for the period stated.   This is 1/3 of Morse's estimate and 1-2/3 times Wagel's estimate.   For the year 1913 the "Review of Russian Trade Statistics" shows an import trade from China of 84,000,000 roubles (say 56,000,000 taels) while the Chinese figures show 45,000,000 taels, or a difference in favor of China of 11,000,000 taels (disregarding any differences in valuation methods).   This would indicate Wagel's estimate too low.   Post-war Russian trade statistics are not available. References: Cf. *China Year Book*, 1921–2, p. 1020; 1925, p. 306.

[20] Wagel's estimates increased from 15 to 45 per cent.   Legation guards in Peking total 950; foreign garrisons total 4,120 men.   Cf. *China Year Book*, 1925, p. 1205–6.

TABLE J—*Continued*

	H. B. Morse Estimate for 1903	S. R. Wagel Estimate for 1912	C. S. See Estimate for 1913	Average Annual Estimates for 1920–1923
Expenditures on foreign Missions, Schools, Hospitals, etc...........		13,500	15,750	25,000 [21]
Expenditures of foreign tourists in China.....		15,000	15,000	22,500 [22]
Remittances from Chinese abroad.........	109,500	60,000	115,000	150,000 [23]
Expenditures on foreign merchant ships and repairs.............		30,000	30,000	45,000 [24]
Expenditures on railways and mines.......	40,500	30,000	30,000	10,000 [24]
New capital invested by foreigners in trade and in treaty ports.......		120,000	120,000	150,000 [25]
New indebtedness of Chinese Government by new foreign loans.....				60,000 [26]
Totals............	$661,627	$925,824	$1,027,005	$1,605,300

[21] John H. Nelson estimates this at $35,000,000 in 1924 in Trade Information Bulletin No. 312, p. 6. Dr. C. H. Robertson, Research and Lecture Section, Y. M. C. A. of China, Shanghai, in personal interview estimated this item at nearer $50,000,000 (Dec. 20, 1926). The figure given in the table is conservative.

[22] Wagel and See estimates increased 50 per cent since more than a 50 per cent increase in tonnage carried by foreign ships in Chinese trade since 1913.

[23] This is the same as Morse's figure for 1906. Number of Chinese abroad probably no less now than then. Nelson cited $100,000,000 figure. Dr. Remer estimates carefully that 80,000,000 taels per year ($120,000,000) represents conservative figure for Chinese emigrant remittances. Cf. Remer, *The Foreign Trade of China*, pp. 218–221.

[24] Reduced because of difficulties of internal strife and curtailment of construction in post war period.

[25] Increased 25 per cent. Probably larger if compared to the increase in imports into China.

[26] New indebtedness for the years 1920–1923 inclusive as calculated from lists in F. E. Lee's handbook, *op. cit.*, pp. 190–198, averaged for the four years.

for the other items in my estimate are explained in the subjoined notes of the table. It is not claimed that these are accurate. The material is definitely conjectural as regards the invisible items, but not without some basis for such conjecture, it is hoped. The table leaves unaccounted for a balance of $50,150,000, which presumably is somewhere among the credit items, since silver has been imported continuously into China.

One's attention is drawn immediately to the large net import of specie or treasure, largely silver—an average of $73,700,000 for each year. This absorption has been possible because of the invisible credit balance, both current and capital. Of course some importation of silver tends to occur for currency and industrial uses. Whatever payments the Chinese Government has made in interest and amortization in the past has been made possible largely by the investments of foreigners in trade, in the treaty ports, or as expenditures on railways and mines, or by expenditures of foreigners on missions, hospitals and schools, as well as by the continued interest of Chinese abroad in the homeland. The new indebtedness itself of the Chinese Government has been for several years about two-thirds, annually, of the payments upon debt service made. The cessation of this item, now virtually accomplished (by force of circumstances rather than by choice) makes the dependence for debt payments fall on the commercial and capital movements. The removal of the item of $60 million from the credit side would leave the credit side failing to balance the debit accounts. Payments must, in the long run, be made out of net income and not out of loans. For the future, temporarily, some payments may be made out of foreign loans; but this is not payment. It is postponement. Further the borrowed funds themselves give rise to new interest obligations which act to increase the installments of succeeding years.

But it might also be argued that this paying off of the Chinese Government obligations, made possible by the increased investments of foreigners in China, is making the Chinese as a people no less indebted. There is basis for the argument. The creditor position of foreign countries is being changed from that of bondholder of Government obligations to that of bondholder of or investor in private enterprises. The remittances of foreigners in China to foreign countries may be expected to increase. This is now probably the largest of all the invisible debit items. But there is this difference between these two forms of national indebtedness. In the first place it is good to relieve the government of its indebtedness that it may take on more constructive functions. Further, not all of the principal of such investment by foreigners will have to be repaid. In all probability most of it is for permanent investment. And lastly, probably not all of the profits earned by foreigners in Chinese enterprises will be remitted out of China. Some profits will remain in China for reinvestment. The foreign population may increase. It must be expected, however, that this item of remittances will increase as the investments of foreign capital increase, though the rate of increase may not be the same. From the viewpoint of China this influx of capital need not be bad. Other nations have experienced the same thing—the development of industry and transportation with the assistance of foreign capital. The Chinese are interested—and indeed it is an international interest—that this investment be unaccompanied by political power or encroachments. In spite of all of these qualifications, however, it must not be forgotten that the substitution of bonds of private enterprise held abroad for government obligations now held does not increase the nation's capacity to pay its national indebtedness to foreign agencies.   Interest and amortization upon these private obligations, and even dividends or profits accruing from permanent investment in Chinese undertakings, can be met only if exchange is available. Thus the problem comes ultimately to the net income of China on international account from goods and services sold.   The development of a trade export surplus becomes ultimately necessary if China in the future is to liquidate all its obligations, both governmental and private.

The treatment of loan payments and the means by which they have been accomplished has been reckoned on the basis of what has been paid.   But the requirements of debt payment are greater than $90,150,000 annually.   Indeed considering the figures given in Chapter VII for 1925 and 1926 of £ 14,933,000 and £ 15,146,000, respectively, required to be paid abroad, (or between $140,000,000 and $160,000,000, depending upon the rate of conversion used), the burden upon China's international accounts and exchange would be very much greater, and it is doubtful whether recent tendencies in the development of the items of credit to China warrant the belief that there would have been a surplus of exchange to such required amounts had China from a revenue standpoint been able to pay all the secured debt charges and interest only on the unsecured foreign debt.   If a consolidated debt scheme is adopted for the unsecured indebtedness the total surplus of exchange annually needed for several years would be at least $155,-000,000 [27] with the further consideration that within a very few years (according to the plan proposed) the amortization of the consolidated issue would begin raising this re-

[27] Calculated at $10.50 to the £ sterling.

quirement to $190,000,000 or perhaps $200,000,000. From where is such a surplus of credit on international account for China to come?

The economic capacity of China to pay the government indebtedness which has been paid in the past has been dependent, as already stated, not upon current income from sales of Chinese goods and services, or other necessary items of credit. These do little more than provide for the imports of goods which China takes from the world. The point is that China's economic capacity to pay at this time depends upon the continuance of the flow of capital to China including the remittances of emigrants' savings and other remittances from Chinese abroad, as well as the investments of foreigners; and upon the continuance of the interest in foreign missions and humanitarian enterprises. The latter, particularly, do not require the payment of dividends, interest, or profits. But for the future the development of a surplus of exchange must fall upon the development of export trade. China has no investments abroad. She has but few services such as shipping, insurance, or banking facilities to sell but in these lines she will be dependent upon outside agencies for some time. The development of banking in China is perhaps the most noteworthy of these services yet the immediate prospects for contributions to the financing of foreign trade are not great. Much is still dependent upon foreign banks or joint foreign and Chinese banks operating in the field.[28]

Interest chiefly attaches to the development of export trade. In later chapters the development of trade in specific commodities will be treated. Suffice it here to consider certain general problems relating to Chinese trade.

One of these has to do with the methods by which ex-

[28] Cf. F. E. Lee, *op. cit.*, Ch. VI–XI inclusive, *passim*.

ports are accomplished. Much of Chinese export trade is brought about through the medium of foreign compradors, who buy from the Chinese producer and either dispose of the goods abroad or sell to some foreign buying house. Chinese organization for internal trade is much more direct. It is possible that as the Chinese become more acquainted with the possibilities of foreign markets that they will themselves organize their own foreign trading establishments and deal more directly. In fact this movement is already under way. Syndicates of Chinese sellers are being organized. The Japanese have done just this. A competent observer remarks, however, " The Chinese will have to develop their internal resources before they become a factor themselves in direct foreign trade." [29]   Direct Chinese participation in the selling and financing of their own products will ultimately be realized, and any movements in that direction will probably react to increase the interest in export trade on the part of the Chinese producer.

Another consideration is the influence of the price of silver. It has been repeatedly noted that China is a silver using country. The price of silver is the important variable factor in Chinese exchange. In recent experiences of trade with countries on a depreciated paper basis it has been found that a depreciation in the exchange on a given country will stimulate exports from that country, though it has been emphasized that the stimulus is temporary, and that such continued stimulus is apt to contribute to the demoralization of governmental finances and the general economic organization of the country.[30]   What is the effect

[29] Julean Arnold, in *Annals*, Nov. 1925, p. 193.

[30] H. G. Moulton and C. Lewis, *The French Debt Problem*, p. 276. Also H. G. Moulton in *American Economic Review*, Dec., 1925, pp. 711–712, 715–716.

upon Chinese export trade of a fall in the price of silver? Some mention has been made of the effect of a falling price of silver on the financial burden of debt for the government. Here our interest is in trade.

In 1896, Walker stated,[31] " Fluctuations in the relative values of the two money metals continually involve international trade in embarrassment and disturbances of a most serious character, and often reduce it to mere gambling." C. A. Conant wrote in 1905,[32] " After a generation of almost steady decline in the gold price of silver a survey of the influence upon the silver countries of the rupture of the par of exchange does not indicate that large benefits are derived by these countries from their monetary policy." (The countries referred to are British India, China and Mexico.) He further stated, upon the question of whether a declining monetary standard does or does not stimulate exports, that " the statistics fail to afford evidence of a direct and powerful stimulation of exports, . . . (this) failed to materialize in an actual increase of gold values." [33] The Commission, which, in 1893, made an investigation of a proposed change of system for India, observed,[34] " Although one may be inclined, regarding the matter theoretically, to accept the proposition that the suggested stimulus would be the result of a falling exchange, an examination of the statistics of exported produce does not appear to afford any substantial foundation for the view that in practice this stimulus, assuming it to have existed, has had

[31] In *International Bimetallism*, p. 139, quoted by C. A. Conant, *Principles of Money and Banking*, p. 344.

[32] *Op. cit.*, p. 347.

[33] *Ibid.*, p. 347.

[34] Report of the Indian Currency Commission, par. 27, quoted by Conant, *op. cit.*, p. 347. Reaffirmed in 1898 by the subsequent Commission on International Exchange, cf. Report, 1903, p. 306.

any prevailing effect upon the course of trade; on the contrary, the progress of the export trade has been less with a rapidly falling than with a steady exchange." In regard to China expert observers remarked it could not be claimed " that the decline in the gold value of silver had done anything to stimulate the growth of China's exports to gold-using countries, while on the other hand it has not checked an expansion of imports from these gold countries." [35]   Dr. Jeremiah W. Jenks, in 1910, speaking of studies made in reference to the trade of Mexico and of China, stated, " The results seem to show that it is impossible to establish the fact that China has made any real gains from the declining value of silver." [36]   In 1926, Professor Chas. F. Remer pointed out that a fall in Chinese exchange is followed after an interval by a rise in the silver prices of Chinese exports, that in this interval there are great profits to be gained by exporters, but not for long. He points out however that if wages and other costs do not go up also there is a " bounty " upon exports which lasts longer.   A fall in Chinese exchange means a rise in the silver prices of Chinese imports, i.e. imports from gold-using countries.   The net result of these two influences, he points out, is an increase in the total exports from China, measured in money value of silver and a decrease in the total imports into China, measured in money value of silver, bringing a more " favorable " (rather less unfavorable) balance of trade, with silver flowing into China.   This increase of exports stimulated by the " bounty " which develops is not necessarily desirable for China, in fact, it

[35] Views of officers of China Association, May, 1903, cf. Report of Commission on International Exchange, 1903, p. 259, quoted by Conant, *op. cit.*, p. 348.

[36] In *China and the Far East*, G. H. Blakeslee (Ed), p. 126; cf. also comment in E. W. Kemmerer, *Modern Currency Reforms*, p. 480.

may be disadvantageous.[37] The views of these various writers would lead us, then, to expect no substantial assistance in the problem of export development from a fluctuating or possibly falling price of silver.

Other considerations in regard to trade development would be in reference to the treaties controlling commerce with foreign nations which China has signed. The control over the tariff recently exercised by treaty Powers has been pointed out. It is not necessary to discuss tariff autonomy at this point. Some mention of the tariff will be made in the next chapter. The commercial treaties providing for extraterritoriality, open ports, and unilateral advantages for foreign nations all affect the development of commerce. For the full development of trade the restrictions of the tariff on foreign merchants beyond treaty ports must be lifted and any existing commercial privileges enjoyed by foreigners but not enjoyed by Chinese operating in the same field of activity should be modified in the interest of equality of position. This raises the whole question of extraterritoriality and treaty revision. In this presentation one can do no more than note the relationship of these partly political problems to the fundamental problems of the economic development of China, and to note that " the removal, so far as possible, of all economic barriers and the establishment of an equality of trade conditions " [38] is a factor of great importance in Chinese capacity to pay, as well as in the maintenance of peace between nations.

[37] " International Trade between Gold and Silver Countries " in *Quarterly Journal of Economics*, August, 1926, p. 601 ff.

[38] President Wilson to Congress, Jan. 8, 1918.

CHAPTER XII

THE DEVELOPMENT OF EXPORT TRADE

China's balance of international accounts has already been treated. It has been pointed out that China as a nation in relation to the rest of the world can obtain annually credits abroad sufficient to meet her annual foreign debt charges only if certain credit items at least continue undiminished, if not in most cases actually increase. Such a condition contains danger to economic stability, and to the credit of the Chinese Government. Debt payments cannot be made if these credits are not available. Many events, mostly internal, but of course those external as well, may operate to upset the flow of capital to China, or the movements of individuals to that country. Further, the debit items of remittances out of China can be expected to increase as this credit item of capital movements increases. At least for the present, however, China's need calls for a continuance of these credit items of foreign investment, foreign tourists in China, and expenditures on foreign missions, schools and hospitals. But such invisible items are not as assured as the visible items are apt to be. In comparison with the visible items of trade they are somewhat more susceptible to variations in the internal security of China, occasioned by political and social disturbances. This is not to say that trade does not suffer but it appears to suffer less. Movements of merchandise, coming from native producers who have in some areas become accustomed to disturbances, will often be delayed only by the interruption of transportation facilities. In 1917 there was a period of great internal strife but it is not apparently reflected in total trade returns. The value of the import and export trade of several ports in 1923 showed increases above 1922, in spite of continued disturbances in and around those ports and cities. " The internal ordinary life of the people and the interests of trade have been much less affected than one would reasonably have supposed," writes one observer regarding the effect of internal fighting on trade,[1] " and except where actual fighting is going on, commerce and industry continue to be carried on without serious disturbance." There has been some diminution of trade, however, as indicated by the fact that the 1925 trade (and customs revenue) did not increase as much over 1924 as had been evident in the immediately preceding years. To minimize the great economic loss which the lack of domestic peace and stability entails would be to lose sight of a great gain which can come to China with the return of order and regularity. The point of interest here is that it is important for China to encourage and develop her export trade since such is apt to be a more stable element in her balance of international accounts than certain other items. Foreigners may become less willing to invest permanently in Chinese industry, as disturbing political changes occur;—and even that which does occur will make greater the remittance item among debits;—so that increased exports of Chinese produce becomes one controlling principle in the solution of the economic aspects of the Chinese debt problem. To the extent that export trade is developed and industrial expansion is achieved China may be able to provide more of her own capital and thus reduce the dependence upon foreign capital now evident.

[1] Report, 1919, *The Prospects of British Trade with China*, Dept. of Overseas Trade. (Cmd. 853) 43, 1920.

There is much in the way of economic change which necessarily accompanies such production for export. The development of trade particularly depends upon the rapid extension of internal communications, more especially the railways, but also the inland waterways, and the telegraphs. Politically, the very continuance of a national existence appears also to depend upon this important factor. Political unity and financial stability upon the part of the Central Government together with numerous related problems may be solved in time by the statesmen of China. But another problem, equally serious, but not as well recognized as some of these others, is and will be to devise means by which exports may be encouraged and developed so that the international balance of exchange may be maintained during debt repayment without bankrupting the nation.

In regard to the export trade in the past one finds that the growth has been fairly steady, with notable exceptions. During the decennial period ending 1913 exports averaged annually 41.4 per cent of the total trade of China while in the decennial period ending 1923 the exports averaged 44.3 per cent. Between 1896 and 1913, the period of China's large expansion in foreign indebtedness, the exports increased at a more rapid rate than the imports. Further, comparing 1923 with an average for the years 1894, 1895 and 1896, which for imports was 178,700,000 taels and for exports was 134,100,000 taels, the year 1923 showed exports as 560 per cent of 1894–6 but imports only 510 per cent of the amounts in those years.

During the years 1915 to 1919 inclusive, the surplus of imports over exports fell below one hundred million taels, to as low as 16,188,270 in 1919. This was due to the falling off of imports and the stimulus afforded to exports by the war in Europe, calling for food and other supplies. This stimulus reached a peak in 1919. The very high gold price of silver in 1918 and 1919, as well as in 1920, served, through the greater purchasing power enjoyed abroad by silver, to sustain an import trade which might otherwise have suffered. The recession in foreign demand in 1920, evidenced in a marked decline in exports, saw imports not only sustained but even rise to a new high point. The growth of imports continued to be greater than that of exports until 1923. In this year exports were 119 per cent of 1919 while imports were 142 per cent of 1919. In spite of this failure to keep up on the part of exports it is to be noted that in 1923 China's exports did increase by 100,000,000 taels over 1922, while imports declined about 22,000,000 taels.

Specifically, what are the leading exports of China? What contributions is each industry now making, what possible contributions can certain industries be expected to make to the export trade? Since China's burden of debt repayment will persist for many years even long run possibilities in trade expansion are worthy of consideration.

Silk and Silk Goods

The principal item of export from China is silk. In 1923 silk constituted 23 per cent of the total exports. This figure includes silk goods and makes a total export value of 170,000,000 Hk. taels. The product of the silk-worm and the mulberry tree has contributed much to the economic life of China. In the foreign trade it has taken the dominant position once held by tea. It is now the largest factor determining China's buying power abroad. In 1860 China furnished one half of the world's supply of raw silk. In 1880 and in 1900, 40 per cent of China's

exports were exports of silk. By 1919 however this proportion had fallen to 22 per cent and it was noted above
that in 1923 this proportion was 23 per cent. A little
over 3 per cent only was in the form of silk goods.[2]

Though the percentage relationship to other exports has
fallen the actual amounts do not reveal any permanent
decline. From the Maritime Customs Statistics the trend
in exports of raw and wild silk and silk waste has been as
follows:

	Weight—Thousands of Piculs	Value—Millions of Hk. Taels
1905	228	
1910	305.3	
1915	337.2	
1919	345.6	113.9
1920	229.7	76.9
1921	275.7	121.2
1922	306.5	148.4
1923	344.4	154.3
1924	382.2	122.4
1925	401.5	153.0

From 1910 to 1917 China obtained only about 30 per
cent of the world's raw silk trade, Japan increasing in
that period from 38 per cent to 51 per cent.[3] China's
formerly dominant position in the world's silk trade was
taken away by Japan, France and Italy, in part because
these countries have adopted more acceptable methods in
silk culture and manufacture, while China has continued
to use the methods of centuries ago. With the pressure
of Japanese competition in the wild silk trade based on
the raw material obtained from Manchuria, Shantung's

[2] Cf. *China Year Book*, 1923, p. 245 for certain of these com-
parisons; also in *The Annals*, November, 1925, Julean Arnold,
" China's Post War Trade."

[3] *China Year Book*, 1923, p. 1212.

pongee and tussore industries came near a crisis, production having been diminishing for several years. In this case the great competitor is the Japanese machine woven pongee made from a scientifically reeled, prepared and partially twisted thread from the Manchurian grown cocoon. The Japanese are even using increasingly the far superior cocoon grown in the very province of Shantung, whose silk industries are feeling the pressure of Japanese competition.

In an article on " China, An Economic Survey " (1923) prepared by Dr. F. E. Lee,[4] one finds it reported that " ancient methods of sericulture are gradually being replaced by scientific instructions, bettering production and enabling China to take a still more important world position in this trade than it has in the past." But Mr. John H. Nelson, Trade Commissioner of U. S. Dept. of Commerce, remarks, " Little tendency is noted of attempts to increase the economic value of China's silk products as a means of balancing foreign trade or improving the economic status of the people, and no well defined movement is apparent either toward increased quantity or improved quality." [5] The statistics of silk exports given above do not reflect any great impetus in that industry towards greater production. China has failed to keep up with the rest of the world's demand for silk. At the present time Chinese governmental agencies are to some extent encouraging and directing farmers. Mr. F. Hayley Bell, Commissioner of Customs of Chefoo in his annual report for 1924 writes, " Four new training and experiment stations are to be opened up in the leading producing centers "

[4] For the Commission on Commerce and Marine of the American Bankers Association, p. 3.

[5] In *Trade Information Bulletin,* No. 312, Jan. 1925, "Changing Factors in the Economic Life of China," p. 20.

14

near his district. Further mention is made by the same
writer of plans for afforestation of waste lands with scrub
oak for feeding purposes.[6] Attention directed towards
better organization in the collecting of cocoons, an increasing establishment and operation of silk filatures with
modern machinery, greater attention to preparing the raw
silk in a manner suited to meet the needs of foreign high-
speed looms, and the development of factories for manufacturing silk products will bring increasing economic results.
In the manufacture of silk goods the Chinese people possess an artistic ability which it is as important to consider
and foster as cheaper processes. This fact in itself can
be significant in increasing the value of the silk and silk
goods which China sells to the world. With the employment of scientific methods the Chinese export trade in silk
and silk goods could at least be doubled in quantity within
a few years and perhaps this would bring an equal increase
in point of value.

The Soya Bean Industry

Second place among the exports of China is now taken
by the soya bean industry. Beans, beancake and bean oil
constituted 15 per cent of exports in 1923, as against 8
per cent in 1910, an actual increase in the annual value
of the export of these commodities of over 100,000,000
taels in the thirteen year period just mentioned. The aggregate value in 1923 of these products was 127,400,000
taels.[7] The beans and beancake have become important
in the trade with Japan and Europe where they are used
for fertilizer and cattle food. The bean oil is used in the
Orient for cooking purposes. This remarkable expansion

---

[6] Cf. *Chinese Economic Bulletin*, May 9, 1925, p. 267.
[7] *The Annals*, Nov., 1925, J. Arnold, p. 89.

in the soya bean industry was given a great impetus by the European War, and the continued increase of export of these commodities in post war years indicates that the industry will probably continue as a leading one.

The three northern provinces are the center of the soya bean industry. Seventy per cent of China's soya beans are produced in this area, which comprises Manchuria. In fact the soya bean is Manchuria's most important commercial crop. Several varieties are raised, some more adapted for cake and oil, others for bean sauce, the salty liquid used widely as a condiment. The area under cultivation in the three northern provinces is as follows in millions of mow (one mow equals .151 acre): [8]

Area	Fengtien	Kirin	Heilung-kiang	Total
In Beans.....................	55.7	27.7	31.7	115.1
In all cultivated crops..........	215.9	156.3	118.1	490.3

Twenty three per cent of the cultivated area of these three provinces constituting Manchuria is devoted to beans. In the absence of complete statistics it is difficult to estimate the total yield either for all of Manchuria or for the balance of China. The northern section of Manchuria (including the producing districts of Tsitsihar, Anta, Harbin, Fuyu, Sungari, and the southern and eastern sections of the Chinese Eastern Railway) raised a bean crop in 1922 of 138,900,000 poods,[9] equal to about 2,500,000 tons, which was an increase of 6.4 per cent over the crop of 1921 for the same area.[10] In 1922, after local consump-

[8] *Chinese Economic Monthly*, Jan., 1926, p. 2. " Economic Resources of Manchuria."

[9] The *pood* is a Russian unit equal to 36.11 American pounds.

[10] *Chinese Economic Monthly*, Oct., 1925, p. 13, " Bean and Wheat Production along the Chinese Eastern Railway."

tion was cared for there remained available a surplus which was " exported " [11] to the amount of 1,350,000 tons.   In pood units, the increase of this " export " surplus of beans from this area, as carried by the Chinese Eastern Railway and the Ussuri-Chita and the South Manchuria Railway, is seen from the following data: [12]

```
1920.....................................16,497,000 poods
1921.....................................40,409,000
1922.....................................55,167,000
1923.....................................60,792,000
```

This represents an increase of over 370 per cent in the importance of this section of China as an area producing beans for shipment into the balance of China or for export from China.   These figures on railway shipments can be supplemented by those of bean cakes and bean oil showing that in these products as well the increase of production has been marked: [13]

EXPORTS FROM SECTIONS OF THE CHINESE EASTERN RAILWAY

	Beancakes	Bean Oil
1921	8,670,000 poods	344,000 poods
1922	12,870,000	1,174,000
1923	18,448,000	(not available)

The port of Dairen in the Province of Fengtien has become the center of the distribution of beans, and for the export of beancakes and bean oil.   In Dairen there was in 1923 a total of 84 mills, engaged in the beancake and bean oil industry, having a capital of at least $19,000,000 (Mex.) and a total maximum daily output of over 261,000 pieces of beancake, and of over 1,250,000 catties [14] of

[11] The term " export " used here means export from producing area only.

[12] *Chinese Economic Monthly*, Oct., 1925, pp. 14 and 15.

[13] *Chinese Economic Monthly*, Oct., 1925, pp. 14 and 15.

[14] A *catty* equals 1–1/3 lbs.

bean oil. Of these 84 mills only 69 are now operating, 58 by Chinese and 11 by Japanese, 15 having been suspended (1925). This decline in operations occurred probably in response to local conditions. The very thriving position enjoyed by the bean oil industry during the war and post war years will probably be held. From material given in the Chinese Economic Monthly for October, 1925, I have calculated that the industry in 1925 was running at 85 per cent of capacity in beancakes and 92 per cent of capacity in bean oil production.[15]

All of the material presented here, for certain areas of Manchuria, and for the port of Dairen, in the various phases of the soya bean industry, would indicate an increasing production in China. The trend of the most recent years shows an increasingly large contribution to export trade both as to weight and as to silver value of the products themselves. In 1924 soya bean exports increased 58 per cent over 1923 in point of value, bean cakes exports remained about the same, while bean oil increased about 25 per cent. In addition Chinese exports of all other kinds of beans increased by over 50 per cent. The Japanese and European markets continuing strong for these commodities,—and there is no apparent likelihood of loss of these markets—an increasing export trade in beans and bean products can be expected.

Vegetable Oils

In addition to bean oil, China produces other vegetable oils which have become important articles of commerce. In 1910, vegetable oils were $3\frac{1}{4}$ per cent of total exports, in point of value, while in 1923 vegetable oils, exclusive of bean oil, constituted over 5 per cent of exports. Among

[15] *Chinese Economic Monthly*, Oct., 1925, pp. 27–30.

vegetable oils are included peanut oil, tea oil, and wood oil. Exports of all of these oils, including in this case bean oil, have increased materially in the last twenty years: [16]

Average 1898–1902	330.2 thousands of piculs [17]
1903	421.4
1907	454.6
1911	974.3
1913	1,212.0
1915	1,689.7
1917	2,841.3
1919	4,256.2
1921	2,045.5
1922	2,624.9
1923	3,443.9

The place taken by vegetable oils in China's exports in the war and post war years is thus seen as being gradually regained. Wood oil alone increased in 1924 over 1923 by 9 per cent in point of value, and bean oil increased about 25 per cent.

There is a very definite differential between the prices of imported kerosene oil and native vegetable oils, which, if exceeded very materially reduces kerosene oil consumption and increases native oil consumption insofar as there is possibility of substitution of such oils for the purposes which kerosene satisfies. In time kerosene will undoubtedly displace the native vegetable oils for illuminating purposes, particularly if there develops a greater market abroad for Chinese vegetable oils. At the time when China was exporting such large quantities of oils as noted in the table above, the imports of kerosene into China increased markedly, assuming third place in the imports of China in 1923.

[16] *Trade Information Bulletin* No. 312, Jan., 1925, p. 20, from *Maritime Customs Trade Statistics of China*, 1923.

[17] A *picul* equals 133–1/3 lbs.

Raw Cotton

The most important cotton producing countries of the world in the order of their relative importance in commercial cotton production are the United States, India, Egypt and China, according to Leslie A. Wheeler, Special Agent of the U. S. Dept. of Commerce.[18]   In 1916 China ranked third as a producer of cotton.[19]   According to Mr. Wheeler's figures, however, China has exceeded Egypt since 1921, thus making China appear as third in importance.   It is almost impossible to arrive at an accurate estimate of the total production of cotton in China.   Cotton is grown in a wide area, on small farms, widely scattered, often being planted along with other crops.[20]   For this reason the total area under cultivation for cotton is unknown.   The Chinese Ministry of Agriculture and Commerce has however estimated the area at 26,000,000 mow.[21]

Some indication of China's production can be ascertained by taking cotton mill consumption plus exports.   This is done by Mr. Wheeler and his figures are reproduced here in the following table: [22]

[18] L. A. Wheeler, " International Trade in Cotton," *Trade Promotion Series* No. 13, p. 2, 1925, U. S. Dept. of Com.

[19] According to Ralph M. Odell, " Cotton Goods in China," *Special Agent Series* No. 107, p. 199, U. S. Dept. of Com.

[20] Cf. *Chinese Economic Monthly*, March, 1926, " Cotton Cultivation in Chekiang," p. 108.

[21] A *mow* equals .151 acre; estimate found in *China Year Book*.

[22] Figures taken from *Census Bulletins*, " Cotton Production & Distribution," cf. Wheeler, *op. cit.*, p. 2.

COTTON PRODUCTION IN CHINA—MILL CONSUMPTION PLUS EXPORTS
(In Thousands of bales; one bale equals 478 lbs. net)

1914–15	788
1915–16	887
1916–17	851
1917–18	865
1918–19	940
1919–20	1,150
1920–21	1,045
1921–22	1,175
1922–23	1,300
1923–24	1,450

According to these figures there was an increase of 67 per cent in 1923–24 over the average of the years 1914–19, the period of the war; and the post war year average is 36 per cent greater than the average of 1909–14, 1,224,000 bales as against 898,000 bales. These figures based on mill consumption plus exports are but partly indicative since imports of cotton have increased materially during the same period.

There have been various estimates made of the total annual production of cotton in China in the years before the war which can be compared with the material above:

	Bales
U. S. Dept. of Agriculture Yearbook	3,473,000
Shepherdson's Cotton Facts	4,385,000
Jones Annual Cotton Handbook	4,032,000
Chinese Ministry of Agriculture and Commerce [23]	3,683,000

Thus it has been quite generally accepted that the commercial cotton production of China has been in the past between 3,500,000 and 4,225,000 bales in the pre-war years. The actual production is larger for much of the

[23] The Ministry estimated 15,680,000 piculs = 933,000 tons = 3,683,400 bales. Cf. *China Year Book*, 1923, p. 200.

cotton raised does not reach the commercial markets. "The common practice of Chinese farmers of retaining relatively large quantities of cotton for padding their winter garments, bedding, etc. and for home spinning when cotton prices give a low return for their labor" is one factor which prevents full knowledge of the cotton crop of China. The evidence of exports alone, though by no means increasing as much during the past fifteen years as raw cotton imports, combined with a very much larger use of cotton as reflected by mill consumption, would seem to indicate an increasing production of cotton in China.

It is interesting that China should be an exporter of raw cotton and at the same time consume increasingly larger quantities of foreign cotton. China's cotton is a short staple of kinky fiber and finds a ready market in the United States since it is well adapted for the manufacture of blankets. Further, it is used by cotton mills in Japan where it is mixed with Indian and American cottons. On the other hand China must now import foreign cottons to obtain certain qualities and also the quantity, not supplied by her own production, but needed by her constantly expanding cotton milling industry.

The exports and imports of unmanufactured cotton both by weight and by silver value is shown by the following table: [24]

[24] Source: The official Statistics of the Maritime Customs of China.

CHINA'S FOREIGN TRADE IN RAW COTTON

Year	Exports		Imports	
	Bales of 478 lbs. Thousands	Value Hk. Taels Thousands	Bales of 478 lbs. Thousands	Value Hk. Taels Thousands
1909–13.	Aver. 240	19,451		
1914....	188	12,715	37	2,917
1915....	202	13,700	102	6,652
1916....	237	17,091	114	8,069
1917....	232	20,036	84	6,406
1918....	360	37,887	53	6,071
1919....	299	30,253	67	6,499
1920....	105	9,225	189	17,993
1921....	170	16,483	469	35,867
1922....	235	22,861	497	41,956
1923....	272	32,606	450	53,816
1924....		42,284		49,836
1925....		31,809		70,852

Note: Exports include re-exports direct to foreign countries. Imports are net, exclusive of re-exports.

One notes the decline in exports immediately preceding the war, an increase during the war, a decline of pronounced character in 1920, and a period of steady growth since that time, almost attaining the peak of 1918–1919. The year 1924 indicates an export of over 300,000 bales and an increase in the value of such over 1923 of 34 per cent. The 1925 report shows a decline in value to 31,809,000 taels in exports and a remarkable increase of imports to 70,852,500 taels. While there was a declining tendency after 1918 in exports it is now probable, however, that this is not going to remain true. Soil, climate and labor supply favor the production of cotton in China. China can grow her own cotton of a variety suitable for modern machinery.

In certain Provinces such as Kiangsu, Hupeh, and Honan some special attention and encouragement has been given to the crop by provincial authorities. " If a systematic effort were made or sponsored by the Chinese Government to improve the cultivation of cotton there would be but little doubt that China would become an outstanding factor in the world cotton situation." [25] This would add greatly to China's possibilities in export trade, while possibly, if other types of cotton than are now produced were introduced Chinese imports of raw cotton would be reduced. " It is possible for China to develop an industry ultimately free from dependence on an outside supply of the necessary raw materials." [26] The export of cotton in 1923 constituted 4 per cent of total exports while the import of cotton in the same year totalled 6 per cent of imports.

Eggs and Egg Products

Eggs and egg products are exported chiefly to Japan, Hongkong and Great Britain. These products are assuming increasing importance in Chinese trade. In 1910 the export trade in these goods was valued at 4,000,000 taels while in 1921 the value of this trade had increased to 24,-677,000 taels, and in 1923 to 29,600,000 taels, or 4 per cent of the total export trade for the latter year. During the war the Far East became an important source of food supply in certain lines of foodstuffs. China was called upon to supply an increased quantity of eggs and egg products. Strangely this was done and continues to be done without industrial organization. " There is no poultry industry in China, the eggs being collected in small quantities from

[25] L. A. Wheeler, *op. cit.*, p. 21; also cf. *China Year Book*, 1923, p. 221 for further discussion on " Cotton Growing in China."
[26] H. M. Vinacke, *Industrial Development in China*, p. 15.

market centers to which they are carried from the family farms, each of which keeps a few hens," writes Julean Arnold, American Commercial Attache in China.[27]

Tea

Tea is produced principally in the southern Provinces of China where the tea plant is grown. The growth of these plants is generally not carried on on a large scale by any one producer, the plantation system being as yet unknown. Individual peasants raise small plots of tea plants and the first stages in the preparation of tea for market use are still in the stage of domestic economy. Tea has been a large factor in Chinese production for many years and its cultivation and preparation is one of the most important industries of the country. According to the Ministry of Agriculture and Commerce the total yearly output of tea is over 2 million cases of a value of 40 million dollars (Mex.).[28] Tea has figured to a varying extent in China's export trade. In 1820, tea constituted 75 per cent of the exports of China. China practically supplied the world with tea for 50 years after that. But tea showed a declining relative importance in the total exports as evidenced by the following percentages: 1867, 60 per cent; 1882, 48 per cent; 1899, 16 per cent; 1902, 11 per cent; 1919, 4 per cent; 1923, 3 per cent.

The actual figures by weight reveal a similar decline in the part taken by tea exports:[29]

[27] In *The Annals*, Nov., 1925, p. 89.

[28] Cf. *China Year Book*, 1924, p. 535.

[29] Report of Trade, 1922, Abstract of Statistics, p. 127; also 1923; also *China Year Book*, 1928–1929, p. 123.

EXPORTS OF TEA DIRECT TO FOREIGN COUNTRIES

1913	1,442,109 piculs *
1914	1,495,799
1915	1,782,353
1916	1,542,633
1917	1,125,535
1918	404,217
1919	690,155
1920	305,906
1921	430,328
1922	576,073
1923	801,417
1924	765,935
1925	833,008

* These are inclusive of re-exports.

Looked at from the viewpoint of values, tea exports in 1913 were 25,278,000 haikwan taels and in 1922, 16,-622,000 taels. The latter, however, calculated at the 1913 average values would be 18,125,000 hk. taels, not as great a reduction as would otherwise appear.[30]

China's tea trade has been wrested from her by India, and Japan. One significant factor in this was the high cost of production as caused partly by the inland tax on tea as well as the export duty. Methods of cultivation and preparation for market were also important, the Indian teas particularly being produced on a larger scale and being better advertised and marketed.

The tea trade, though apparently on the decline, has possibilities for the expansion of export trade. There is a large world market. The restoration of trade relations with Russia, which before the war took over 60 per cent of China's export of tea, should increase tea exports. Brick tea, which is made of tea dust, broken leaf, and stalk

[30] *Ibid.*, 1922, p. 19.

pressed together with machine power into the form of a brick, has generally been largely destined for the Russian market via Siberia. On account of the unfavorable conditions in Siberia this business was in 1925 practically at a standstill.[31] The continuance of prohibition in the United States, where tea-drinking has, according to reports, increased,[32] the development of better marketing methods and the education of buyers to the superior qualities of certain Chinese teas, the increasing attention of the Chinese Government and local bodies to the cultivation and production of those qualities of tea in which China excels, are all factors in this improvement in export of tea. Since 1919 the export duty has been remitted in whole or in part. Since 1920 tea exports have increased from the low point of that year. The reduction in 1924 and 1925 was 20 per cent of the regular tariff as concerns the tea destined for ports in China, while teas for export are duty free except for conservancy dues.[33] A continuance of this policy would be wise.

Wool

North China produces large quantities of wool, the annual exports of which are valued at about 13,000,000 taels (1923), a large portion of which is exported to the United States. If some of this wool, in increasing amounts, is kept at home for manufacture, as there is at present a tendency, woolen manufacturing will tend to be independent of an outside supply. Until that time an expansion in wool exports is to be looked for.[34]

[31] *Chinese Economic Monthly*, Jan., 1925, p. 21.

[32] The year 1923 showed increased exports of tea to the United States over 1922 of 50 per cent.

[33] Cf. *China Year Book*, 1924, pp. 533–537; also 1925, pp. 498–502.

[34] Julean Arnold, *Commercial Handbook of China*, II, p. 364.

Hides and Skins

The export trade in skins and hides has been becoming increasingly valuable. To be sure the war period accentuated the demand and value of these articles as shown in the following figures of the export trade in undressed hides and skins:

```
1910...................................16,000,000 taels
1913...................................19,700,000
1917...................................27,000,000
1923...................................19,100,000
```

In addition there is trade in dressed skins and furs as well as leather. The trade in all of these goods is capable of great expansion. The almost untouched trade possibilities of Mongolia in these commodities is as yet only appreciated to any great extent by Russian traders.

Oil Seeds

China exports many kinds of seeds of commercial value: cotton seed, rape seed, sesamun seed, linseed, melon and apricot seeds, and in addition seed cake. The contributions of these many items to export trade has varied considerably since before the war, the war causing several to fall off noticeably. In 1923 the export of sesamun seed was 12,200,000 taels and of rape seed 2,000,000 taels. All of these seeds together constitute about 2½ per cent of total exports.

Grains and Cereals

During the war years China became a large exporter of wheat and flour, and the flour milling industry made great strides. But this was not to last. The recession in prices consequent to the war made China again an importer of these commodities.   In 1923 the import of wheat was 9,100,000 taels and the export was 2,100,000 taels, and the import of flour in 1923 was 27,200,000 taels. China did however, export millet and kaoliang to the amount of 12,000,000 taels.   For a country as needful of food as China, with its susceptibility to famine, and its large population, the encouragement of exports of foodstuffs would not appear wise.   To a certain extent this will take care of itself.   The increased production of China along all lines is fundamental to increased consumption and these foodstuffs if needed in China will not be exported if the Chinese themselves develop a market for them.   As matters now stand " bad internal conditions of communications " and " antiquated farming methods militate against China's rapid emergence in to the category of a regular exporter of flour." [35]

Coal

Formerly and until 1922 China imported more coal and coke than she exported, in point of value, and this in spite of the fact that China is the richest country in coal on the Pacific outside of the United States.   In 1923 China's total export of coal was 20,300,000 taels but deducting coal imports the net export of coal becomes 7,300,000 taels.   The coal mines of China produce from 20 to 25 million tons annually compared to America's 550,000,000 tons.   The 1924 figure of Chinese coal production was 23,711,000 long tons, an increase over 1912 of over 75 per cent.[36] The import and export of coal as follows, in thousands of tons:

[35] *Annals*, Nov., 1925, Julean Arnold, p. 87.
[36] Cf. *China Year Book*, 1925, p. 127; 1928, p. 80, and *Commerce Year Book*, 1925, p. 621.

	Imports	Exports
1919	1,172	1,744
1920	1,338	1,970
1921	1,361	1,886
1922	1,151	2,377
1923	1,366	3,108
1924	1,610	3,202
1925	2,752	3,002

The coal resources of China have been variously estimated, some conservatively, and others probably not so.
Dr. Sun Yat Sen, one time Provisional President of China,
spoke of " a country most rich in coal deposits—scarcely
scratched." " If China is as equally developed as the
United States she should have an output (in proportion
to population) of 4 times that of the United States " or
about 2200 million tons.[37]   The total area of coal mining
registered with the Ministry of Agriculture and Commerce
up to June, 1924 was 3,805 square li or 390, 775 acres.
In contrast to this the total resources have been estimated
conservatively at between 40 and 50 billion tons.[38]   Other
estimates have been given.   Prof. Fernald of the University of Pennsylvania, estimates China's coal resources
at 1,200,000,000 short tons,—this in reference to that of
commercial value.   The China Year Book, 1921–1922,
gives the various grades of reserves but notes 23,435 millions of tons, a figure which the editors admit is not complete.   In an article by E. M. de Villa, Consulting Mining
Engineer, in " Readings in Economics for China "[39] one
finds an estimate of 300 billion tons available.   There are
about fifteen principal companies operating, of which six

[37] In *International Development of China*, p. 224.

[38] *China Year Book*, 1925, pp. 122–123.

[39] C. F. Remer (Ed.) *Readings in Economics for China*, p. 209,
article on " Examination of Mines in China, 1919."

are Chinese, four are joint Chinese and foreign undertakings, and the others are foreign.   The total capital
investment of all these fifteen largest companies is in the
neighborhood of $100,000,000 (Mex.), of which slightly
less than half is Chinese.   There are now many small mining concerns, which are scarcely worth mentioning, though
their number is quite large.[40]   Shansi Province has particularly rich deposits of coal of which only a very small percentage has yet been mined.   Transportation difficulties
form the chief deterrent to the development of these mines.
To the extent that China can increase production in coal
there will either be a curtailment of imports or an increase
of exports or possibly both.   In this development much depends upon the facilities of transportation and improvements in methods.[41]

Other Minerals and Metals

In regard to the production of iron ore and other minerals it can also be said that much depends upon the development of internal transportation.   Nature has en-
dowed China with an abundant supply of iron and copper,
and also supplies of tin, lead, zinc, gold, quicksilver, antimony, tungsten, and other minerals.   These resources are
at present practically untouched.   China's known iron reserve has been estimated by the Geological Survey at
677,000,000 tons, this authority estimating this amount
as probably about one-half of China's total reserve of iron
ore, and conservatively places the total at 1,000,000,000
tons, one half of which is capable of being worked by mod-

[40] *China Year Book*, 1925, pp. 126–127.   A list of coal mines in
China is in *Chinese Economic Monthly*, Nov., 1925, p. 3.
[41] Cf. description of "Coal Mining in Shansi," *Chinese Economic
Monthly*, Nov., 1925.

ern methods.[42]   The present annual production of iron ore
in China is about 1,500,000 tons of which about two-thirds
is smelted in China.   The value of the export of pig iron
and iron ore in 1923 was 8,800,000 taels.   The exports
are gradually increasing.

China is the leading producer of the world in antimony
and tungsten.   " Regulus "   or   pure   antimony   and
" crude " or antimony sulphide are included.   In 1918
China reached a peak of 15,985 tons of regulus exported
which in 1923 had fallen to 11,587 tons, though the latter
year was greater than the low years of 1919 and 1920.[43]
In 1923 exports of antimony were valued at 1,500,000
taels.   The strength displayed in the recovery of this trade
indicates a probable continuance of this trade as an important one.

In tungsten production, China in 1923 produced 70 per
cent of the world's supply.   The export in tons in 1923
was 4,016.[44]   The foregoing statement of the resources
of China in iron and other minerals and the present production makes evident that the present contribution to export trade of all of these commodities is but a small frac-
tion of what it can and should be.

To enumerate every commodity which enters into the
export trade of China would be impossible.   The " sun-
dries " item both of imports and exports has been including
a continuously larger number of items.

Specifically in regard to the year 1924, there were increases in the value of the following important exports:
silk piece goods, soya beans, other beans, raw cotton, egg
albumen and yolk, ground nuts, coal and coke, bean oil,

[42] Cf. *China Year Book*, 1921–1922, p. 170.
[43] Cf. *Ibid.*, 1925, p. 137.
[44] Cf. *Ibid.*, p. 137.

wood oil, millet and sorghum, cigarettes, sheeps' wool, and pig iron and iron ore.

The conclusions from such a limited survey of the possibilities of Chinese export trade are encouraging. In such commodities as silk and silk goods, tea, raw cotton, beans and related products, coal, and iron, and many other raw materials, both agricultural and mineral, it is seen that there are not only future possibilities but that development of a steady character is already under way. In the next chapter further treatment will be made of the imports of China and the development of other industries.

Exportation from China cannot fail, however, to feel the crippling effect of export taxes. Until a few years ago an effective 5 per cent was applied. Since that time irregular increases in export taxes have been made gradually until there is great variance among the different ports, with some ports of North China levying a tax of 20 per cent quite indiscriminately on all goods.[45] For commodities which have to compete in world markets this will have a decidedly limiting effect, more especially for those of a non-luxury character. This disregard of economic principles is a hardship for Chinese industry and cannot fail to have an effect on China's balance of international accounts.

[45] According to press dispatches. Cf. *Christian Science Monitor,* July 20, 1929.

CHAPTER XIII

China has been characteristically an importing nation. Imports into China have shown a continuous increase, broken, however, in some years, as 1915 and 1923, by declines. The relation to total export trade and the figures on total import trade were given in Table J (Chapter XI). Interest in the future movements of import trade is important because a consideration must be given to the possibilities of curtailing imports as a means of developing an export surplus and because of the importance of imports in the continuing expansion of industry within China.

The principal items among Chinese imports together with the value of the trade in each and the relative position of each in the total import trade is found in the following table on page 218: [1]

This table registers notable increases in certain imports in 1924 over 1923 as for example in sugar, flour, and wheat. Foodstuffs vary in trade demand considerably, reflecting changed production yields and changing prices, as for example in rice, as well as changing tastes. The whole list of China's imports is too long to give in full. There is wide variety. This table indicates that the trade is very broad in character since no single group of commodities is predominant.

Internal development has been going on continuously, but in the last few years particularly, in certain lines of production which affect specific imports. Notable here is the cotton textile industry. It has been noted that cotton goods are now the chief item in the import trade and with cotton yarn make up 18 per cent of total imports. China

[1] 1923 data from *Annals*, Nov., 1925, p. 84, based on Customs Statistics, article by J. Arnold.

Item	Value in millions of Hk. Taels—1923	% of 1923 Total Imports	% Increases 1924 over 1923
Cotton goods.............	132	14	2.6
Rice..................	98	10½	— 33.
Kerosene..............	58	6	6.
Raw Cotton...........	54	6	— 1.3
Sugar.................	50	5½	57.
Cotton yarn...........	42	4½	— 10.
Cigarettes and Tobacco..	41	4½	
Metals................	41	4½	
Machinery.............	35.7	4	
Flour.................	27.2	3	19.
Marine Products........	25	3	
Dyes.................	22.1	2½	
Wheat................	9.1	1	125.
Woolen goods.........	19	2	
Paper................	16.6	1.9	
Coal.................	13	1½	
Clothing and hats.......	12.8	1½	
Lumber...............	9.6	1	

has been one of the world's largest markets for cotton yarn, as well as for cotton piece goods. The enormous population of China depends largely upon cotton goods as a material for clothing. Through the years 1880 to 1914 the imports of cotton manufactures averaged 33 per cent of total imports in each year.[2] In recent years the development of the cotton spinning industry in China has accounted for a great increase in the amount of raw cotton imported into China, elsewhere mentioned. This item alone was 54,000,000 taels in 1923 and 70,000,000 taels in 1925. The development of the cotton spinning has also accounted for the decline in cotton yarn imports from 61,500,000 taels in 1910 to 42,000,000 taels in 1923, and even lower

[2] " Cotton Goods in China," *Special Agents Series,* No. 107, U. S. Dept. of Com., p. 26.

in 1924. In the six years closing with 1925 the number
of spindles operating in China has increased by over 183
per cent, with a total of 3,414,062 operating spindles, and
173,916 not yet operating;—making a total of 3,587,978
spindles in China. Of these spindles 55 per cent are Chinese owned. The total production of yarn for 1925 was
719,215,000 lbs, of which 65 per cent was from Chinese
owned mills.[3] The European war gave a considerable impetus to the cotton spinning industry, because of the high
prices which developed, and because also of the strong anti-
Japanese boycott, which served to stimulate Chinese industry.

In regard to the import requirements of this industry
little decline in import demand for raw cotton can be looked
for immediately since China can not yet supply certain
qualities of cotton and her own production is not yet sufficiently large to meet the needs of this industry. It has
already been indicated, however, that China can in time
reduce this importation. There is sufficient arable land
to grow the raw cotton needed. Imports of cotton yarn
may be expected to decrease as the cotton spinning industry
develops, but the complete answer to this question cannot
be given without considering the demand within China for
such yarn for weaving. If the cotton piece goods industry
develops more rapidly than that of spinning there can be
expected little decline of imports of yarn.

The cotton piece goods industry is developing quite rapidly. The total number of operating looms in 1925 was
25,934; of those not yet operating, 4,090; making a total
of 30,024 looms in China. Of the looms in operation 63
per cent are Chinese owned. The total production of

[3] *Chinese Economic Monthly*, Feb., 1926, pp. 83–88, " List of Cotton Mills in China."

cloth in 1925 was 120,023,000 yards of cloth of which
Chinese mills produced about 5/6ths.   (This does not however make allowance for varying width of cloth.)   In
six years the number of looms has increased by over 500
per cent.[4]   Here reference has been made to power looms.
The hand loom industry is very old in China, and the use
of hand looms is more extensive in that country today than
in any other country in the world.   The hand loom industry consumes a large amount of yarn.   The output
of cloth cannot be stated.   By far the largest amount of
the production of hand looms is in the homes of the farmers
but there are establishments with from 50 to 300 hand
looms.   Thus whenever the price of foreign piece goods
rises considerably the hand weaving industry has an increased demand.[5]

Whereas cotton yarn imports have increased but slightly
in recent years, cotton piece goods imports have increased
more rapidly, standing at 132,000,000 hk. taels in 1923
and over 150,000,000 hk. taels in 1924.   The cotton piece
goods industry is making progress towards supplying the
Chinese domestic needs in this line of production.   It is
not, however, developing with quite the same speed as the
cotton spinning industry if one judges on the basis of the
degree to which the home market needs are being supplied.
To the extent that this home market demand is supplied
at home China's unfavorable balance of trade will be reduced.   It thus appears that if the cotton spinning industry can continue to develop equally with the demands
of the weaving industry and this with the needs of the

[4] *Chinese Economic Monthly*, Feb., 1926, p. 83 ff; *Chinese Economic Journal*, Nov., 1928.

[5] Cf. "Cotton Goods in China," *Special Agents Series* No. 107, p. 185 ff., also *Chinese Economic Monthly*, Nov., 1925, p. 22, "Weaving Industry in Wuchang and Hankow."

home market that China's economic position will be more secure. With the improvement of the economic position of the masses, coming as a result of industrial development the consumption of cotton goods will undoubtedly increase. It is a matter of doubt whether the cotton weaving industry can keep pace with such increased demands consequent to improved economic conditions. For the time being then one must expect a continuance of imports of both cotton yarns and cloth, but probably in successively decreasing amounts.

Some measure of forced readjustment in this connection would have been occasioned by the imposition of the 50 per cent increase in the customs tariff rates had the $2\frac{1}{2}$ per cent surtax been imposed at the Peking Tariff Conference. It had been stated that such would have provided a measure of protection, though not complete protection, to mill owners in China. Under tariff autonomy China may impose protective duties on cotton piece goods and cotton yarns, thus assuring the development of these industries, and a consequent reduction of the imports of such goods.[6] There will not probably be, for some time, a reduction of imports of the finer shirtings and sheetings from Great Britain and elsewhere in anywhere near the same proportions which may occur in coarser productions since it is in the latter products particularly that China is now working. It appears that even now China is able to meet some foreign competition in this field, particularly that of Japan, as imports of the latter have increased but slightly in recent years. Certain goods of finished character and of certain dyed qualities will probably continue to be imported.

[6] The tariff rates for 1929 as promulgated are admittedly provisional, for one year's trial, and the statement has been made that these rates will probably be further increased. Cf. W. H. Mallory, "China's New Tariff Autonomy," *Foreign Affairs*, Apr., 1929, p. 498.

" The principal factors that have contributed to the establishment and growth of the Chinese cotton-goods industry have been the following: (1) a supply of native-grown cottons of sufficiently good quality for spinning low counts; (2) an enormous domestic demand for the production of the mills; (3) low cost of power; and (4) an abundance of very cheap labor, which makes the cost of production lower than in any other part of the world." [7]

Turning to the investment in the cotton milling industry, both yarn and cloth, one finds, in 1925, 118 mills in operation with a total capital of roughly $290,000,000 (Mex.). About 57 per cent of the capital is from foreign sources, and 40 per cent or 49 of these mills are foreign owned. Of these 49, 45 are Japanese owned and 4 are British owned. Some of the capital in Chinese companies may be from foreign sources. The statistics given above for spindles and looms indicates that 55 per cent of the spindles and 63 per cent of the looms are Chinese owned. The production in Chinese owned mills is keeping pace with the production in foreign owned mills. The Chinese plants are operated by electricity. In Chinese and foreign mills, both yarn and cloth, 6,776,847 piculs of cotton were consumed, of which 60 per cent was in Chinese owned mills.[8]

In close connection with the cotton weaving industry is the importation of dyes. In 1924 artificial indigo constituted 2 per cent and aniline dyes 1 per cent of total imports. Artificial indigo is of recent importation. The war caused the decline in imports of aniline dyes, causing a reversion to the use of vegetable dyes. The continuing development of the cotton textile industry will make necessary an increasing importation of dyestuffs.

[7] Julean Arnold, *Commercial Handbook of China*, Vol. II, p. 322.
[8] *Chinese Economic Monthly*, Feb., 1926, p. 83 ff.

Another industry which has been developing rapidly in recent years has been that of cigarettes and tobacco. In fifteen years the imports of cigarettes and tobacco have increased 400 per cent. Both of these facts indicate that the Chinese market for cigarettes has grown very rapidly. It has been estimated that the people of China consume annually 60 billion cigarettes. In 1924 the imports of cigarettes totalled 3 per cent of total imports, and with tobacco and other tobacco products constituted 5 per cent. The Chinese have long been tobacco producers. Recently improved tobacco of American seed has been produced. During 1909–1913 China's exports of tobacco (leaf) exceeded imports but from 1920 on the opposite has been true. China's exports of leaf tobacco in 1924 were about 24,000,000 lbs. while imports were in 1923, 42,000,000 lbs. and in 1924 91,000,000 lbs.[9] Likewise the value of these imports of tobacco increased over 1923 by 109 per cent. It is thus evident that her own production of tobacco is not sufficient to meet the needs of the cigarette industry. Not only have imports of cigarettes increased but also home production of cigarettes has increased.

The textile and cigarette industries are " the only two commodities of importance in China's import trade which can be produced economically in China." [10] These might be encouraged by some measure of protection.[11] In 1924 the total importation of cotton goods, cotton yarn, and cigarettes totalled 215,000,000 haikwan taels, while China's

[9] *Commerce Year Book*, 1925, p. 224.

[10] Frank R. Eldridge, of U. S. Dept. of Com., in paper at Johns Hopkins (Baltimore) Conference on China; cf. Proceedings, p. 77.

[11] The tariff rate established in Feb. 1, 1929 was 40 per cent on tobacco products including an excise of 32½ per cent on cigars and cigarettes. Cf. W. H. Mallory " China's New Tariff Autonomy " in *Foreign Affairs*, Apr., 1929, p. 498.

net unfavorable balance of trade for that year was 268,-
000,000 taels, and the average 1922–1924, inclusive, was
243,000,000 taels.   If China supplied her own needs in
these commodities there would be a marked reduction in
the imports, tending to reduce the unfavorable balance of
trade.

The inspiration for such a policy of protection comes
not from the "self-sufficiency" argument.   There is already a large amount of self-sufficiency in China, but this
is not the present concern.   Some measure of protection
is often valuable for a nation for the purpose of setting
to work, against competition already well organized, latent
economic possibilities which later can survive without aid
but which require assistance to overcome the obstacles
found in the task of getting under way.   Such a policy
is justifiable since the industries (cotton and cigarettes)
are capable of economical production.   It would not be
wise to apply this universally to all undeveloped industries
in China since not all are capable today of economical
production.   Sometimes it occurs that a nation possesses
all the natural advantages for carrying on a certain line
of production but due to lack of organization, and the
pressure of competition from industry well established elsewhere, it is unable to effect arrangements whereby its advantages can be drawn together, without the aid of artificial trade barriers.   Investors require special encouragement to overcome these initial difficulties.[12]   Such is the
case with China in the textile and cigarette industries, and
it is being suggested that a limited use of protection, possibly not even complete protection, would be beneficial to
China, in that such would provide a greater impetus for

[12] Cf. H. R. Seager, *Principles of Economics*, pp. 393–8; R. T.
Ely, *Outlines of Economics*, p. 366.

industrialization than now exists, would make possible a reduction of imports of certain kinds, build up the productive forces now latent, and through increased production make possible improvements in standards of living. China will probably be wise, however, if the application of protection is confined only to those in which economical production is definitely possible. Many writers have concurred in the thought that a scientific tariff for China would have a large free list and very few protective duties.[13] The new tariff includes on the free list only cereals and flour and books, maps and periodicals.

But Marshall says, " Protection to any one industry tends to narrow the markets, especially the foreign markets, for other industries." [14] In what ways would exports be affected? If the curtailment of imports by certain tariffs meant that the supply of London bills of exchange arising out of Chinese exports became abundant it would cause exchange rates to become less favorable to the buyer of Chinese goods. If, however, some other sources of demand for London bills (i.e. other than imports) sustain the rates this would not be probable. Imports would not be unduly encouraged.

Chinese trade is carried on to a large extent by means of London bills of exchange. Foreign buyers of goods provide letters of credit addressed to the exporters in China authorizing a London bank to accept the four months' or six months' draft of the Chinese exporter up to a certain amount. The exporter sells it to a bank in China which will sell its amount to Chinese importers or sends it to London for collection. As the volume of these bills drawn

---

13 Cf. *Proceedings*, Baltimore Conference, p. 82, also *passim*.
14 A. Marshall, *Principles of Economics*, VII Edition, p. 465.

on London increases relative to the demand the exchange rates rise or become easier for Chinese importers. A rise in exchange is followed by a fall in the silver prices of Chinese imports, which is followed by an increase in total imports into China, measured in money value of silver. But if a demand for exchange occurs equal to the loss of demand due to the original declining imports, then no such marked change in exchange, or prices, need take place and exports can continue unrestricted.

Thus there need not occur a reduction of Chinese exports of all commodities since foreign markets would not necessarily be narrowed. A decrease in imports could be accompanied by an attempt to increase interest and amortization payments upon China's foreign debt. (Indeed such demand for exchange would occur if financial readjustment were accomplished by the government as previously discussed.) Such would operate, provided no more than the surplus of exchange were absorbed, to sustain the exchange between China and other countries in the same manner as imports of commodities and prevent an even greater flow of silver to China than now takes place.

Of course, the development of certain industries may mean that imports may remain the same in amount but different in character. To the extent that these imports, however, tend to be machinery and other forms of capital goods China's industrial production can be enhanced and further exportation made possible.

But to return to other imports. One notes that capital goods of a constructive character are figuring increasingly in Chinese imports. In 1923 the following items appeared:

Metals	41,000,000 taels
Machinery	35,700,000
Railway Materials	9,000,000
Copper Ingots and Slabs	3,800,000
Building Materials	3,400,000
Cement	3,300,000
Motor Cars	2,200,000
Telephone and Telegraph Materials	1,000,000
Scientific Instruments	1,000,000
Window glass	2,000,000
Paints	2,500,000
Lubricating Oil	3,300,000
	110,200,000 taels

These items of imports are but indicative of the demand for certain commodities which will increase as the industrial development of China continues. It would be a short sighted policy which would tend to discourage such imports. Dyestuffs and leaf tobacco have already been mentioned as necessary to such development. Kerosene was mentioned, in discussing vegetable oils, as figuring increasingly in Chinese imports, offsetting exports of vegetable oils. The development of industry will call for increasing amounts of electrical equipment for power and light, for machinery, for iron and steel products of all kinds, and for automotive equipment. The exploitation of China's now unused sources of hydroelectric power, the development of transportation and other internal communications will necessarily be accomplished largely through importations. Some influx of foreign capital will undoubtedly accompany these changes. Some contributions may be expected from the iron ore and pig iron production of China but not much in the form of manufactures of iron or steel since these cannot yet be produced economically in China. It is hoped that any increases of the tariff will not impose protective duties on most of the commodities just considered, since they are in large part not obtainable in China, or are not, except with tremendous effort, capable of economical production there.

China imports foodstuffs. In 1923 imports there are found the following:

Rice	98,000,000 taels
Sugar	50,000,000
Flour	27,200,000
Marine Products	25,000,000
Wheat	9,100,000
Condensed Milk	1,600,000
	210,900,000 taels

The importation of sugar, flour, and wheat is increasing. This has been called a " dietic revolution in the making." China's consumptive possibilities along lines of food are enormous. The population is 440,000,000, in the total area of China.[15] But the satisfaction of these consumptive potentialities depends upon production and trade. It is not even on productive capacity, for China has the capacity for much greater production if only her whole economic system were organized and developed, particularly along national lines. As it is now China's production of foodstuffs may develop a surplus in one portion of China while another suffers from a famine.

China is predominantly agricultural. There is a wide range of climate, a rich soil, and the wants of millions of the population are simple. Many have said that the country, from a food standpoint, can be self-supporting. The number of people engaged in agriculture, according to a report of the Ministry of Agriculture and Commerce in the 5th Year of the Republic (1917),[15] was 49,028,864

[15] Found in C. F. Remer, *Readings in Economics for China,"* p. 209.

families. The land not under cultivation was 388,645,355 mow, and forest land was 389,261,043 mow, thus indicating possibilities of development. There are large areas of land capable of reclamation from the devastating inroads of floods.

Until China's internal transportation is improved, and the agricultural output increased, it would not be wise to pursue a policy which might act to restrict Chinese imports of foodstuffs. Rice is still an essential part of the diet of the masses, and northern provinces are able to import rice from Japan more cheaply than they can with present facilities bring it from other parts of China. That country has for so long faced the imminence of famine in certain areas that no immediate reduction in imports of foodstuffs should be expected.

In regard to much of the balance of the commodities now imported into China, most of which are now unobtainable in China, or if produced there in certain parts are relatively unavailable in other parts, no market reduction should be expected.

The conclusion of this treatment of Chinese production and import trade is largely that import trade will not decrease in amount,—it will increase—though it will probably decrease relative to exports. There will probably be some increase in raw cotton for a short time, a gradual decrease in cotton yarn, perhaps however only relatively, no great increase in cotton piece goods (which will cease if protection is given), an increase in dyestuffs, a relative decrease in cigarettes, (absolute if protection is given), but at least no marked increase, some increase in tobacco, which may actually decline as Chinese production continues, an increase in constructive capital goods, and a continuance of the same relative volume in foodstuffs and many

16

items not obtainable in China. To the extent that the character of the imports brings contributions to industrial organization and development, the economic fabric of the nation will be strengthened, the purchasing power of millions stimulated, and all phases of trade, internal and external, increased. China will gain but so will those who trade with her. The possibilities of increasing home production, for home consumption as well as for export, in silk, and silk products, tea, cotton, beans, eggs and egg products, and other commodities treated in the previous chapter must not be forgotten. Chinese export trade will probably develop more rapidly than import trade in total amount as the industrialization of China proceeds. In the near future, however, considering the dependence of China upon foreign countries for the goods necessary for this transformation, no export surplus of goods can be expected. China will do well if the gap between imports and exports is narrowed rather than increased. To the extent that this is done China will be less dependent upon the continuance of foreign capital investment in China, or foreign missions' and cultural expenditures, as a means of balancing her international accounts and of securing the gold credits necessary to pay interest and repayment charges upon the government foreign debt, or as a means of supporting in the way of capital investment this very development of industry itself. But this is a long run rather than an immediate consideration. Immediately China will be compelled to depend upon these " invisible " items of credit to China on international account. Hence, though looked at over a long period China does have the potential economic capacity to meet her indebtedness, in the present years, China's economic capacity is conditioned upon the continuance and increase of capital movements towards China, and upon certain non-economic activities rather than upon current income derived purely from the sale of goods and services abroad.

The next consideration could very well be certain general aspects of the industrial development of China.

CHAPTER XIV

Industrial Development

Many writers have dwelt upon the industrial development of China. The transformation of this great agricultural state into an industrial state has caused much discussion of the problems which are incident and consequent thereto. Some have spoken of China as transforming itself; while others have thought of it as being transformed. Some have envisioned the industrialization of this part of the Orient as equivalent to Occidentalization, while others have spoken of industrialization quite apart from any implied change in the balance of the individual and social, institutional characteristics above and beyond the distinctly economic. The problem is far too broad and important to be treated lightly and, for that reason, it is suggested that our attention should be centered here mainly on the economic aspects. Some writers look with apprehension upon the industrialization of China, but for different reasons,— some because of the fear of keen economic competition were this great people to capture the markets of the world, others, because they wish China to avoid the evils that have come in Europe and America from industrialism. The former is a selfish expression, but this latter group believes it better, for China's own sake, to reduce to a minimum any pressure which would seem to force China to industrialize, believing that China will best serve herself and the world by continuing as she has continued, and by making only such economic, political and social, institutional and other changes as gradually come to pass from

232

within her own resources and life. There is the problem of population however—440 millions—with a very marked density in certain areas. One writer states " Such large numbers of people can only be ultimately provided for at a higher standard of living through the progressive industrialization of China." [1]

The facts are that, good or bad, there is a strong tendency toward industrialization in China today, and as conditions are now industrialization has become an international question. The international aspects may in time be changed, extra territoriality may be removed, the tariff has become politically a domestic issue, but the industrialization is bound to continue.[2] Industry in China in one sense is as old or older than in any of the other countries of the world. It is modern industry which forms the problem. As Prof. Vinacke says, " Thus it is quite in order to make a study of the possibilities of development rather than of origination of industry in modern China." [3] An enumeration of all existing industries in China would be a long list, since there are at least 34 different kinds : Factories devoted to the production of cotton goods and yarn, albumen, matches, leather, bean cake, tobacco products, woolen goods, vegetable oils, flour, and for rice cleaning, and smelting.[4]

While recognizing that there is danger in a too rapid transformation, it is to be recognized that much will probably be gained in economic wealth through a hastening of industrialization. There are many things that can

[1] H. M. Vinacke, *op. cit.*, p. 3.

[2] Cf. *Baltimore Conference Report*, pp. 91 ff.

[3] P. 19.

[4] Cf. *China Year Book*, 1925, pages for full statement of such industries.

be done to effect these changes in a sound and organized way. This is China's great opportunity.

A repetition need not be given of the resources which China possesses in natural wealth awaiting development. It is interesting to note, however, what China's wealth has been estimated to be, which in American dollars is as follows: [5]

Land	$43,344,441,562
Houses, godowns, etc.	2,766,611,112
Furniture, art goods	863,854,106
Cattle, animals, etc.	827,219,905
Minerals	249,631,404
Marine Products	124,815,702
Salt	709,077,235
Gold and silver	731,051,550
Public utilities, Rys.	53,652,328
Ships and Vehicles	45,806,787
Commercial Cos., Banks	35,781,300
Merchandise	2,103,664,408
Rivers and Harbors	996,278,008
Total	$52,851,885,410

In the discussion of the financial aspects of China's indebtedness and capacity it was noted that everything depended on the establishment of strong governmental authority. In discussing the possibilities of the development of export trade the assistance of the government was noted as important in the silk, cotton, and other industries, in the form of education, information and experimentation, and in the form of a well planned tariff serving the needs of China's growing industries. The importance of the

[5] Estimate made by Baron Takahashi, sometime Premier of Japan, and quoted in article by Prof. Chas. Hodges in *Baltimore Conference Report*, pp. 72–73—already changed from yen to U. S. currency, hence will not convert to Chinese currency. In reference to 18 Provinces of China Proper, only.

problem of government in the general problem of industrial development must be recognized. Although it is true that trade and industry have continued to develop in spite of political instability and internal disorder, the full development of industry rests upon political stability. In the present conditions the retarding influence of disorganization will soon be seriously felt, for, in competition with countries already well organized industrially, the failure to keep pace in many of the essential accompaniments of industrial development will probably react seriously to impede progress.

The most important consideration is the development of internal communication and transportation. A glimpse at the present extent of development has been gained through the discussion of the railway loans and the telephone and telegraph loans. China has about 7000 miles of railways completed and in operation. There is almost an equal number of miles under contract or awaiting completion. An even greater mileage has been " projected." The total capital investment of the Government railways is given (1923) by the Chinese Government Bureau of Economic Information as $635,279,486. There are 80,-000 miles of telegraph lines, 13 wireless stations and 28 telephone offices. But today, due to the breakdown of central authority the communications of China are in a serious plight. The railways have been made to serve the interests of military leaders, both financially and as military agencies, to the detriment of government revenue on the one hand, and the development of trade and industry on the other. The necessity for centralized administration as an agency of a strong united government is evident, not alone if further extension is carried out, but also if that mileage which exists is to serve a useful economic function.

The Diplomatic Corps on February 12, 1925 addressed a note to the Government on railway conditions, pointing out not only the danger to economic development but also the possibility of insolvency and close relationship of foreign interests.[6]   With the failure to live up to loan agreements comes the possibility of a proposal for an international control of railways in China.   At the present juncture of internal conditions, such a proposal might have serious consequences.   As to the technical condition of the railways, the Minister of Communications reported in 1925 as follows, " Bridges are decaying and falling. Rolling stocks are broken down and sadly in need of repairs.   Work on incompleted lines is interrupted and deterioration overtakes the existing lines, which are gradually becoming useless." [7]   All discussion of methods of organizing the administration, or of bringing financial readjustment of the railways and communications is useless until such government authority is established as can prevent further misappropriation of equipment and funds and can restore an efficient system.

As to the future, the building of further railways will undoubtedly follow upon the completion of political stability.   China's present railways, with certain notable exceptions, as the Peking-Kalgan Railway, have been built by foreign capital.   Further employment of foreign capital, if divorced from political influence so that international complications are avoided, as is contemplated in the Second Consortium, and if not granting special privileges to foreigners in trade as opposed to the Chinese them-

---

[6] This note is quoted in part in the Report of the Minister of Communications given in the *Chinese Economic Monthly*, Nov., 1925, p. 36.

[7] *Ibid.*, p. 39.

selves, will be not only wise but probably necessary. The problem of repayment of such increasing indebtedness need not concern us as much as the other forms of indebtedness since (1) such loans are productive, creating income yielding assets, capable of yielding not only interest and repayment but also a surplus to the Government (2) the railways are vital to other economic development and such development bids fair to provide both sufficient bases for taxation and commercial expansion in the more distant future as to make possible the repayment of the debts.

The Second Consortium

The treatment of the foreign loans to China which was given omitted discussion of one event which bears quite directly upon the future history of loans to China, and in particular upon this question of further railway loans. This was the formation of the Second Consortium. It was not earlier treated, largely because no loans have been contracted by the Chinese Government through its agency.

It was mentioned that during the European War the Consortium then existing was unable to play its full part and Japan was able in that period to supply large quantities of funds to China. It became evident to the State Department at Washington that the American policy in regard to Chinese loans should be changed. The war had created a community of interest theretofore not so completely realized by the Wilson administration. The result was that in July, 1918 negotiations were begun between the Department of State and American bankers relative to a loan to China, and by the former also with the Governments of Great Britain, France and Japan for the reorganization of the old Consortium. These negotiations continued until October 15, 1920, when a final agreement

17

for the Consortium was signed for five years.[8]   The agreement has been continued with rights of withdrawal upon 12 months' notice, but with no other change in the terms of agreement among the banking groups.   The old Consortium had excluded in 1913 from its scope all but political and administrative loans but in the new Consortium scope has been extended to include all existing options or loans upon which substantial progress has not been made, as well as industrial and financial loans.   The Consortium as now organized includes many options for future railway construction and this pooling arrangement should go far to avoid many of the complications that have resulted from international competition in this field, which have been evident in the past, from the treatment that has been given. These options now held by the Consortium are:[9]

1. Hukuang Railways, second series and further loan
2. Pukow-Sinyang Railway Loan, 1913
3. Nanking-Hunan Railway Loan, 1914
4. Jehol-Taonan Railway Agreement
5. Tsinan-Shunteh, Kaomi-Hsuchou, 1914
6. Chinchowfu-Aigun Railroad, 1910
7. Hengchowfu-Nanning Railway, 1916
8. Fengcheng-Ninghsia   "   "
9. Ninghsia-Lanshowfu   "   "
10. Chungchow-LuKwei   "   "
11. Hangchow-Wenchow   "   "

China seems unwilling to utilize the resources of the Consortium.   The result is that China's ability to borrow is restricted.

    [8] Cf. *The Consortium,* published by Carnegie Endowment giving negotiations, 1921. Cf. also Correspondence re "New Consortium for China," *Parliamentary Papers,* 1920. Cf. also pamphlet, " Preliminary Report on New Consortium," T. W. Lamont, 1920.
    [9] Letter of T. W. Lamont to writer, 1926.

In the question of expenditure China objects to foreign control of loan fund expenditure, yet it would seem that through joint Chinese and international activity in this regard, as well as in the matter of security, pledged for any loan, that the economic interests of China are thus to be furthered. It may politically have its disadvantages but they will be mainly internal. However, the financial interests involved working with their respective Governments, let us say in the Consortium, have a responsibility in addition to such things as concern control. One reason for the large costs to China of obtaining funds has been the risk involved in loaning to a Government which because of internal difficulties, for some time has not appeared stable. Were agreement to be reached on questions of security it would seem, that, the security of the loan being thus enhanced, more favorable terms as to initial discount, commissions, or interests could be granted.

If questions of security and supervision of loan expenditure which have been the basis of Chinese objections, were made unnecessary by a general financial reorganization of the country, the Chinese Government could hope to obtain further loans without encountering internal opposition. In the present political situation much can be done. The Nationalist Government claims to speak for all of China. Thus the problem of developing transportation and communications is fundamentally one of political initiation and negotiation.

Conclusion

What has just been said of communications and transportation can also be said of currency reform, industrial organization, commercial and financial organization both investment and banking, commercial education and the administration of justice—all come ultimately for solution to the question of government. Yet, all are factors in industrial development. They are also all related to that important task of developing export trade and China's international balance of accounts. Further industrial and commercial economic development is the fundamental basis for Governmental financial capacity. It is unnecessary to repeat much of what has already been said in regard to these various phases of China's capacity to pay. Both in regard to the financial problem of securing a budget surplus and the economic problem of securing an exchange surplus the present condition is one of incapacity, more definitely as concerns the government's revenues and expenditures, than in the field of international exchange. But this is not to say that the future does not hold promise of greater capacity. The present limiting factors cannot be overlooked by one who would appraise China today, but equally so the potentialities of that country must not be forgotten in appraising the economic future. As a preliminary to everything else and underlying all other problems is the difficult task of uniting politically the divergent political groups and forces of China sufficiently to carry through the elements in the program of financial and industrial stabilization as outlined. Unless this can be done any discussion of the future growth of China (at least as China) is idle. Whether or not this can be done is the essence of the Chinese problem today. The complicating part of this—the political problem—is that international commitments of China are important internal political questions—such as extra-territoriality, the foreign loans and foreign financial control.

Will disintegration in China be the next political development? The Nanking Government's authority (Nanking is the " recognized " Government in China) is not complete. The answer to the question of disintegration is difficult. There are disintegrating as well as integrating political forces still influential in Chinese affairs. Whatever group succeeds in uniting China, if in point of time that success is not too far removed, can, if it will, meet China's foreign indebtedness.

BIBLIOGRAPHY

I. Government Publications

1. China—Ministry of Communications, C. C. Wang, Railway Loan Agreements, Peking, 1917; published in Chinese and foreign languages, including English.
2. China—Official History of the Sino-Japanese Treaties, 1915, Peking, 1915.
3. China—Commission on Readjustment of Finance—Preliminary Report, April 16, 1924.
4. China—Commission on Readjustment of Finance—Revenues of Central Government and Likin, October, 1925, Peking.
5. China—Commission on Readjustment of Finance—Tables of Inadequately Secured Loans of the Ministry of Finance, Peking, November, 1925.
6. China—Government Bureau of Economic Information—The Foreign Loan Obligations of China, by J. R. Baylin, Tientsin, 1925.
7. China—Inspectorate General of Maritime Customs—Returns of Trade and Trade Reports, Abstracts of Statistics, etc.; annually.
8. China—Government Bureau of Economic Information—The Chinese Economic Monthly, now The Chinese Economic Journal, cf. The Chinese Economic Bulletin; periodicals.
9. France—Documents Diplomatiques, Chine, 1898–99.
10. Great Britain—Foreign Office, Parliamentary Papers by Command—CIX, 1899, 1; 1900, 1; 1912, 1, 2, 3, (Cd. 6148, 6446, 6447); 1913, (Cd. 7054); 1918, 1, (Cd. 8895); 1920, (Cmd. 853), No. 43; 1921, (Cmd. 1214). Accounts and Papers and Reports, Committees.
11. United States—Department of State—W. W. Rockhill, Treaties and Conventions with and Concerning China, 1904.
12. United States—Department of State—U. S. Foreign Relations, 1905, 1909, 1912, 1913, 1914, 1916.
13. United States—Conference on Limitation of Armaments—Text of Nine Power Treaty re China, Treaty Series No. 723.
14. United States—Department of Commerce—Miscellaneous Series No. 84, Commercial Handbook of China, by Julean Arnold, Vols. I and II. 1919 and 1920.

15. United States—Department of Commerce—Special Agent Series No. 186, Chinese Currency and Finance, by A. W. Ferrin, 1919. List of loans.

16. United States—Department of Commerce—Special Agent Series No. 107, Cotton Goods in China, by Ralph M. Odell, 1916.

17. United States—Department of Commerce—Trade Promotion Series No. 13, International Trade in Cotton, by Leslie A. Wheeler, 1924.

18. United States—Department of Commerce—Special Consular Report, Railway Situation in China, by G. E. Anderson, 1911.

19. United States—Department of Commerce—Trade Promotion Series No. 27, Currency, Banking and Finance in China, by Dr. F. E. Lee, 1926. Lists of loans.

20. United States—Department of Commerce—Trade Information Bulletin No. 299, Budgets of Far Eastern Countries, by James A. DeForce, December, 1924.

21. United States—Department of Commerce—Trade Information Bulletin No. 312, Changing Factors in the Economic Life of China, by John H. Nelson, 1925.

22. United States—Department of Commerce—Trade Information Bulletin No. 400, Budgets of Far Eastern Governments, by E. E. Groseclose, December, 1925.

23. United States—Department of Commerce—Commerce Yearbook.

II. Books

1. Bau, M. J.—Foreign Relations of China, New York, 1921. Chapters on the New Consortium.

2. Bau, M. J.—The Open Door Doctrine in China, New York, 1923. Political aspects of loans considered.

3. Blakeslee, G. H. (ed.)—China and the Far East, New York, 1910.

4. Blakeslee, G. H.—Recent Developments in China, New York, 1913.

5. Bland, J. O. P.—Recent Events and Present Policies in China, Philadelphia, 1912. Bland was British representative of First Consortium.

6. Buell, Raymond L.—The Washington Conference, New York, 1922.

7. Carnegie Endowment—The Consortium, New York, 1921; gives correspondence re New Consortium.

8. Chang, Ying Hua—The Financial Reconstruction of China, Peking, 1923; Chang was sometime Minister of Finance, and a member of Commission for Study of Financial Problems of Chinese Government.

9. Gibson, Rowland R.—Forces Mining and Undermining China, New York, 1914; More "undermining" than "mining."

10. Hornbeck, Stanley K.—Contemporary Politics in the Far East. New York, 1916.

11. Hsu, M. C.—Railway Problems in China—New York, 1915. Problems of finance treated; reflects a Chinese view of foreign control.

12. Huang, F. H.—Public Debts of China, New York, 1919. Appendix of loans to 1918.

13. Kimber, A.W.—Foreign Government Securities.

14. Latourette, K. S.—The Development of China, Boston, 1924.

15. Li, Chuan Shih—Central and Local Finance in China, New York, 1921.

16. MacMurray, J. vA.—Treaties and Agreements with and Concerning China, 1894–1918, published by the Carnegie Endowment. MacMurray is Minister to China (1929) and was Secretary of the Legation in Peking formerly. Contains contracts for most loans in secured group and many in unsecured group.

17. Moore, Frederick—The Chaos in Europe, New York, 1919. Chapter on "The Backward State." Moore was formerly Associated Press representative in Peking.

18. Morse, H. B.—An Inquiry into Commercial Liabilities and Assets of China in International Trade, Shanghai, 1904.

19. Morse, H. B.—International Relations of the Chinese Empire. Vol. III, Shanghai, 1910, 1918.

20. Morse, H. B.—Trade and Administration of China, London, 1921 Edit.

21. Millard, T. F.—Our Eastern Question, New York, 1916.

22. Millard, T. F.—Conflict of Policies in Asia, New York, 1924.

23. Overlach, T. W.—Foreign Financial Control in China, New York, 1919. Good treatment of relation of economic factors to political problems.

24. Pan, Shiu Lun—The Trade of the United States with China, New York, 1924.

25. Parker, E. H.—China, Past and Present, London, 1903.

26. Parker, E. H.—China, Her History, Diplomacy, and Commerce, London, 1917.

27. Reinsch, P. S.—An American Diplomat in China. Chapter XVIII on "American Entrepreneurs in Peking" re Siems Carey projects; Chapter XXV on "The Chinese Go A-Borrowing" re Nishihara loans.

28. Remer, C. F.—Readings in Economics for China, Shanghai, 1922.

29. Remer, C. F.—The Foreign Trade of China, Shanghai, 1926.
30. See, Chong Su—The Foreign Trade of China, New York, 1919.
31. Sun, Yat Sen—The International Development of China, New York, 1922.
32. Spalding, W. F.—The Eastern Exchanges, Currency and Finance, London, 1917. Loan statistics not comprehensive.
33. Straight, Willard, Chinese Loan Negotiations, New York, 1912.
34. Tyau, M. T. Z.—China Awakened, New York, 1922.
35. Vinacke, H. M.—Industrial Development in China, Princeton, 1926.
36. Wagel, S. R.—Finance in China, Shanghai, 1914.
37. Williams, E. T.—China Yesterday and Today. New York, 1923.
38. Willoughby, W. W.—Foreign Rights and Interests in China, 1920. Chapters on loans and good appendices.
39. Willoughby, W. W.—Washington Conference Reports, 1922.
40. Woodhead, R. G. W. (ed.)—The China Year Book, Tientsin, 1913 to 1928. Contains much material from official Chinese sources with excellent statistical compilations.

III. REPORTS, PAMPHLETS, PERIODICALS

1. Johns Hopkins (Baltimore) Conference 1925, " American relations with China," Baltimore, 1926.
2. Institute of Pacific Relations, Honolulu, 1925. Papers to Members No. 25. Industrialization of China, by A. W. Au-Young. No. 30—Development of National Resources of China, by Jeremiah W. Jenks. No. 73—Loans and Investments in the Countries of the Pacific, by J. W. Jenks. No. 38 —Foreign Loans in China, by L. T. Chen. R-12—Advantages and Disadvantages of the Industrialization of China, by S. T. Wen. R-43—Customs Control, Tariff Revenues, and Foreign Loans, by Tsurumi.
3. Padoux, G.—The Financial Reconstruction of China and the Consolidation of China's Present Indebtedness. Peking, 1923—pamphlet.
4. (Lee F. E.)—China, An Economic Survey, 1923—published by the American Bankers Association—pamphlet.
5. Lamont, T. W.—Preliminary Report on New Financial Consortium for China, New York, 1920.
6. Annals of American Academy of Political and Social Science, November, 1916—Denby, Chas.—Foreign Debts of China.
7. Annals of American Academy of Political and Social Science, November, 1925—Arnold, Julean—China's Post War Trade.

8. Annals of American Academy of Political and Social Science, November, 1925—Lee, F. E.—Significance of Foreign Financial Control in China.
9. Commerce Reports—May 18, 1925, E. E. Groseclose, The Gold Franc Settlement.
10. Commerce Reports—June 7, 1926—Chas. K. Moser, Likin—China's Inland Trade Tax.
11. Chinese Economic Monthly—Peking (now Chinese Economic Journal), October, 1925—China's Finances under the Republican Regime.
12. Chinese Economic Monthly—Bean and Wheat Production along C. E. R.
13. Chinese Economic Monthly—Treasury Note Issues of the Chinese Government.
14. Chinese Economic Monthly, November, 1925—China's Finances—A Summary.
15. Chinese Economic Monthly—Development of Communications in China—A report of Min. of Communications.
16. Chinese Economic Monthly—Chinese Tariff Law.
17. Chinese Economic Monthly—Weaving Industry in Wuchang and Hankow.
18. Chinese Economic Monthly, January, 1926—Economic Resources of Manchuria.
19. Chinese Economic Monthly—1925 Customs Revenue.
20. Chinese Economic Monthly, February, 1926—List of Cotton Mills in China.
21. Chinese Economic Monthly—Notes on Chinese Native Customs System, by F. G. Otte.
22. Chinese Economic Monthly, March, 1926—Cotton Cultivation in Chekiang.
23. Chinese Economic Monthly—List of Secured Loan Payments, 1926.
24. Chinese Economic Monthly, April, 1926—Silver in 1925.
25. Chinese Economic Monthly, September, 1926—Commercial Statistics in China.
26. Chinese Economic Monthly—Cotton and Cotton Yarn in Shanghai.
27. Chinese Economic Monthly, October, 1926—Silk Filatures in Shanghai.
28. Chinese Economic Bulletin—Peking.
29. Foreign Affairs, April, 1925—MacMurray, J. vA., Problems of Foreign Capital in China.
30. Foreign Affairs, April, 1929—Mallory, W. H., China's New Tariff Autonomy.

31. Far Eastern Review, December, 1918—a list of Japanese loans. December, 1919—re loans.
32. Japan Advertiser, March 12, 1925—re Nishihara Loans.
33. Japan Weekly Chronicle, May 21, 1925—list of Chinese loans in default.
34. L'Europe Nouvelle, September 5, 1925—Les douanes en Chine et la prochaine conference des tarifs, 1187–9.
35. Quarterly Journal of Economics, August, 1916—Winston, A. P., Chinese Finance under the Republic.
36. Quarterly Journal of Economics, August, 1926—Remer, C. F., International Trade between Gold and Silver Standard Countries.

INDEX

248